JAMES

RUNNING UPHILL
INTO THE WIND

JAMES

RUNNING UPHILL INTO THE WIND

DON ANDERSON

LOIZEAUX BROTHERS

Neptune, New Jersey

Library of Congress Cataloging-in-Publication Data

Anderson, Don, 1933-
    James : running uphill into the wind / Don Anderson.
        p.   cm.
    Includes bibliographical references.
    ISBN 0-87213-007-X
    1. Bible. N.T. James—Commentaries.   I. Title.
BS2785.3.A53   1990   90-31385
227'.9107—dc20   CIP

The author wishes to acknowledge the editorial assistance of Jane
Rodgers.

10 9 8 7 6 5 4 3 2 1

To Julea,
our youngest.

You're about halfway up the hill and still
running. Go for it, Doll!

Dear Dad,
I sit among your charts and papers at your desk
in the evening all alone. My heart knows well
what it wants to convey to you. I learn more and
more from you about *never giving up*. Dad, you
fight your way through and I learn from that. I
guess I've always believed you were right for
"pressing on" in all areas of your life, but now I
have reasons to believe. The number one reason
is because of the rest I have in my relationship
with God. I love you, Dad, for showing me the
way to the gift.

Julea

אֲנִי לְדוֹדִי֙ וְדוֹדִי לִי֔

I am my beloved's and my beloved is mine
Song of Solomon 6:3

πάντα χαὶ ἐν πᾶσιν Χφιστός

Christ is all and in all
Colossians 3:11

Contents

Foreword

I have known Don Anderson and his ministry for thirty-four years. We were next-door neighbors during seminary days, and you really get to know each other's families when their back door and your front door are just a few feet apart.

Whether as a Young Life director, or a Christian conference director, or a pastor, or a Bible study leader, Don Anderson has always had a strong desire to take good theology, built on solid biblical exegesis, and make it relevant for the man on the street. This practical exposition of James mirrors the ministry Don has had for many years. It will warm you, instruct you, convict you, and build you up in the Lord Jesus Christ—the focus of Don Anderson Ministries.

EARL D. RADMACHER
PRESIDENT, WESTERN SEMINARY

Going for It

Texas is famous for its blue northers. When the "gate" is left open in the panhandle, temperatures can drop from 85 to 35 degrees throughout much of the state in a matter of hours. I awoke in Fort Worth several years ago to be greeted by such a cold, gray, norther-spawned morning. I had stayed the night at the home of my running buddy Doug and family, in order to train with him for our mutual goal, the Houston marathon.

Training for Houston was vital. Doug and I had run our first marathon together in Las Vegas a couple of years before, and both of us thought we would die before finishing. We started too fast, and hit the wall at the twenty-mile mark. Our muscles cramped, making each step a gigantic, excruciatingly painful effort of the will. Thousands of reasons to quit bombarded our brains, and like so many runners who do not pace themselves properly, we nearly became casualties along the route.

We both completed Las Vegas that year, but it took every shred of energy and determination we had to make it across the finish line. We wanted to do better in Houston. I was particularly eager to do well there because a loss of body fluids had forced me out of the White Rock Marathon in Dallas earlier that same year.

At 5:00 a.m. Fort Worth time, Doug rolled me out of bed and explained the training course we would run that day. We set off through the streets of the city, working hard to get warm. Keeping comfortable was tough, since temperatures had dropped to the low thirties and the wind was gusting at twenty miles per hour. My wind suit, socks, gloves, and hat all seemed pitifully inadequate against the bitter, piercing chill.

Then it happened. We came to Fort Worth's version of Heartbreak Hill. Suddenly the street in front of us seemed to reach for the stars. Quadriceps screaming, I grunted and groaned, straining to make it uphill. About halfway up, the wind blowing fiercely in my face, I heard Doug's cheerful (yes, *cheerful*) voice: "Don! When you reach the top, the rest of the way will be a piece of cake!"

I dug a little deeper, sucked it up, and kept going. At the crest of the hill, the sun peeked over the horizon. The day's first warming rays exploded into visibility, showering the distance with glowing pinks and yellows. I cannot describe the joy and well-being felt at a moment like that—the wonder of a brand-new day after the struggle of a long, steep, rugged ascent. Dawn breaks as an obvious gift of the Lord, a twenty-four-hour challenge in which there are more mountains to climb, more work to be done, a new race to be run.

The Christian life is like that. It is running uphill into the wind. Every step of progress is costly. Advancing and taking new territory involves sacrificially spending ourselves. Cresting a summit means facing new challenges. I am convinced that champion Christians are those who have been spent and are still going on. Can you hear the hymn they sing?

> I'm pressing on the upward way,
> New heights I'm gaining ev'ry day;
> Still praying as I'm onward bound,
> "Lord, plant my feet on higher ground."
>
> Lord, lift me up and let me stand,
> By faith, on Heaven's tableland,
> A higher plane than I have found;
> Lord, plant my feet on higher ground.
>   (Johnson Oatman, Jr.)

Higher ground should be the goal of every believer, the end result of a life lived for Christ, a life that is progressively changed to conform to the image of the Savior. Becoming Christlike involves steep ascents, struggles, detours, successes, and failures—because it is basically a battle to change our behavior. So much of growing up in Jesus involves running uphill into the wind.

THE WRITER

The New Testament book of James is a practical manual for running the race that is the Christian life. It is a guide to going for higher ground.

The author, James, was evidently the half brother of Jesus Christ. Following the virgin birth of Jesus, Mary and Joseph had children of their own. The oldest and firstborn son of their union probably was James.

Imagine growing up with the Lord Jesus Christ as your big brother. He was perfect. He could do no wrong. I have known big brothers who thought they were perfect, but none of them could really pull it off. Nothing was ever Jesus' fault. He never lied or cheated. He never got mad. His IQ was off the charts.

Surely while growing up, James noticed that his older brother was different from other people. It would be wonderful if I could tell you that James recognized Jesus as the Son of God right from the start. But it wasn't so. John 7:5 tells of Christ that "not even His brothers were believing in Him" (NASB). Sadly, throughout the Lord's entire earthly life before the cross, none of his brothers acknowledged him as the messiah. James, a Pharisee, was probably embarrassed more than once by Jesus' attacks on the Jewish religious leaders. Surely it repulsed him that his own brother would associate with sinners, tax collectors like Matthew and Zaccheus, prostitutes, and half-breed Samaritans. James had probably spent the three years of Jesus' public ministry apologizing for his older brother's actions and words, secretly wishing that He would keep quiet or leave the country, longing for the day when the family would no longer be ridiculed because of Jesus' behavior and the company He kept.

One day all of that changed. A cruel execution silenced Jesus.

But the grave could not contain him. On the third day after the cross, the Lord rose again and during the next forty days appeared to hundreds of eyewitnesses. Among them was James. First Corinthians 15:7 tells of this encounter between James and Jesus, which happened sometime after the Lord's resurrection and before his ascension into heaven. The Bible doesn't give specifics about this meeting. We don't know what was said. We don't know how or where Jesus appeared. We do know that James was never the same. No longer cynical, he was completely convinced of the truth of who Jesus Christ was. He became a 110 percent follower of the Lord, a leader of the early church, one of its "pillars," as the apostle Paul wrote in Galatians 2:9. Eventually James's commitment would be pushed to the edge of human endurance. Tradition tells us he would die a martyr for the cause of Christ—first shoved off the pinnacle of a temple, then stoned, and finally viciously clubbed to death when he still showed signs of life.

THE LETTER

As I write these words, two Wycliffe missionaries are being held captive by South American guerrillas, another independent missionary working in Central America has not been heard from for three months, and two Christian missionaries in Mexico have recently been stoned to death for their faith. They are but a few of the war-zone stories of suffering lived by those on the front lines for Jesus (see Matthew 5:10-12; 10:28).

Although we are grieved when we hear about such situations, I wonder how real the concept of being persecuted for our faith is to most of us twentieth-century Christians. Do we truly understand what it means to suffer for the sake of Jesus? Oh, we may endure some social ostracism. We may find that certain career choices must be avoided. We may lose money in a business deal because we must choose to be ethical beyond the shadow of a doubt. We may find that our opinions and standards are ridiculed, our convictions cannon fodder for the audiences of talk-show hosts. If we want to see some real flak coming our way at a party, all we have to do is point out the scriptural teachings on abortion, open marriage, premarital sex, or homosexuality. But so far in America at least, the odds are we won't be fired from our jobs, forced out of our homes, disinherited, thrown into prison, or stoned to death because we are Christians. The original readers of the epistle of James could not say the same.

The individuals to whom James wrote were primarily Jewish Christians scattered because of persecution. As one of the earliest epistles, the letter of James can be dated around A.D. 45-48 and thus was penned within three decades of the time Christ actually walked the earth. Many of James's readers had become believers on the day of Pentecost and had returned to their communities to be greeted coldly. They were rejected by their own people for believing in Christ; they were reviled by the Romans because they worshiped a king other than Caesar. Often their property was seized and they were separated from families, forced to make fresh starts as penniless refugees in foreign lands among hostile peoples. James wrote a broad letter to these displaced Hebrew Christians with the goal of instructing them in how they should live. By application, James's words should also encourage us to godly living—in good times and bad, when everything fits and especially when it doesn't.

THE REASON

The goal of James's letter is growth in godliness. James knew, and desired his readers to know, that it is God's wish for every Christian to grow up in Jesus Christ.

I am reminded of our number-one family project in years past. We used to spend weekends each spring and fall planting and tending our vegetable garden. Each Friday when I would return home after a week on tour, teaching Bible classes, one of the first things I would do was walk out to see the garden. My wife Pearl usually commented to our kids, "There goes your father, the city slicker farmer." It was exciting to see small sprouts turn into leafy vines, then blossom, finally to be filled with ripening tomatoes. One week my green beans would be tiny shoots; the next, small tendrils curling up toward the poles I had set. Before too long, we would be picking, stringing, snapping, and freezing them. The growth process was wonderful to watch because there was usually visible progress week to week.

Some seasons though, things did not go so well. My okra bushes withered under the scorching Texas sun; my tomato plants went to vine and never bore blossoms and fruit; my green beans yellowed and played out before season's end. Those times, walking out to the garden was a venture in futility. My hopeful eyes searched for lush green plants and found only unproductive sticks and stalks.

Often I have thought about how many times God comes to his garden and goes away similarly disappointed because He sees so little spiritual growth in those of us who are Christians. How often He searches for healthy vines, for blossoming tendrils, for signs of fruit in our lives, only to find that production is at a standstill. God did not bring us into his family just to give us "pie in the sky by and by." He has designed our lives as believers so that we might grow more and more like his Son *right now*. It is the Father's supreme desire to conform us to the image of Jesus Christ. The Lord wants to pursue a daily maturing process in our lives.

James knew all about that. And he wanted to encourage his readers concerning the whole program of progress God desires for his children. We are going to look closely at his letter, taking an essentially verse-by-verse approach as we examine the text. I am convinced that taking God's word as is, unaltered and in context, is the most effective way to learn about his will.

MARKS OF MATURITY

I believe that the book of James shares with us twelve points for progress, or marks of maturity, characteristic of the Christian life. These dozen guidelines for growth form a framework about which his letter is organized. Here is a preview of the rich wisdom that James, through the inspiration of the Holy Spirit, recorded for us.

TWELVE POINTS FOR PROGRESS

1. The Christian grows taller through testing. God uses the tough times in our lives to produce growth (James 1:1-12).

2. Spiritual growth is stunted by sin. Tests may promote growth, but yielding to temptation paralyzes progress (1:13-18).

3. Growth is produced by reading God's word. The consistent intake and application of scripture causes us to grow spiritually (1:19-27).

4. Our maturity is shown by whether or not we have learned

to love the unlovely. Part of godliness is the capability to care for others without prejudice or partiality (2:1-13).

5. Our faith is dead without deeds. Salvation does not result from works, but if we have the real thing, our faith should be showing itself in our lives (2:14-26).

6. We are to be striving for tongue control. The maturing Christian is one who is increasingly able to tame his or her tongue (3:1-12).

7. The progressing believer should also be growing in good judgment. A person who is manifesting the wisdom from above is growing up in Jesus Christ (3:13-18).

8. Part of the process is lifelong—it is an ongoing war against the big three: the world, the flesh, and the devil. We can count on participating in the fight if we desire to grow up in Christ (4:1-12).

9. Our maturity is reflected in our daily dependence on the designer. Our lives should give evidence of an increasing reliance on the Lord, a gradual yielding of our independent spirits to him (4:13-17).

10. Another indicator of growth is our ability to be discerning about wealth. Although it is not sinful to be rich, it is sinful for a Christian to have much yet not use it properly, for God's glory. We will eventually be accountable for our bank balances, stock portfolios, and giving (5:1-6).

11. Part of growing in Christ is to have an increasing awareness of his prophetic timetable. The Lord's reappearing is right on schedule, and should be an event we eagerly anticipate as we come to know more of him (5:7-12).

12. A growing Christian is a praying Christian. James exhorts us, as a mark of maturity, to pursue the power of prayer (5:13-20).

There you have them. Twelve points for progress. Twelve marks of maturity.

RUNNING WELL

The other day I found myself angry, depressed, bitter, and resentful toward three Christian brothers I felt had dealt with me unfairly. The details are not important. Let me just say that my reaction to the situation was pathetic.

After stewing and fussing emotionally for a good bit of time, my thoughts and feelings ran the gamut of possible responses. I imagined sweet revenge as giving them a piece of my mind (which I can't afford to lose) or even getting physical and punching out some lights (which at my age could be dangerous). Thank God that He brought me up short.

Sometime ago I made a personal commitment to the Lord that I would not let a day pass without spending some personal quality time in his word, in addition to my regular Bible study and sermon preparation. I longed for the type of rich relationship with God that motivated the prophet Jeremiah to write:

> When your words came, I ate them;
>> they were my joy and my heart's delight,
> for I bear your name,
>> O Lord God Almighty (Jeremiah 15:16 NIV).

As I finally turned to the scriptures after fuming about the episode with the three men, two passages ministered to me and helped to set right my orientation. Both deal with Christ's silence before his accusers:

> He was oppressed and afflicted,
>> yet he did not open his mouth;
> he was led like a lamb to the slaughter,
>> and as a sheep before her shearers is silent,
> so he did not open his mouth (Isaiah 53:7 NIV).

> And the high priest stood up and said to Him, "Do You make no answer? What is it that these men are testifying against You?" But Jesus kept silent. And the high priest said to Him, "I adjure You by the living God, that You tell us whether You are the Christ, the Son of God." Jesus said to him, "You have said it yourself; nevertheless I tell you, hereafter you shall see the Son of Man sitting at the right hand of Power, and coming on the clouds of heaven." Then the high priest tore his robes, saying, "He has blasphemed! What further need do we have of witnesses?

> Behold, you have now heard the blasphemy; what do you think?" They answered and said, "He is deserving of death!" (Matthew 26:62-66 NASB).

Okay, God's word had spoken. What was I going to do with my bitterness and resentment? Was I going to do what I wanted to do, or was I going to follow Proverbs 3:5-6?

> Trust in the Lord with all your heart
> > and lean not on your own understanding;
> in all your ways acknowledge him,
> > and he will make your paths straight (NIV).

And in the crucible, could I afford to ignore the wisdom of Hebrews 12:14-15?

> Pursue peace with all men, and the sanctification without which no one will see the Lord. See to it that no one comes short of the grace of God; that no root of bitterness springing up causes trouble, and by it many be defiled (NASB).

The choice I was to make touched on all the issues treated in the epistle of James. I realized that God was using the experience of trial for my personal character development. It was a temptation to do the wrong thing. I would receive a blessing from the situation only if I pursued the path of obedience to his word. The Lord was giving me an opportunity to learn to love the unlovely. The fruit of my faith would be demonstrated in my response. My tongue was going to fail me, if the Spirit of God did not control it. I had the option of choosing to follow the wisdom from above, or that from below. The big three—the world, the flesh, and the devil—were waiting in the wings screaming at me, "Nail them. Let them have it. You're right; they're wrong. They deserve what they get." I knew I had to depend on the Lord to handle the circumstances. I knew I couldn't buy my way out of the trouble. How important was it all, anyway, in view of his imminent reappearing? Could I pursue the power of prayer, starting with that of the Lord Jesus on the cross, "Father, forgive them, for they are not knowing what they are doing"?

What joy and peace flooded my soul as I saw the situation

from God's perspective. I thought of the hundreds who surround us daily with the Lord's love, affirmation, and support. Besides, what could I learn from the words and opinions of those three who had disagreed with me? What lessons could the episode teach?

Satan loves to see us so depressed and defeated over little irritations that we forget the big picture. I realized I am one of those people who wants everything just right—and it won't be like that until we get to glory. Bitterness gone, I soon found myself singing Bill Gaither's song, "We Are So Blessed." I hope you'll feel the same way when you get through with this study on James.

> We are so blessed,
> By the gifts from Your hand,
> Just can't understand
> Why You loved us so much.
>
> We are so blessed,
> We just can't find our way,
> Or the words that can say
> Thank You Lord for Your touch.
>
> When we're empty,
> You fill us
> 'Til we overflow,
> And when we're hungry
> You feed us and cause us to know
>
> That we are so blessed,
> Take what we have to bring.
> Take it all, everything,
> Lord, we love You so much.
>
> We are so blessed,
> Take what we have to bring.
> Take it all, everything,
> Lord, we bring it to You.

1

Gut-check Christianity

James 1:1-12

The sweat-soaked jersey clings to his body like a moist second skin. His well-muscled arms glisten with slippery wetness. Streams of salt water pour off his forehead and face, running down his neck and back. The glare of the lights suspended above reflects off the highly polished wooden floor and forms a tiny sliver of light partly encircling the orange rim facing him. The ringing slap of leather against hardwood echoes throughout the hushed arena as he dribbles the ball once. Twice. Eyes unblinking, fixed on the hoop, mind replaying a video of the perfect arching trajectory of free throws past, he cradles the ball loosely in his hands till it feels just right against his fingertips. He mentally freezes out the sights, sounds, and smells of the packed auditorium and its people pressing in hungry and close. He stares straight ahead and up, forgetting the six men whose eyes are attuned to his slightest move as they watch the ball in his hands. Dots of light coalesce on the game clock to show fourth period, 00.02—two seconds left, score tied. A free throw wins it.

He draws a deep breath, exhales. Can he do it? Does he have what it takes? Will he come through in the clutch or will he choke? Gut-check time. Time to reach inside to see if you have the right stuff. Time to give it all you've got. The last ounce of energy, accuracy, willpower. The last shred of courage and ability. The skill and performance honed in years of disciplined practice. With a quick upward thrust and snap of the wrist, the ball sails toward the rim.

Gut-check times come for Christians too.

Heartaches, headaches, hassles are everyday things with us. Raindrops keep falling on our heads, as B. J. Thomas sang. Sometimes the raging floodwaters of trial rise so high that we think survival is impossible. "It's too much!" we cry. "Lord, stop it!" Those are the gut-check times.

Trials and tests take a measure of us. To make it through and to learn from them, we have to reach deep inside, but not for some magical untapped power or ability of our own. Gut-check time in the Christian life is a spiritual exercise. We have to dig down for the courage to lean on the God who can conquer for us. The Lord gives us the winner's edge. In the game of life, staying by the stuff means staying by the Savior.

SHAPING UP

Staying in shape physically has always been important to me. I've done it by playing high school and college sports. Through the years, being involved in Christian camping has also helped: hiking, skiing, swimming, horseback riding, and climbing are good for keeping trim. But when middle age came on, things changed, particularly my mid-section, so I took up running. Now an arthritic hip has made my doctors see red, and I no longer run to keep fit. I cycle, which makes the doctors, my hip, and my wife Pearl a whole lot happier.

Why do I want to stay in shape physically? There are many reasons. I want to live a long, healthy life, and exercise helps that. I have never thought that heart attacks sounded like fun, and I realize the importance of cardiovascular workouts as prevention. Perhaps the main reason is that I want to be able to keep up a busy schedule of ministry: teaching, preaching, counseling, writing, conference speaking, and serving others. Sweat plus strain equals strength. I can't be constructively involved in the lives of other people if I am always flat on my back, physically exhausted because of my schedule. Keeping in shape gives me more energy and, I'm convinced, makes me less susceptible to sickness. Shaping up is a key to keeping on keeping on in the daily grind.

But what about when the daily grind turns vicious?

What about when the pieces don't fit? When our worlds crumble? When, unprobable winners at best, we face the impossible? Cancer strikes. The plant closes. The corporation squeezes us out two years before retirement. A car accident claims the life of a precious son. Alzheimer's drains away the mind of a once-bright loved one. Those major disasters sap our strength. So do the little, everyday garden variety ones: leaky plumbing, dead batteries, smart-aleck kids, project deadlines. The list could go on and on. When enough of the "minor" problems hit at once, life can seem just as hopeless and broken as when we face a crisis.

When the hassles become too heavy to handle, it's gut-check time. To be ready for it, we have to stay in shape spiritually, and shaping up spiritually means growing up in Jesus Christ. James gave us the signs of this growth in his letter.

How tough it can be to tackle the test. How often we fail. How little, sometimes, we find that our spiritual survival skills have grown. Our ability to cope seems to have hit rock bottom. Instead of the wings of eagles, we find ourselves with feet of clay. But that shouldn't be surprising. The problem of growing up in Christ is a universal one. The writers of the New Testament tried to spur their readers to spiritual maturity, just as they desired that for themselves. The apostle Paul put it this way in Philippians 3:13-14:

> Brethren, I do not regard myself as having laid hold of it yet; but one thing I do: forgetting what lies behind and reaching forward to what lies ahead, I press on toward the goal for the prize of the upward call of God in Christ Jesus (NASB).

As Paul indicated, there is a sense of urgency in the heart of a Christian who genuinely longs to get into spiritual shape. To grow up in Christ Jesus should be a burning desire of our hearts, a tangible goal of our lives.

Why should we want to mature? I think of my garden again. Why should I want my radish plants to mature? It's so they can be productive. Believers in Christ should want to grow up in their faith so they can bear fruit in the lives of others. A growing process must be in progress in our lives before God will use us to our fullest potential.

Don't misunderstand. I am not saying that the Lord never uses immature believers to work his will. Sometimes baby believers are the most effective witnesses for the kingdom. Occasionally, even Christians who aren't poring into God's word, who aren't deeply concerned with making spiritual progress, who don't thirst for Jesus to change their lives, may still be used by God. God uses whom He chooses. But the scriptural attitude toward lukewarmness is not kind. Jesus said of the believers in Laodicea, "I know your deeds, that you are neither cold nor hot; I would that you were cold or hot. So because you are lukewarm, and neither hot nor cold, I will spit you out of My mouth" (Revelation 3:15-16 NASB). Literally, spiritual lukewarmness makes the Lord want to vomit.

The truth, as we see it from scripture and experience, is that the men and women most greatly used by God are often those who are not lukewarm, but who are growing up in him: Abraham, Jacob, Joseph, Moses, David, Peter, Paul, and the list goes on. Notice, I did not say those who are *grown up*, but those who *are growing up*. Christians who are willing works-in-progress in the hands of the master are often those who accomplish the most for the kingdom. These are believers who want to shape up spiritually, who want him to shape them up.

What joy there is in being shaped up. In serving him. Paul knew it, as he let God transform him from persecutor to preacher. Peter knew it, as God took a rough, tough, two-fisted fisherman and turned him into a dynamic leader. John knew it, as God changed him from a hot-tempered son of thunder into an apostle of love.

LIFE IN THE PRESSURE COOKER

At 8:31 on the warm, hazy morning of August 31, 1988, Delta flight 1141 took off from Dallas-Fort Worth International en route to Salt Lake City. When the plane was only thirty feet above the runway, three backfiring noises alarmed passengers and crew. A burst of flame exploded in the left engine, followed by a sudden stall. Pilot Larry Davis and crew were forced to make an extraordinary emergency landing, skidding some 1,000 feet down the runway as the jet hit the ground on its right wing and snapped open in two places. Tragically, thirteen people were killed in the fire that followed, but experts agree that much worse devastation was averted by the quick thinking and actions of the pilots and crew. Shocked at hearing of the disaster, I wrote to Larry, who is a friend from our Bible class in Greenville, Texas.

The aftermath of the fiery crash had brought with it a blazing inferno of a different kind: a firestorm of investigations, meetings with attorneys, interviews, news reports. The pressure was intense. But Larry is a special man, a committed Christian, a survivor. It was a challenge and blessing to see him grow spiritually in those darkest of hours. As Larry put it in a recent letter, God is making "me realize I must place my full confidence in him if I am going to survive."

Part of God's plan for growing us up in Jesus Christ is to permit tests and trials to enter our lives. Life in the pressure cooker has a way of boiling away the fat, waste and superficiality. It can reveal, and increase, the depth of our commitment to Christ. In the pressure cooker is where Larry Davis still is at the moment. And it is where we find the Jewish Christians to whom James wrote his letter.

I mentioned in the introduction that the epistle was intended for the Hebrew Christians who had been persecuted and scattered throughout the Roman empire. Those Jewish believers were displaced persons, rejected by their relatives for their new-found faith, distrusted by the Roman authorities because of their worship of a heavenly king rather than Caesar. Many of James's readers were homeless, jobless, without possessions or property, forced to make new starts in strange lands. They knew what it meant to suffer. Life in the pressure cooker was real to them. Trials and tests were chronic.

To those sufferers, James, under the inspiration of the Holy Spirit, penned a message of hope and a challenge to persist in faith in the midst of it all. He provided them with twelve pointers for progress, for surviving and soaring in the Christian life, beginning with an exhortation to persevere with patience.

His words ought to hit home with all of us. Like the Christians of A.D. 45, we too face our shares of hassles. We are seldom lifelong strangers to hardship. Tough times eventually hit us.

The principle of Christian growth that James stressed is this: *We grow taller through testing.* Don't forget, pointers for progress become practical only when they are actually applied to our lives. Let's turn now to James and see what he had to say. For the purposes of this book, we will be using my personal translation of the Greek text. I hope you will compare it with your own Bible.

THE LETTERHEAD—JAMES 1:1

> James, a bondslave of God and the Lord Jesus Christ, to the twelve tribes, those in dispersion, be rejoicing.

Most businessmen I know correspond on letterhead. Along with corporate logos, their titles are displayed prominently at the top of page one: executive vice president, director of marketing, managing partner. James started off his letter with his credentials too, although they are not what we might expect.

His credentials? Like Paul in his letter to Titus, James began by identifying himself as the "bondslave of God and the Lord Jesus Christ." He was, by his own admission, the property of another, a slave of Christ. When you stop and think about it, his words are pretty amazing.

James, remember, was the earthly half-brother of Jesus Christ. They had grown up together. James had spent more time with Jesus than most people, over thirty years in the same family. Wouldn't that information have been impressive to some of the believers to whom he was writing? People are generally more concerned with whom we know than what we know—and James humanly knew the Lord more intimately than any of his readers. He could have played on the ties of brotherhood to wow his audience, but he didn't.

James was also a respected leader in the early church. Eventually he would preside over the debate on circumcision in the Jerusalem council (see Acts 15). The apostles paid attention to him. Like E. F. Hutton, when he spoke, people listened. But he still called himself the bondslave of God.

If I had been writing the letter, I would have been tempted to begin by referring to myself as something like "The Right Reverend Bishop James, the brother of Jesus Christ, God's Son." I would want my readers to know I had a right to speak. I would want them to be aware that I was a SVIP, a SPIRITUALLY

VERY IMPORTANT PERSON. I wouldn't want anyone asking, "James *who*?" I would mention every degree, honorary and earned. I would play up my family tree for all it was worth.

But James didn't start off that way.

Instead he humbly called himself a "bondslave" of the Lord Jesus Christ, giving Jesus his entire messianic title. James had no question about the deity of Christ. He knew that Jesus was God's Son. He knew, as Paul did, that all things in his own life were "loss in view of the surpassing value of knowing Christ Jesus" (Philippians 3:8a NASB). So James began his epistle with honest humility. His words reflected his conclusions about life. This term *bondslave* conveys at least three ideas.

1. *Absolute obedience*—the slave in the Roman empire had no choice except to obey his master. Working the will of the master was a way of life.

2. *Absolute brokenness and humility*—there were few opportunities to get puffed up as a bondslave. Total obedience demanded total submission.

3. *Absolute loyalty*—there could be no equivocating; the slave had to look out for the interests of his master. No double-crosses, no divided attention, no mixed loyalties. The commitment had to be complete.

Obedient. Broken. Loyal. Such adjectives are not what I would have chosen for myself when opening a letter to a huge group of men and women, many of whom I had probably never met. What about you? James desired the focus to be on the master.

Just the fact that James was totally convinced of Christ's deity is tremendous evidence of the truth of it. No one knows your weaknesses and shortcomings better than a member of your own family. Yet James, one of the people closest to the Lord, recognized that Jesus is God.

Notice also that James exhorted his readers to "be rejoicing." He explained this command in the verses that follow.

THE JOY DIRECTIVE—JAMES 1:2-3

> Deem it pure joy, my brethren, whenever you fall into various kinds of trials, knowing that the testing of your faith is producing endurance [patience].

How do you respond in the gut-check times of life? When the hurt is so real and so heavy that you can't stand it? When the walls close in? James started his letter by telling us how to respond. His words are tough medicine, hard to swallow. They run contrary to what we think we really want.

A trial or test is an experience allowed by a sovereign God to enter our lives to measure our progress toward Christlikeness, or to hasten the development of Christlike character in us. If we are not believers, trials often come to nudge us toward belief. If we are believers, they come to grow us up. Remember the principle: We grow taller through testing.

The other evening while driving home I jokingly said to my wife, "Honey, guess what? We are working on a manuscript on James." Her sigh and statement nearly made me drive off the road: "Lord, help us all! You know whenever you preach on James, we *always* get to practice it. When will you ever learn?" It's true. Opportunities to practice what we preach do increase as the Lord works his message in our lives before we proclaim it to others. Pearl and I are no strangers to the gut-check times.

What does God want from us when things get tough? James says we are to consider it "pure joy . . . whenever [we] fall into various kinds of trials" (1:2). Note the word *whenever*. Not *if*, but *whenever*. Trouble is inevitable. It will happen to us, although we belong to Christ. Remember, James was writing to Christians. Tough times are unavoidable, even though the modern trend in the church is to present the abundant life in Jesus as a fun-packed adventure, guaranteeing health, wealth, and prosperity. This is what J. I. Packer called "hot tub religion":

> The hot tub experience is sensuous, relaxing, floppy, laid-back: not in any way demanding, whether intellectually or otherwise, but very, very nice, even to the point of being *great fun*. . . . Many today want Christianity to be like that, and labor to make it so. The ultimate step, of course, would be to clear church auditoriums of seats and install hot tubs in their place; then there would never be any attendance problems (Packer 69).

God never promises that the Christian life is floppy, laid-back, and undemanding. His directive is that in the midst of trouble, we consider each heartache and trial to be pure joy.

REAL JOY

What does it mean to deem trials and tests pure joy? First of all, let me tell you what it does not mean. It does not mean that when tough times hit, we plaster Cheshire cat smiles on our faces and show everyone how spiritual we are by holding back the tears. God doesn't expect us to exclaim cheerfully, "Oh, good! I lost my job. My teenage daughter is pregnant. My mother has Parkinson's disease. My husband is seeing another woman. I am *sooo* happy!" God doesn't desire us to display hypocritical happy faces, masks disguising our hurt, questions, rage, and emptiness. He isn't looking for steel-clad saints who refuse to feel, who deny their sorrows, who never own up to their struggles.

He *is* looking for us to reach the point in our walk with him where we can have joy in the midst of the fiery furnace, financial disaster, debilitating illness, family tragedy. The joy isn't a show of phony bravado or fake happiness. It is a genuine peace, a right attitude, a heart of contentment, an honest submission to the Father's purpose and plan. It requires total trust in what He is doing in our lives. It is the joy of expectation and anticipation regarding the outcome. It is the confidence in what Paul affirmed: "For I consider that the sufferings of this present time are not worthy to be compared with the glory that is to be revealed to us" (Romans 8:18 NASB).

Joy is past as we experience sin's forgiveness.

Joy is present as we sacrificially serve and give of ourselves to others.

Joy is future as we eagerly anticipate what is in store.

Real joy is the result of what is on the inside; it has nothing to do with what is happening on the outside. Real joy can be found only in Christ, and not in our circumstances. In the words of Jude, "Now to Him who is able to keep you from stumbling, and to make you stand in the presence of His glory blameless with joy" (Jude 24 NASB). Jesus said, "These things I have spoken to you, that My joy may be in you, and that your joy may be made full" (John 15:11 NASB).

Notice that James told us to deem it pure, unmixed, unadulterated joy when we "fall into various kinds of trials." Some versions translate the term *fall into* as "face" or "encounter" (NIV, NASB), but "fall into" is more accurate. The original word is the same one Jesus used when He described the parable of the good Samaritan. You know the story: A man walking along *falls among* thieves and robbers who strip him and leave him half dead (Luke 10:30). We too fall among trials and troubles. They surround, envelop, pummel, and pound us. They draw blood and tears. James was not telling us to be joyous *for* those trials, but to be joyful *as* we fall into them. There is a major difference. Like Paul, he was exhorting us to be joyful *in* the trials, "in everything [giving] thanks; for this is God's will for you in Christ Jesus" (1 Thessalonians 5:18 NASB).

WHY THE CRUCIBLE?

How do we do it? How can we be joyful in the midst of hassles, pain, and sorrows? In order to understand the *how* of it all, we must look at what the Bible tells us about suffering. Many of us have no idea why bad things happen to good people. Those who are not believers argue that if a loving God exists, He would never allow the human horrors—war, starvation, rape, murder, injustice—that we see splattered across the television screen each evening on the nightly news.

Even those of us who are Christians may not understand suffering. Trained by our culture and the modern "prosperity gospel" to expect to have our cake and eat it too, we are confused when we enter the crucible, when we share in sorrow. We question the Lord's wisdom. We wonder what we have done to deserve his disfavor. We feel abandoned. We assume that Satan has gotten the upper hand, and his demons are at work. God is surely not the author of *this*.

Do we ever think that God must be mad at us when we get knocked to the canvas a few times? What about when suffering happens to someone else, particularly another Christian? How easy it is to assume they have done something wrong. The Lord is mad at them. He has zapped them. They are getting what they deserve. A divorce? You must have failed to be a godly husband or wife. God is going to let you have it. You have been compromising; now he is reaching down to mash you. Oh, we may not say it, but sometimes we think it. In the Old Testament, Job's friends surely did.

Remember the story? Within a matter of minutes, the godly Job lost his livestock, property, and fortune. Worse than that by far, his beloved children were killed as the home of his eldest son collapsed. Soon Job also fell victim to a devastating disease that ravaged his body. Three friends came to comfort him. The three started out fine, but then began to question Job about what he might have done to deserve such judgment. "Examine yourself!" they cried. "Where have you sinned? Confess it. Get things straightened out with God and the bad stuff will all go away."

The fact is, the *why* of the matter had nothing to do with Job's unfaithfulness, and had everything to do with his unwavering trust in God almighty. The trials were permitted by God for his own purposes and for his glory. Job's trust in the midst of it all served as a sharp rebuke to Satan. And eventually, Job received blessings. In this case, it was a second family and increased possessions. It was also a lesson learned well about the faithfulness of a God who cares and who is always there (see Job 42:10).

> Because of the Lord's great love we are not consumed,
> for his compassions never fail.
> They are new every morning;
> great is your faithfulness
> (Lamentations 3:22-23 NIV).

How easy it is for us, like Job's comforters, to assume that our Christian friends are suffering because of some unconfessed sin in their lives. God is spanking them (or us). He is applying the board of education to the seat of knowledge to draw us up short. He is giving us a good licking because He feels we need it. Let us never reduce God to the level of some unflinching, unloving disciplinarian. He is no prison camp commandant. He is a heavenly Father. Satan is a defeated foe who will ultimately fall before God's sovereign purpose—even when that purpose involves our personal trials.

So, why does God allow suffering in our lives? Why do "bad" things happen to "good" people?

It is because a sovereign God knows what is necessary to bring into our lives to grow us up in Jesus Christ. Trials don't come simply because the Lord is unhappy with our behavior.

They come because He desires us to become spiritually mature. In John 15, Jesus spoke of himself as a vine and of us who know him by faith as the branches. Any gardener worth his green thumb can tell you that in order for branches to bear sufficient fruit, they must be pruned. When we as Christians get our branches nipped through trials, it smarts. But it also causes us to bear fruit for Christ. We can have joy in the midst of trial because each trouble, each heartache, comes with the Father's intention of pruning us. We should rejoice in the fact that He is not through with us yet. Indeed, the troubles we encounter should convince us of that.

We Christians can legitimately rejoice in difficulties because they prove that God is still working in our lives. My wife Pearl put it this way in an article she wrote years ago:

> At the times in my life when I seem to reach a new level of spiritual commitment, I think the Lord is going to reach out and tap me on the back and say, "Well, isn't that sweet? Now let's just go on. I'll bless you more." Instead, when I reach that level of new commitment, the Lord reaches out and touches me because He realizes that I am at a level of new productivity. So He orders new trials and events in my life to produce greater fruit and quality.

Isn't that going the way of the cross? Why should we be scared of it? God will never order a trial in our lives without sustaining us through it. Remember that He took the three Hebrew men *through* the fiery furnace, not around it (see Daniel 3:19ff). When trials come, the Lord desires to increase our trust in his ability to handle the circumstances in our lives.

Leonard and Sandy Wells are in the congregation at Hide-A-Way Lake Community Church. A motorcycle accident left their nineteen-year-old son Marty unconscious. Now bills are mounting and Marty is making excruciatingly slow progress. Leonard and Sandy's entire future has been affected by this tragedy. Leonard said it well, and I love him for it, "I guess we are just going to have to dig a little deeper." There was no bitter outcry toward God, no "Poor me!" or "Why me?"—just a recognition of the need to draw more deeply on the resources in Christ that are available to us at a time like this. Sandy shared that the scriptures are coming alive to her, and she is seeing things in the word through new eyes. Marty's condition hasn't changed much through these many weeks, but Leonard and Sandy have, and sometimes that is God's whole purpose.

SUFFERING 101 IN THE DIVINE CURRICULUM

Are you still not convinced that God permits troubles and trials in our lives? Do you realize that permitting them is his sovereign prerogative? Do you still doubt that trials can work for our ultimate good? To some degree or other, Suffering 101 becomes part of the divine curriculum for every believer. Look at what other sections of scripture tell us about the presence and purpose of trial:

> Sorrow is better than laughter,
>> because a sad face is good for the heart
>> (Ecclesiastes 7:3 NIV).

> Although the Lord gives you the bread of adversity and the water of affliction, your teachers will be hidden no more; with your own eyes you will see them. Whether you turn to the right or to the left, your ears will hear a voice behind you, saying, "This is the way; walk in it" (Isaiah 30:20-21 NIV).

> When you pass through the waters,
>> I will be with you;
> and when you pass through the rivers,
>> they will not sweep over you.
> When you walk through the fire,
>> you will not be burned;
>> the flames will not set you ablaze.
> For I am the Lord, your God,
>> the Holy One of Israel, your Savior
>> (Isaiah 43:2-3 NIV).

> I know, O Lord, that your laws are righteous,
>> and in faithfulness you have afflicted me
>> (Psalm 119:75 NIV).

> A righteous man may have many troubles,
>> but the Lord delivers him from them all
>> (Psalm 34:19 NIV).

> "Have pity on me, my friends, have pity,
>   for the hand of God has struck me"
>   (Job 19:21 NIV).

> But he knows the way that I take;
>   when he has tested me, I will come forth as
>   gold (Job 23:10 NIV).

> Furthermore, we had earthly fathers to discipline us, and
> we respected them; shall we not much rather be subject
> to the Father of spirits, and live? For they disciplined us
> for a short time as seemed best to them, but He disci-
> plines us for our good, that we may share His holiness
> (Hebrews 12:9-10 NASB).

> Beloved, do not be surprised at the fiery ordeal among
> you, which comes upon you for your testing, as though
> some strange thing were happening to you; but to the
> degree that you share the sufferings of Christ, keep on
> rejoicing; so that also at the revelation of His glory, you
> may rejoice with exultation (1 Peter 4:12-13 NASB).

> So that no man may be disturbed by these afflictions; for
> you yourselves know that we have been destined for this.
> For indeed when we were with you, we kept telling you
> in advance that we were going to suffer affliction; and so
> it came to pass, as you know (1 Thessalonians 3:3-4
> NASB).

> For to you it has been granted for Christ's sake, not only
> to believe in Him, but also to suffer for His sake (Philip-
> pians 1:29 NASB; see also Colossians 1:24; Revelation 2:10).

The united testimony of these verses is that a loving God has
the prerogative to do what He deems necessary in our lives to
accomplish his ultimate objective, which is to make us more
like his Son. What happens to us is Father-filtered. It comes
for his glory and with his goal, our good, in mind. Nothing
catches God by surprise. Things may hit us on the blind side,
but they are known beforehand by the Lord. To paraphrase
Andrew Murray, when we experience difficulty, we should
remember who brought us here.

Drawing further from the ideas of Murray, this is what the

process entails when you're suffering, when the wheels have fallen off, when the wagon has flipped.

1. Remember it is by God's will that you are in this situation. Rest in that fact.

2. Realize that He is going to keep you in his love and give you the grace to behave as his child in the midst of the difficulty.

3. He is going to make the trial a blessing, teaching you lessons that He intends you to learn, working in you his grace.

4. He is going to bring you out of the trial eventually. The results may not be what you expect. His methods may be surprising. But inevitably there will be an exit.

IN TRAINING

We can joy in the fact that trials and tests show us that God is not through with us yet. We can also rejoice in the truth that the suffering, designed by a loving Father, is doing a good work in us. It is increasing our ability to endure it. James put it this way in 1:3, "The testing of your faith is producing endurance [patience]."

Believers are spiritual athletes in training. Think of how serious athletes treat their bodies, and you'll get the picture. The stress athletes put their bodies under is incredible. Pumping iron, swimming, running laps, sticking to special diets—each facet in a training program is geared toward developing the athlete's body to its maximum potential.

I remember a Bible class that one of the Dallas Cowboys attended. The man was a mountain of muscle. He was enormous. I told a joke that tickled him, and in his laughter he reached over and slapped his wife on the leg. He didn't mean to hurt her, but she just about went through the floor. He didn't know his own strength. That strength, that power, that physical brawn, was a direct result of his regimen of training. His disciplined life produced a tremendous specimen of tough humanity. He was ready to do battle on the football field.

Like that pro-football player, stressful circumstances can toughen us. They increase our endurance as we move through life. God designs the tests with consideration for our capacity to take them. He will never overload us. He will not exceed our limits, and we cannot exceed his. Paul said, "And He has said to me, 'My grace is sufficient for you, for power is perfected in weakness.' Most gladly, therefore, I will rather boast about my weaknesses, that the power of Christ may dwell in me" (2 Corinthians 12:9 NASB).

Often when we are being wrung through the wringer, we pray desperately that the Lord will change our circumstances. Sometimes that happens. But more often, God desires to change us through the circumstances. He does not design our lives necessarily to be calm, comfortable, materially prosperous, problem free. He does design them to enable us to grow. Just as I prepare the soil before planting my garden each spring, the Lord creates the perfect environment for our maximum growth and productivity.

To grow taller through testing—it can be done. And with the concept comes a responsibility, as we will see in the rest of the passage. How does God use tests and trials to change us? Let's read on and see.

THE RESPONSIBILITIES—JAMES 1:4-8

> But let patience be having its complete work in order that you may be fully developed and complete, lacking in nothing. And if any of you is deficient in wisdom, let him keep on asking from God who is giving to all generously [without reserve], and who does not reproach, and it shall be given him. But let him be asking in faith, without any doubting, for the one who is doubting is like the surf of the sea, moved and tossed by the wind. For let not that man be supposing that he shall receive anything from the Lord. A double-minded man is unstable in all his ways.

What are our responsibilities in the process of trial and testing? The first is to realize the truth of James 1:4: "But let patience be having its complete work in order that you may be fully developed and complete, lacking in nothing." James was exhorting us not to rebel against the circumstances, but to allow the testing process to go on to completion so that we will receive the maximum benefit of a particular circumstance at a particular time.

Convinced of God's word, challenged by prayer, the prophet

Elijah came courageously into the presence of wicked King Ahab, then ruler of Israel, with a message straight from the Lord that there would be neither dew nor rain in the land for the next few years (1 Kings 17:1 NIV).

Following that brief moment in the spotlight, Elijah followed God's orders and fled to the brook Kerith (Cherith). There, God had promised to provide him water from the brook and food specially delivered by ravens. That was fine for a while, but then something unexpected happened. The brook dried up. What did Elijah do? He sat there. The stream of water became steadily smaller each day. Soon there were only puddles. Still he sat. He had no marching orders, so he waited on God until the creek was bone dry. I would have been tempted to leave sooner, but not Elijah. He knew that lessons were to be learned in a drying brook. This was a test, and in patiently waiting it out, learning all he could learn, he passed with flying colors. In the nick of time, the orders came through: Go to Zarephath and find a widow there. She will have only a handful of flour and a little oil, but it will be enough, because I have commanded her to feed you. And it was enough. The widow's jar of flour and jug of oil never ceased to produce (see 1 Kings 17:1ff).

Sometimes we have to wait on God, as Elijah did, to finish the test. It may take months or even years for the Lord to complete the process of testing a particular area of our lives to teach us what He wants us to know. It took him years, for example, to convince me that my hopes and aspirations for my children were basically selfish. Was that a hard one to learn!

I used to think that the perfect Christian home was one in which the sons went into the ministry and the daughters married missionaries. If seminary was good enough for Dad, it was good enough for the boys, right? To realize that Bobby and Andy were not inclined toward fulltime ministry, although they both love the Lord, was traumatic for me. I had the hardest time trusting that God knew what He was doing. Finally, after years of wrestling with reality, I was convinced that I had been wrong to doubt God. Bobby is in engineering; Andy, in medicine. They love their respective careers and are good representatives of Christ in the secular world. We need to keep our fingers out of things and let God work.

No Pain, No Gain

My daughter Julea tells me that Jane Fonda encourages those who exercise to her aerobic videotapes to "Make it burn!" "No pain, no gain" is the philosophy. Growth, whether physical or spiritual, in the life of any individual is going to mean change, and change often brings pain. It was painful for me to come to the realization that my sons were not going to be preachers (although God graciously gave me a son-in-law who is). The problem was not Bobby's or Andy's or God's; it was mine. But the "pain equals gain" principle still rang true.

It is essential that we realize the place of pain in the process of spiritual growth, and that we are willing to learn all that God has for us to learn anyway. Growing up in Christ is no gravy train to glory, but it is the most worthwhile goal I know.

But how can we make it? What should we ask for when we're up against the wall?

James gave us a clue in 1:5. When we are in the crucible, we shouldn't necessarily pray for God to change the circumstances, because we need to learn all that He would have us to learn before it is all over.

Getting the Big Picture

God's wisdom is perhaps the single, greatest tool for growth we Christians need in the midst of human suffering. That wisdom enables us to know what God is trying to do in our lives. In the midst of trial we need to know God's purposes as much as possible. We need to know where He desires to direct us. As we are willing to open up, He will give us the wisdom we need. We may never know the reasons why certain things happen, at least not until we get to glory, but we can know the route to go to pass the test.

Paul wrote: "For now we see in a mirror dimly, but then face to face; now I know in part, but then I shall know fully just as I also have been fully known" (1 Corinthians 13:12 NASB). Someday we will have all the answers. For now, the lens is fuzzy. Some reasons for the crucible won't be made perfectly clear, and we must accept it. Just jot down your questions in a notebook and when you get to heaven and sit in on the great Bible study in the sky, you can ask the Lord, Why the meningitis? Why the car accident? Why the break-in? Why the stock market crash? The reasons will become obvious. We will wonder why we didn't figure it out down here. We will marvel at the wisdom behind it all. We will know that everything which happened to us was totally consistent with God's love and character.

When we ask the Lord for wisdom, we are opening our lives to learn about the overall perspective. Many Christians don't grow to maturity in Jesus Christ because they fail to seek the big picture. Instead they allow trials to make them bitter. Why did God give me such a crummy deal? Here I am, one of his choice children. I've been a faithful Sunday school teacher. I've given my money. I've witnessed for Jesus. Now God reaches down and squashes me. My hopes, my dreams, are dashed. I don't deserve it. And frankly, Lord, I'm angry.

Such feelings are natural. They shouldn't be suppressed, but they also shouldn't be allowed to fester. The problem is that many people never get past them. They never look to the immensity of a God who is working all things together for good for them that love him, as Romans 8:28 says. It is usually wrong to isolate an event in our lives and form a judgment against God in light of that event. We have no right to an opinion until all the facts are in.

Right now, many of us who have been Dallas Cowboys fans for years are still shell-shocked by the firing of Tom Landry. The man is a legend, the only coach in the team's twenty-nine-year history, a producer of Super Bowl champions. Landry is also universally respected for his controlled demeanor and solid character. Committed to Jesus Christ, Coach Landry's actions on and off the field are honoring to God. It seems grossly unfair that the team's new owners would replace him so abruptly.

Before we become too riled up about Landry's treatment, let's remember something. We see through a tiny knothole in the wooden barricade. God sees the whole picture beyond. He knows the construction that is taking place in Coach Landry's life. He knows what new opportunities for even greater ministry will open up now that the coach is free of the Cowboys. May God give us the wisdom to have wide-angle lenses—or to wait on him to reveal his plan before we become angry or frustrated.

As Christians we will face human sorrow. We will be tempted to rail at God for it. But we will never be wrong to trust the Lord and wait for him to vindicate himself (see Psalm 27:14).

ASKING IN FAITH—NOT ON A ROLLERCOASTER

How do we ask God for wisdom in the midst of challenging circumstances? When we ask for wisdom, we must ask in faith, not doubting that God can and will give it to us (1:6). We may first have to ask him for faith! But that will come.

Ever ridden on a rollercoaster? I have. My son Andy talked me into going on the Shock Wave, billed as the largest double-loop rollercoaster in the world. I should have known better. I did know better as we hit the first loop and I lost my keys and glasses, but by then it was too late. What a ride. Incredible heights followed by sheer drops, dips, dives, and belly-flopping twists. The giddy ups and crashing downs of a rollercoaster resemble some people's faith—exultant and energetic in the good times, rock-bottom in the bad.

There is no place for rollercoaster Christianity in the midst of suffering. Some believers find it easy to be thankful and trusting when their kids are healthy, their mortgages are paid, their cars are either running well or still under warranty. They crest the heights on the rollercoaster. When the bottom drops out, their faith hits the ground. James urged consistency. When we come to the Lord and ask for wisdom, we must not doubt his goodness, mercy, and power. When things are bad, we must come to him with the same confidence, the same trust, that we had when things were smooth and easy.

I speak from experience. I remember a particularly devastating time in our family. After she had battled severe diabetes for years, our daughter Becky began to experience one of the disease's dreaded side effects: kidney failure. Watching Becky suffer through dialysis, my faith in God concerning her condition started a slow decline. Thankfully, Becky was accepted into a transplant program at a major Dallas hospital. My trust began to build again.

After months of anxious waiting, a suitable donor organ was found. The doctors and nurses were alerted, the operating room prepared for a transplant. Everything was ready. The only problem was that nobody had bothered to tell Becky about it. When the hospital finally phoned us, it was time to wheel her into surgery. But we were two hours away at our home in Tyler; it was impossible to get Becky to Dallas in time. The organ was given to someone else. Becky's tear-filled eyes were all it took for my faith to crash. The rollercoaster hit rock bottom.

I was having trouble trusting God to see us through. Then He caused me to realize some things. It was almost as if He told me, "Listen, Anderson, can't you trust me? I can handle it. Lean on me. You are already depending on me for your eternal destiny. Can't you trust me for the next twenty-four hours? Can't you trust me with Becky's life?" Talk about rollercoaster faith. But I realized that while I might make a mess, God can make a miracle. I was like a wave of the sea, tossed and turned in every direction, doubting God's goodness and ability to see us through. I realized that I was wrong. In fact, I was the type of man James described as "a double-minded man, unstable in all his ways" (1:8).

The double-minded man is one who asks something of God without faith, who is inclined to lean on himself, to seek wisdom, satisfaction, and strength on his own terms. He desires to pull himself up by his own bootstraps. As admirable as that may be in Hollywood westerns, that attitude doesn't cut it with God, who desires us instead to depend. Double-minded persons have a desire to depend on themselves, but strangely enough they also long to look to God for help. They vacillate between trust and trying to go it alone. They hesitate. Decisions are tough. And godly wisdom will not come until they are ready and willing to depend only on God. Jesus said that no one can serve two masters. We cannot trust the Lord one minute and doubt the next. If we do, it means that our commitment is only half-hearted, and part-time allegiance benefits no one. It does not please God. It does not bring us wisdom.

Today we thank God that Becky eventually received another donor organ and is doing well. And I thank him for what He taught me in the process.

THE GREAT LEVELER—JAMES 1:9-11

> But let the lowly brother be glorying in his high position and let the one who is wealthy [glory] in his humiliation,

because as the flower of the grass, he shall come to an end. For the sun rises with its scorching heat and the grass dries up and its flower falls off and the beauty of its appearance is destroyed, so also the wealthy person will fade away together with his pursuits [projects, undertakings, investments, holdings].

Suffering is the great leveler. It strikes us all in the human family regardless of our position or prominence. Law clerks get cancer, as do high-powered attorneys. The mechanic's father dies, just like the father of the owner of the Rolls Royce in the garage. Babies are born with spina bifida no matter what their parents' bank balances are. Sudden Infant Death Syndrome claims the lives of both rich and poor babies.

The bottom line of human suffering is that we all experience it. In 1:9-11, James gave practical advice on how we can grow taller through testing, regardless of our background or economic status.

When suffering, the poor Christian, the "lowly brother," can "be glorying in his high position" (1:9). The high position is his position in Christ. It refers to his status as righteous in the sight of God the Father because of faith in Jesus Christ as Savior. Nothing can take that away. Poor individuals may not be what they ought to be or wish to be, but after coming to Christ, they are no longer what they were. When faced with a tough situation, the poor can cling to that promise although all else is swept away. No matter how humble our circumstances, we have the promise of the divine presence while we are going through trial and tribulation.

Very often those who are not materially wealthy are spiritually rich. James later referred to this when he wrote, "Listen, my brethren, beloved ones, did not God choose out for himself those who are poor in the world to be rich in faith and heirs of the kingdom which he promised to those who love him?" (2:5). Earthly possessions often cloud the issue. They interfere with our fellowship with God. They demand our attention. They claim our affection. Indeed, if we are wealthy, when the inevitable trials come, our money and property often make things even more complicated. We worry about losing the things we have accumulated. It is very easy to substitute mate-

rial goals for spiritual goals when thin[
used to the cushy life, we tend to think t
our journeys all downhill, the wind at
founded when we discover it doesn't \

James warned that when tough tim[
should glory in their humiliation (1:9)
the fact that they are able to be depend
should comfort prosperous Christian[
happens to their bank balances, God is there to lean on. Cars,
summer homes, yachts, and stock portfolios are all temporal.
The vital, sustaining relationship one can experience with God
is eternal. Yet how easy it is to slip off track, especially if we
have been blessed with much materially.

Well-to-do Christians going through trial often settle for the
secondary. They become super concerned about what's happening to their possessions. They become entangled in main-
taining the status quo, forgetting to focus on the future. The
apostle Paul saw some of his closest followers fall by the wayside when the going got tough. Of one who evidently succumbed to the lure of the material world, he wrote, "Demas,
having loved this present world, has deserted me and gone to
Thessalonica" (2 Timothy 4:10 NASB).

James cautioned that, in the end, wealth will prove temporary. It will all fade away. Money can pay for a fancy funeral,
but it cannot follow us into eternity. When trouble strikes, the
first choice for wealthy Christians should not be the protection
of their possessions, but instead the goal of depending in
humility on the master (see Matthew 6:33).

THE RESULT—JAMES 1:12

> Happy is the man who, being tested, is holding his
> ground because, having been approved, he shall receive
> the crown of life which God has promised to those who
> love him.

We can rejoice in the midst of our trials. We really can! We can
have joy if we understand that God uses difficulty to produce
growth. We can praise him for trouble, because He is working his
will in us. When the screws tighten severely on both sides, we have
no choice but to look up, and so we grow taller through testing.

are the results of growing taller through testing? We
appy if we are holding our ground (1:12). Holding our
ound means not becoming discouraged or depressed. It
means trusting God and not doubting him. It means giving in
to God, waiting on him to finish the process, not giving up on
him. It means deciding that *yes*, the Christian life is worth it.
It means realizing that whatever happens, God has ordered the
circumstances. It means accepting the fact that God is more
interested in conforming us to the image of Christ and developing our character than He is in making us comfortable. It
means accepting the challenge of Paul: "Therefore, my beloved
brethren, be steadfast, immovable, always abounding in the
work of the Lord, knowing that your toil is not in vain in the
Lord" (1 Corinthians 15:58 NASB).

Perhaps you are wondering, What's in it for me if I do all
those things? What do I gain by keeping on when I'd rather
sell out and quit? Remember, James said that the person who
hangs in there in faith will be happy. He or she will also
become more like Christ through it all. And eventually that
man or woman will "receive the crown of life which He
promised to those who love him."

In heaven, rewards will be issued to believers at what is
called the judgment seat of Christ. These rewards will be rep-
resented by crowns. Not every Christian will receive a crown;
some will receive several. According to my friend Earl Radmacher, "The crown is a symbol standing for position and
privilege which we will enjoy in the reign with Jesus Christ to
the extent that we have endured for him in this life." In scripture we find mention of the crown of righteousness (2 Timothy
4:8), the imperishable crown (1 Corinthians 9:25), the crown
of rejoicing (1 Thessalonians 2:19), the crown of glory (1 Peter
5:4), and the crown of life (James 1:12).

Will you receive a crown? Scripture teaches that the answer
is a matter of motivation.

In his first letter to the Corinthians, Paul wrote of two
builders who figuratively build on the foundation of Christ.
The first builds on the foundation with "gold, silver, precious
stones," the second with "wood, hay, straw" (1 Corinthians
3:12). At the judgment seat of Christ, the first believer finds
that his works are pleasing to God; he receives a reward (3:14).

The second believer, although saved because salvation is a gift of God based on faith (Ephesians 2:8-9), receives no reward. His works will be "burned up" (3:15). The principle is clear: what lasts is that which is empowered by God in accordance with his plan and purpose. What will not last is that which we do "in the flesh"—poorly, for our own reasons, under our own power.

Who will receive the crown of life? This crown is given if you have gone through the experience of testing and have hung onto your confidence in God (1:12). You have drained the test experience of all the character you can squeeze out of it. You have begun to learn about life.

Is It Worth It?

Have you ever talked with someone who has suffered a great deal? Has the person become embittered by that suffering? Yes, he has endured it, but his love for God has been lost along the way. He is angry for the raw deal he's been given. I remember such a man. His first wife died of cancer, and he never got over it. It is hard to imagine what is going on inside him now that his present wife also has cancer. He has lived his life for the almighty dollar and he has written off God for allowing the illnesses. The dynamic closeness with Jesus Christ which could be his is missing. It hurts to think of what might have been.

And then there is the opposite, the ones who have become better. Charlie and Marie are such people. Last August a collision proved fatal to their elderly aunt and nearly took Charlie and Marie home, but God spared them. It has been a long tough year of recovery, and it isn't over yet, but I will never forget Marie's tranquility and sweet words in the wake of the disaster. Even in the emergency room, she quoted Romans 8:28, "And we know that God causes all things to work together for good to those who love God, to those who are called according to his purpose" (NASB). God has worked. He is working. He will continue to work until his purpose is accomplished. Already we have seen evidence of his hand. Through the ordeal, Charlie and Marie's son professed faith in Jesus Christ.

Is it worth it? Yes, in the light of eternity. Charlie, Marie, and believers like them are building firmly on their foundation in Christ. They will one day enter into his presence unashamed.

"And now, little children, abide in Him, so that when He appears, we may have confidence and not shrink away from Him in shame at His coming" (1 John 2:28 NASB).

SOMEONE UNDERSTANDS

The cold fact is that, Christian or not, submissive or rebellious, we are all going to suffer. Trial is an inevitable part of the human condition. I ask you, would you rather be wrung through the wringer with God, or without him, by your side? The choice is yours.

It might comfort you to know that whatever your circumstances, suffering, or personal traumas, the Lord Jesus Christ knows all about it. You see, He has been there too. Hebrews 2:17-18 says of Jesus that "He had to be made like His brethren in all things, that He might become a merciful and faithful high priest in things pertaining to God, to make propitiation for the sins of the people" (NASB).

For thirty-three years Jesus Christ walked the earth as God incarnate, God made man. In that time He knew human rejection. He had friends, yes, but more people spit on him than sat down to fellowship with him. Even his friends turned tail and deserted him at the end. His family didn't understand him. His brothers were embarrassed by him. He was unjustly arrested, convicted, and sentenced to die. The people to whom He had been sent as messiah clamored for the release of a murderer named Barabbas rather than for the freedom of the Son of God.

After a morning in which He was beaten, stripped, mocked, spit on, a crown of thorns shoved on his head, a mock scepter thrust into his hand, his flesh ripped open by the cat-o'-nine tails, Jesus Christ stumbled along the road to Golgotha. Nine a.m. found the Roman soldiers pounding nails through his hands and feet and the cross thrust viciously upward and roughly dropped into a hole in the ground. There for six hours the Son of man dangled. His body dehydrated; his skin became swollen; his organs and arteries were ready to burst from the unnatural position. At twelve noon the sky became dark as God the Father put out the lights of heaven, and for three hours Christ became sin for us. For the first time He was totally separated from the presence and love of the Father. He was alone as He took the penalty for our sins. The isolation was worse than the physical horror.

And then, it was finished.

Truly, has ever one suffered more?

If we have trusted Christ as our Savior, God will never withdraw his presence from us in the midst of trial and trouble. We will have him to cling to, no matter what. Things will never be as bad for us as they were for Jesus Christ on the cross.

And no matter what, Jesus will never leave us. He will always understand (see Exodus 33:14; Isaiah 41:10; Hebrews 13:5).

TAKING STOCK

Do we grow taller through testing? You bet we can. Pearl and I have five sons and daughters, all grown now (we even have grandchildren). Marks on the kitchen door bear witness of the physical progress our kids made while growing up. We would measure them at least once a year to see how tall they were and how they compared to last year. It would have grieved us if they had lived an entire year and not grown a bit. We would have carted them to the doctor to see what was wrong.

God is at the kitchen door of our lives. He is looking for signs of spiritual growth in us. He is hoping to see us a little taller each day. He is wanting for us to know him better. He is hoping we will respond properly to the tests and trials He allows in our lives. He wants to make the marks of progress just a little bit higher each time.

I have an opportunity for personal growth coming up a few weeks from now. I am scheduled for surgery for a total hip replacement. Satan would like to keep me dwelling on the negatives, and I have done plenty of that.

1. No more marathons
2. No more racquetball
3. No more horseback riding

I wanted to have this surgery done as an outpatient, but the doctors said, "Eight to ten days in the hospital." I was willing to sacrifice eight weeks for recuperation, but the doctors said, "Twelve weeks." My friends have started praying for my nurses and for my wife, and I hope they keep it up.

God is using this experience to teach me some things, and

I'm sure before it's all through, He will have taught me many more. Right now, He is showing me the positives about the situation:

1. Time for reflection and evaluation of goals
2. Time to grow in the Lord
3. Time to pray
4. The promise of new and better things the Lord has for me.

Some things are gone, but good things are on their way. "'For I know the plans I have for you,' declares the Lord, 'plans to prosper you and not to harm you, plans to give you hope and a future'" (Jeremiah 29:11 NIV).

THE VESSEL

> The Master was searching for a vessel to use,
> Before Him were many, which one would He choose?
>
> "Take me," cried the gold one. "I'm shiny and bright,
> I'm of great value and I do things just right.
> My beauty and luster will outshine the rest.
> And for someone like you, Master, gold would be best."
>
> The Master passed on with no word at all.
> And looked at a silver urn, grand and tall.
> "I'll serve you, dear Master, I'll pour out your wine.
> I'll be on your table whenever you dine.
> My lines are so graceful, my carving so true.
> And silver will always compliment you."
>
> Unheeding, the Master passed on to the brass,
> Wide-mouthed and shallow and polished like glass.
> "Here, here!" cried the vessel, "I know I will do,
> Place me on your table for all men to view."
>
> "Look at me," called the goblet of crystal so clear,
> "My transparency shows my contents so dear.
> Though fragile am I, I will serve you with pride,
> And I'm sure I'll be happy in your house to abide."
>
> Then the Master came next to a vessel of wood,
> Polished and carved, it solidly stood.

"You may use me, dearest Master," the wooden bowl
   said.
"But I'd rather you used me for fruit, not for bread."

Then the Master looked down and saw a vessel of clay.
Empty and broken it helplessly lay.
No hope had the vessel that the Master might choose,
To cleanse, and make whole, to fill and to use.

"Ah! Now this is the vessel I've been hoping to find.
I'll mend it and use it and make it all mine.
I need not the vessel with pride of itself,
Nor one that is narrow to sit on the shelf,
Nor one that is big-mouthed and shallow and loud,
Nor one that displays his contents so proud,
Nor the one who thinks he can do things just right,
But this plain earthly vessel filled with power and might."

Then gently He lifted the vessel of clay,
Mended and cleansed it and filled it that day:
Spoke to it kindly—"There's work you must do . . .
Just pour out to others as I pour into you."

                          (B. V. Cornwall)

Points to Ponder

1. How does James identify himself to his readers in verse 1? What does his use of the term *bondslave* tell us about his attitude toward Jesus?

2. What does 1:3 tell us that tests and trials are producing in our lives, if we are responding properly to them?

3. What, according to 1:12, is the ultimate result of responding correctly to trial? Do you know someone who has suffered a great deal, yet has managed to become better, rather than bitter, about all he or she has endured?

2

Hitting the Wall

James 1:13-18

Have you ever participated in a marathon? I have run in four of them. A phenomenon called "hitting the wall" occurs at about mile twenty.

It is vital that you pace yourself when running a marathon's twenty-six miles. You have only a certain amount of strength to expend, and if you spend it too early, you will play out before the tape at the end of the race. Then Galatians 5:7 will be true of you: "You were running well," and instead of finishing the course, you drop out.

Take it from me, hitting the wall is no fun. Your muscles cramp. Your body starts burning fat, and this hurts. Mentally you want to quit in the worst way. A myriad of reasons to throw in the towel occurs to you. You don't have anything to prove. Why go farther? How stupid of you to try this in the first place.

When hitting the wall, you have a choice. You can give in, surrendering to the temptation to quit, or you can keep going and run through the wall. In the Houston marathon I was able to run through the wall because my friend Pat Hawkins drove down to watch the race. To my surprise, there stood Pat at mile twenty-three, waiting for me, wearing his running gear, carrying a large orange drink which he thrust into my hand as

I came by. Pat then ran the last three miles of the race with me, shouting words of encouragement. No wonder I ran my best time in that marathon.

YOU WERE RUNNING WELL

In the marathon of life, people often hit the wall too. They may be running along smoothly, and then something rears up to sidetrack them from the goal. Temptation proves irresistible, and instead of keeping on, they succumb. Maybe it happens in college, or as children come, or at mid-life, or possibly during retirement. People who are full of potential become powerless to overcome an inclination to sin. All the promise of their lives turns tragically to what might have been.

As I write these words, a young man named Kevin Mitnick is being held without bail in the Los Angeles city jail. He faces a possible thirty years in prison and $750,000 in fines for computer fraud. So adept has this twenty-five-year-old hacker become at stealing and scrambling computer programs over telephone lines, that he cannot be allowed near a phone unless he is under a guard's supervision. Then he is permitted to call only his wife, mother, or lawyer. Mitnick is brilliant, but from the age of seventeen he has used his brilliance and the phone system to steal electronically stored software and information. As a *Time* magazine article put it, to computer whiz Mitnick, a phone is as dangerous a weapon as a gun in the hands of a hit man ("Drop," 49).

Hitting the wall can have even more deadly results. Raised in a Christian home, Ted Bundy grew up to be a bright, articulate, attractive young man. His associates and co-workers liked him. But a vice he indulged in his early teens—pornographic literature—led to sexual obsessions which eventually resulted in a blood lust that Bundy, with his twisted psyche, satisfied by cold-bloodedly murdering at least twenty-eight victims. In everyday life, his serial-killer image was successfully shrouded by his clean-cut wholesome good looks and easygoing personality. As the Focus on the Family film *Fatal Addiction* shows, the web of Bundy's perversion began subtly enough. He had a normal childhood. Then came experiences with soft-core pornography, alcohol, hard-core pornography, all leading to sexual violence and murder.

How subtle Satan is in fogging the links of the chains that ultimately, irreversibly, bind.

UNDER SIEGE

As disturbing as the actions of these individuals are, the fact is that, like them, we are all tempted each day by a variety of external and internal forces. None of us is immune to hitting the wall, although, thank God, few of us become Ted Bundys or even Kevin Mitnicks. In a sense we are cities under siege, struggling to survive amid a hail of enemy fire directed at the chinks in our walls. The bombardment may start slowly: a single shot here, a volley there. A second glance at a pretty young woman, a moment thinking about manipulating the stock market, an impulse to cheat on a tax return, curiosity about the effects of certain chemical substances, resentment harbored against another person—such things ignite desire and give way to wrong action, unbiblical action. Adultery, dishonesty, substance abuse, gossip, envy, bitterness. Let's call them what they really are: sin.

HITTING THE WALL OF TEMPTATION

It is not a sin to be tempted. Jesus himself was tempted. Hebrews 2:18 says of Christ, "For since He Himself was tempted in that which He has suffered, He is able to come to the aid of those who are tempted" (NASB). Matthew 4:1-11 gives the account. Led out into the wilderness for forty days, the Lord listened as Satan taunted him to turn stones into bread, to hurl himself off the pinnacle of a temple that the angels might rescue him, and to worship Satan in exchange for the kingdoms of the world. Christ's humanity rendered him vulnerable to temptation, but He did not give in to this temptation. Instead of doing what the devil asked, Christ rebuked Satan straight from scripture.

As we saw in the last chapter, the maturing Christian is one who is growing taller through testing. Now we learn from James that the growing Christian is also one who, like Christ in the wilderness, is saying no to temptation. Notice: believers are being tempted. They are hitting the wall. The arrows and ammo are being fired. But the maturing believers are refusing to lower their shields and surrender. They are not consistently giving in to sin.

The principle is simple: Spiritual growth is stunted by sin. The believer who falls into temptation, and indulges in the sin that is a result of that temptation, becomes spiritually paralyzed. There can be no growth, no maturing, no progress, until the problem is dealt with. Things must be cleared up with our Father in heaven before we can continue the climb toward Christ-likeness.

The men or women who have made decisions to trust Jesus Christ as Savior, and then trip up, are not permanently lost. They are temporarily sidetracked. They still have a relationship with God, although they are, for the moment out of fellowship.

God does not change his mind about our salvation every time we fail. He does not rewrite his will each time we don't do what He wants. As Jesus said, "My sheep hear My voice, and I know them, and they follow Me; and I give eternal life to them, and they shall never perish; and no one shall snatch them out of My hand. My Father, who has given them to Me, is greater than all; and no one is able to snatch them out of the Father's hand" (John 10:27-29 NASB).

Even though we are eternally secure, the principle of keeping short accounts with God and man is a good one. Ab was quickly beginning to lose his battle with illness when I slipped to his bedside to hear him whisper, "I'm going home!" The statement radiated joy and peace, emotions I had not detected in earlier visits. The reason? Ab and a long-estranged son had finally gotten things straightened out days before. Tears of reconciliation and forgiveness flowed freely as father and son made their relationship right by putting the past behind them.

Like Ab and his son, we must keep short accounts with God, our heavenly Father. First John 1:9 gives us the formula: "If we confess our sins, He is faithful and righteous to forgive us our sins and to cleanse us from all unrighteousness" (NASB). We will be tempted. We will sin. But as Christians we will never be without hope of a restored relationship with the Father who loves us.

THE PROBLEM—JAMES 1:13

> Let no man say when he is being tempted, "I am being tempted by God." For God cannot be tempted to do evil, and He himself is tempting no one.

How does temptation strike us? Usually we are tempted in one of three areas: the physical, the mental, or the spiritual. All three are interrelated, one affecting the other. We can be nailed to the wall with doubts in our spiritual lives. You know the questions that spring up at times. Is there really a God? Maybe I should check out some other religions, just to be sure. Could the empty tomb have been a hoax? Does God love me? Is heaven real? Is there really life after death, or is this life all there is?

We can also come under attack physically. Disease may leave us bitter and angry. Attractive members of the opposite sex may tempt us to forget our wedding vows. The promise of the effects of chemical substances may cause us to indulge when we shouldn't. After all, being drunk never hurt anyone, right? What's one little marijuana joint? A one-time fling with a pretty secretary—it won't really do anybody any harm, will it? How easily we rationalize. How quick we can be to set aside convictions when the allure of the illicit physical becomes powerful. Willfully blinded to permanent commitments and responsibilities, we give ourselves over to the moment, to the temporary.

Please don't take this as an argument for relentless self-denial. God made us physical beings. God gave us physical desires, but He expects us to exercise those desires within the proper bounds. Sex is for marriage (1 Corinthians 7:9); other legal pleasures are to be enjoyed in moderation (Galatians 5:22-23; 2 Peter 1:6; Ephesians 5:18). Overeating, alcoholism, drug addiction, and other such overindulgences are sin. A river that overflows its banks is a force of destruction. So is desire when it is allowed to pour out unbridled and unrestrained. The result is the devastation of divorce, unplanned pregnancy, substance addiction, and scores of other human tragedies.

Then there is mental temptation. In my experience, most temptation hits here first—at least most of my personal warfare in the Christian life occurs in this area. It starts in my thought life.

We get careless about what we allow ourselves to read or watch on television, and we set ourselves up to be tempted. It's the principle of "garbage in, garbage out." A businessman who regularly thumbs through *Playboy* or *Hustler* is ripe for a fall later on, because right now he is filling his mind with images to ignite his lust. A housewife whose day revolves around soap operas is setting herself up to become depressed and discontent with a lifestyle that may seem lackluster compared to what is depicted on *General Hospital* or *As the World Turns*. A teenager constantly tuning in to sexually explicit, drug-oriented rock videos may be tempted to experiment with things he or she can't handle.

The battle of our minds starts the minute we wake up. Think about it. How did you start your day today? When the alarm clock sounded, did you punch the snooze button and roll over in bed, thinking, "Good grief! I've got so much to do today. I'll never get it all done. It's hopeless. I don't want to get up. Why bother? I need an extra half hour in the sack." I used to do that, until I realized that with a beginning like that, I was spiritually defeated before I ever got started. Let me share with you the formula I've found to change my mornings. Instead of beginning with the blahs, I turn off the alarm and start talking to God, praying something like this:

> Father, thank You for this new day. I know You're alive and well, and that You are going to live in me today. Thank You that by divine design You are going to guide me to the people You want me to talk with. I know You are going to allow me to accomplish exactly what You want done today. And what I don't get done today is evidently in your plan for tomorrow. I'm checking in for signals. Tell me what You want me to do. I'm ready to get after it.

You would not believe the difference it makes. By beginning the morning with positive thoughts centered on God and his will for my day, I am actually eager to get out of bed. I can't wait to see what the Lord has for me to do. I am not tempted to complain about having to get up and get going. My mental outlook is fresh and new. Psychologists refer to this as P.M.A.—positive mental attitude.

Try it over the next week and see what happens. You will probably be tempted to shut off the alarm and roll over, but don't. When you see the change that results in your morning attitude, I think you'll be convinced. Keeping a positive attitude was also Paul's advice:

Finally, brethren, whatever is true, whatever is honorable, whatever is right, whatever is pure, whatever is lovely, whatever is of good repute, if there is any excellence and if anything worthy of praise, let your mind dwell on these things (Philippians 4:8 NASB).

TESTING OR TEMPTATION?

Often I have been asked to explain the difference between a test and a temptation. That's easy. You'll like one, and you won't like the other one. The temptation will seem pleasurable; the test will be tough. It's tough to keep on running in a marathon; it's tempting to quit, collapse on the sidelines, and drink Gatorade. The professor comes to class and tells everyone, "Your exam is today." That's a test. The temptation is to cheat. Your wife bakes chocolate chip cookies for the women's association, and tells you, "Don't touch them, dear! They're for tomorrow." That's the test. The temptation is to see how many ways you can arrange them so she won't know that any of them is missing.

In a test, God puts his finger on something in our lives that must go, in order to make us more like his Son. The temptation is to resist, rebel, and hang on as long as possible before responding properly and resigning ourselves to his will. The test demands that we act responsibly; the temptation tells us to run away. Tests call for us to sacrifice our desires; temptations urge us to satisfy them *now*. Submitting to tests grows us tall in the Christian life. Yielding to temptation leaves us spiritual babies, consistent victims of our lack of self-discipline, puppets of our desires, pawns manipulated by the devil on the chessboard of life.

Another difference between a test and a temptation is that one comes from God and the other does not. "Let no man say when he is tempted, 'I am being tempted by God.' For God cannot be tempted to do evil, and He himself is tempting no one," wrote James (1:13). God is never the source of temptation.

When we are tempted, particularly when we give in, our inclination is to want to blame somebody. That is what happened in the garden of Eden. Adam and Eve were given a lush paradise, a beautiful, spotless world of peace and tranquility.

They could roam freely and without fear, since in those days the lion truly did lie down with the lamb. The first couple did not know hunger, thirst, nakedness, danger, or anxiety.

Yet Adam and Eve were curious. They were curious enough, at the insistence of the serpent empowered by Satan, to eat fruit from the one tree God had forbidden them. They exceeded the single limit the Lord had set, and when they did, the darkness of their sin tainted the whole world and the whole race (see Genesis 3:1-7ff). It may have been easy to disobey, but it was tough for the two to own up to their disobedience. When God confronted the pair, Adam blamed Eve for what they had done. As for Eve, she blamed the serpent (see Genesis 3:11-13). Nobody blamed himself or herself. How human. How typical of us all.

When we foul up, we search for somebody to fault. Grant Howard, in *The Trauma of Transparency*, called this behavior "hurling" (31-34). The blame just can't be ours. It's the fault of the husband, or the wife. The boss made me do it. Or the kids; they drive us crazy and make us act before we think. Ultimately, we often blame God. After all, He created us this way. It's his fault that we fail. It's his responsibility for making us the kind of persons we are. What a comedy of errors as we try to pass the buck. What a tragedy of misplaced blame.

We will talk about who is responsible for temptation shortly. For now, let's acknowledge the truth: Temptation does not begin with God.

THE PROCESS—JAMES 1:14-15

> But each one is being tempted when he is taken in tow and lured by his own desires. Then when the desire has conceived, it is giving birth to sin, and this sin, when it has run its course, brings forth death.

From the dawn of time, temptation has been a product of the evil one. As he did first with Adam and Eve, Satan uses our eyes, minds, and internal desires to knock us off course. Let's look at the biblical account of the temptation in the garden and watch the process.

> Now the serpent was more crafty than any of the wild animals the Lord God had made. He said to the woman,

"Did God really say, 'You must not eat from any tree in the garden'?"

The woman said to the serpent, "We may eat from the trees in the garden, but God did say, 'You must not eat fruit from the tree that is in the middle of the garden, and you must not touch it, or you will die.'"

"You will not surely die," the serpent said to the woman. "For God knows that when you eat of it your eyes will be opened, and you will be like God, knowing good and evil."

When the woman saw that the fruit of the tree was good for food and pleasing to the eye, and also desirable for gaining wisdom, she took some and ate it. She also gave some to her husband, who was with her, and he ate it. Then the eyes of both of them were opened, and they realized they were naked; so they sewed fig leaves together and made coverings for themselves (Genesis 3:1-7 NIV).

As he did with Adam and Eve, Satan often starts a bombardment of temptation with two shots. One causes us to doubt God's goodness. The other shows us the attractiveness of the object. Thus, the devil assails our minds and eyes. Speaking through the serpent in Eden, he told the woman something like this: "Eve, you have it made. I wish I could live like you. This is fantastic! What about all these trees here? They're beautiful! I hear there's a special one in the middle of the garden. Bet its fruit tastes great."

"We can't eat that fruit," Eve replied.

"Oh no? That's very interesting. I wonder why you can't, unless God knows something He doesn't want you to know," continued the serpent, dangling the bait. "That's it! God knows that when you eat from that tree, you'll be like him. Isn't that selfish of him to keep you from eating from the most significant tree? He must want to keep the good stuff all for himself."

Eve fell for the lie—hook, line, and sinker. She looked at the tree—*the* tree. She'd probably never given it a second thought before. But Satan had slithered into her thoughts and started her doubting God's goodness. And now the fruit of that tree looked mighty appealing. So she took a bite, Adam tried some—and all was lost.

"Try it, you'll like it," the devil will tell us. Everyone else is doing it. Go ahead. You might as well live a little. No sense in growing old gracefully. You're still young and alive with desires. Go on, enjoy yourself. Live life to the fullest. Grab for the gusto. You only go around once. Get it while the getting's good.

THE BAIT

Quite a few years ago we chartered the *Shawmanee*, a fifty-foot vessel piloted by Phil and Mary Erickson, to sail for a week in the Strait of Georgia off the Puget Sound. Thirteen of us were aboard, including a number of friends of the Ministries. Naturally, I wanted those Texans to enjoy some real living by sitting down to a meal of fresh salmon, eaten the day it was caught. In spite of my hopes, two days passed without a nibble. Our youngest daughter, Julea, prayed for our luck to change, and the one who was famous for filling nets in Galilee answered a little girl's prayer the next day.

At five the following morning, I quietly lowered a small dinghy into the glassy smooth waters of Melody Cove. No sooner had I cast the line than something grabbed at it and then let go. Momentary disappointment turned to instant thrill as he hit again and the fight was on. Have you ever tried to pilot a small craft, fight a fish, and tend a net all at the same time? Thirty minutes later a totally exhausted twenty-five-pound salmon rolled over and fell into the waiting net; the fish was the makings of two beautiful dinners and the fixings of a great salmon salad lunch. I wanted to let out a rebel yell of triumph, but I'd have lost a lot of friends in that sleepy little cove.

In case you haven't guessed, I love to fish, especially for salmon. God has made me a fisher of men too, as I tell others about the good news of his Son. Satan is also a fisherman—it's something we have in common—only Satan goes after human fish for the wrong reasons. Our own desires make us susceptible.

James said we are lured by our own desires (1:14). The picture suggests fishing or hunting. The word is the same one we use when we describe casting a little plastic worm right behind a log. Whack! A big bass hits it. What a thrill for us to reel in a monster.

Satan loves it when we give in to our inner desires and grab the plug, shiny spoon, or spinner which happens to pass in front of our noses. We do not have to take the hook. We have a choice. "The devil made me do it" is a popular catch-phrase, yet as we'll see in James 4:7, Satan cannot force the believer to do anything. The selfish pursuit of pleasure, unchecked desire, unmastered lusts, and undisciplined lives leave us vulnerable to failure. When we say yes when we should say no, the blame is squarely our own, said James.

HOOKED ON A WOUNDED HERRING

If you've never been salmon fishing, let me give you a quick lesson. First you take a large salmon rod and attach a big silver flasher to the line. Behind that you string some hooks, and bait one of them with a good-sized herring. Then you cast the line into the water (I prefer the Puget Sound). The flasher moves back and forth, attracting attention; the herring looks like a wounded herring, easy pickings for a salmon's supper.

Salmon know all about wounded herring. When salmon are hungry and happen upon a school of herring, they swim through the school, using their powerful tails to whack and wound as many small fish as they can. The injured herring straggle behind as the school swims on, and the salmon return to eat the wounded fish.

Let's pretend we're fishing. Once our line is cast, a big old thirty-five-pound salmon swimming nearby catches a glimpse of something flashing to the side. He alters his course, going out of his way to check things out. As he nears the flasher, he notices a treat. Somebody has already wounded a herring for him. Isn't that convenient? Gulp. Any salmon that gulps doesn't stay around long enough to decide whether or not he has made a mistake. With a jerk from above, the hook is set and he has to fight for his life, a battle he will probably lose. The most he can hope for is to break the line and swim away scarred, the hook still imbedded. More likely he will fight, get flipped into a net, find himself fileted, and wind up food for the table.

What happens to a salmon is what happens to us when we're tempted, according to James. Lured by our desires, we change our course of action, our way of life, and follow another course that seems at the moment to be pleasant, enjoyable, scintillating. We know it's wrong, but we find excuses for it. We work up our nerve and go for it. We indulge. And if we're lucky, we walk away with only a few scars. First Peter 5:8 says that Satan is like a roaring lion, seeking whom he may devour. He loves it when Christians wander off alone into dangerous territory (see also 2 Timothy 2:26).

THE ENEMY WITHIN: OUR LUSTS

We are carried away by our own lusts. Jesus says, "For out of the heart come evil thoughts, murders, adulteries, fornications, thefts, false witness, slanders. These are the things which defile the man" (Matthew 15:19-20a NASB). When the enemy attacks, he attacks from within. If we have trusted Christ as Savior, within us resides a new divine nature that will respond to the Holy Spirit. But within us also still dwells our old sinful nature, the inclination toward sin we had before accepting Christ (see Romans 7:14ff; Galatians 5:17). The old nature is standing by, ready to kick in whenever we give it a chance. None of us is immune. Even the apostle Paul admitted to having struggles in his Christian life. "For that which I am doing, I do not understand; for I am not practicing what I would like to do, but I am doing the very thing I hate" (Romans 7:15 NASB; see also 7:19). Like so many others in scripture, he too battled temptation.

We see in the Bible, and also in our own experiences, that temptation involves three essential components.

1. The suggestion of pleasure. A temptation tries to convince you that it will be fun.

2. The idea that it is possible to get away with indulging in the temptation. You will be the exception. You won't get caught. Sure, it's not right to cheat on your wife or on your income tax. But just once won't hurt anybody, will it? No one is going to know.

3. The notion that it is possible to escape unscathed. You will emerge unhurt, and so will everyone else around you. You can walk away from the sin whenever you want. You might even be a better person for having given in.

Temptation always suggests pleasure, and never pain. It promises enjoyment with no strings attached. Only afterward do we hear about the aborted pregnancy, the drug rehabilitation center, the AA meeting.

So much time in the ministry is spent helping others pick up the broken pieces of shattered homes, shattered lives. Temptation finds an answering chord in people's hearts. Lust works with lure. The missing faces from congregations and Bible classes tell the tale. Dad runs off with another woman and leaves a wife and small children behind. Or Mom, tired of drudgery and responsibility, takes off to "find herself." Hearts crumble amid custody battles and property settlements. Another family becomes a statistic.

The formula can be fatal: Our desire plus the devil's suggestion equals destruction. Today the mind-set that it is easier to get forgiveness than to ask permission is in danger of permeating even the evangelical church. May we never forget the consequences of sin.

THE WAGES OF SIN

What are the consequences of sin? According to James, "When desire has conceived, it is giving birth to sin, and this sin, when it has run its course, brings forth death" (1:15). Sin brings *death*. Here James alluded to the marriage relationship to convey his message; he spoke of union, birth, and death. It is an example with an ironic twist.

What is the hope of the union in a real-life marriage? Usually at some point in a marriage we hope there will be conception and birth, bringing life. As I write this, our son Bobby and daughter-in-law Jan are expecting their fourth child, visible fruit of their union.

Witnessing a physical birth is one of the most moving experiences possible. After the final contraction, we wait wordlessly for the baby to draw his or her first breath outside the womb. At last comes the cry that signifies life.

In contrast, a union with temptation gives birth to sin, which brings forth death. We think we will be happy, fulfilled, by saying yes. Then sometime down the pike we find that it isn't so, that Satan is the father of lies. By then, it's too late Sin is the unwanted child of an illicit union, and sin's outcome is death.

David Swartz described the consequences of sin as he recalled an experience from his teens. A *Playboy* magazine

"Playmate of the Year" was making a promotional appearance at a shopping mall, so Swartz and some friends went. After standing for what seemed like hours in a long snaking line, the boys finally stepped up to the table to meet Ms. Playmate, only to be startled by her looks. She was a stunning Scandinavian blonde, obviously used to the glamor of winters in Aspen and summers on the Riviera, one of Hugh Hefner's pampered pets. Yet there was, as Swartz recalls, a "wasteland in her eyes." No glow, no sparkle. An empty, meaningless gaze emanated from that woman who seemingly had it all.

> She was as stripped of human vitality and joy as an ear of corn shucked of its husk and grain. I wish I could say that hers was the last of the vacant stares I've ever seen, but I'm afraid I've seen many since then. That empty, soul-drained look is everywhere. What is especially dismaying is the frequency with which it is found within the church (Swartz 69-70).

What a sharp contrast to such emptiness is the description of Moses from Hebrews 11:24-26:

> By faith Moses, when he had grown up, refused to be called the son of Pharaoh's daughter; choosing rather to endure ill treatment with the people of God than to enjoy the passing pleasures of sin; considering the reproach of Christ greater riches than the treasures of Egypt; for he was looking to the reward (NASB).

DEATH—FOR THE CHRISTIAN AND NON-CHRISTIAN

The consequences of hitting the wall and giving in to sin are serious. Lust is the bud; sin, the blossom; and death, the fruit of our failure.

The death James referred to can be either spiritual or physical. For the unbeliever, who has never come into a relationship with Jesus Christ, the "wages of sin is death" (Romans 6:23). Death—separation from God—is the penalty for our disobedience and unbelief. "Raise the wages of sin" was the message on a bumper sticker I saw one day, but the truth is that the wages of sin can't get any higher. Payday brings death, not life.

If you have been born into God's family through faith in

Jesus Christ, and you consistently yield to temptation and indulge in sin, James's message is different for you. Remember, his letter is addressed to Jewish *Christians*. By habitually straying from the right path, you may be setting yourself up for a great fall. If you are dishonoring God's name, it is the Father's prerogative to take you to glory in physical death. That may sound tough, but it is biblical truth. 1 Corinthians 11:31-32 says, "But if we judged ourselves rightly, we should not be judged. But when we are judged, we are disciplined by the Lord in order that we may not be condemned along with the world" (NASB). It seems that several of the Corinthian Christians had actually died because they had refused to deal with sin in their lives (1 Corinthians 5:5; 11:30). If we, as stubborn children, persist in a routine of saying yes when we ought to say no, we may be in danger of forfeiting our earthly lives. After all, if we are doing nothing for the Lord down here, we might as well be in heaven.

We can be so smug, can't we? We bank on the fact that our God is a God of love and forgiveness. We tell ourselves that surely He won't strike us for a little indulgence. He wants us to have fun, doesn't He? How easy it is for us to forget the awesome power of a just God who hates sin. Jesus told the parable of a wealthy man who hauls in a bumper crop one year. Consumed with greed, the miser plans to hoard it all and take life easy. "And I will say to my soul, 'Soul, you have many goods laid up for many years to come; take your ease, eat, drink and be merry,'" he self-confidently says. God's reply to him? "You fool! This very night your soul is required of you; and now who will own what you have prepared?" (Luke 12:19-20 NASB).

Just like him, just like that, we too can be gone.

In his mercy, however, God often lets us slide. He does not always call us home. Many Christians dishonor the kingdom for long periods of time. Some seem to make careers of it. On the other hand, many believers who lead godly lives are called home while still young, their early deaths not at all connected with sin in their lives. But the possibility of the penalty is there. It's one of the consequences of sin that Satan deceitfully obscures.

AND OTHER CONSEQUENCES

Sin has other consequences. Disease, broken marriages, ruined friendships, substance addictions, prison sentences, financial ruin, marred reputations—such unwanted offspring may also result from giving in. As we see in the Old Testament, King David found that out the hard way.

At fifty years of age David had captured Jerusalem and made it his home and capital city. He brought back the ark of the covenant and consolidated his kingdom. The season for marching to war came, and David, now too valuable to his country to risk the battlefield, remained behind in the capital while Joab led the nation's armies against the Ammonites. Supposedly safe at home, David was soon to face a more devastating personal battle, one he would lose with horrendous consequences.

Arising from his couch one evening, the bored, middle-aged king walked to his window and spied a woman bathing on a nearby roof. He discovered she was Bathsheba, the wife of one of his best officers, a foreigner named Uriah the Hittite. David sent messengers to fetch her, and when Bathsheba came to him, he had physical relations with her. She returned to her home, but their brief one-night stand mushroomed into a national scandal. Bathsheba was pregnant.

After attempts failed to make Uriah appear to be the baby's father, David arranged to have the Hittite slain in battle. An evening's fleeting pleasure set off a chain reaction of life-shattering events: unplanned pregnancy, deception, murder. It was a year that culminated in a public confrontation when Nathan the prophet rebuked the king for his sins of adultery and murder. His reputation ruined, his heart stained with guilt, David faced both immediate and long-term consequences. The son which Bathsheba, now his wife, bore him lived no more than a few days (see 2 Samuel 11–12).

Other children of David saw the weakness in their father's moral character and could not discipline themselves either. One, Amnon, raped his half-sister, Tamar. Another, Absalom, cold-heartedly revenged the crime by slaying Amnon (see 2 Samuel 13). Absalom later led a rebellion against his father and died trying to wrest the kingdom from him (2 Samuel 15–18).

In a sense, David still answers today for that sin of long ago. Although he is called "a man after [God's] own heart" (1 Samuel 13:14; Acts 13:22), his sin with Bathsheba continues to sell novels and movies. It is his adultery, not his battle victories, spiritual commitment, kindness, humility, reverence, or creativity, that publicists promote when plugging books and films about him.

And yet how attractive sin first appears.

Mark and Donna, my son-in-law and daughter, gave me a bug zapper for my birthday a couple of years ago. It has made outdoor living a possibility in our backyard again. The fluorescent light attracts flying insects to an electrically charged wire-mesh shield. Once contact with the shield is made, a sound like "zzzst" or "zap" indicates the fall of another crispy critter.

That bug zapper reminds me of sin. Waiting, enticing, appealing, attractive, sin is ready as we unsuspecting little flies buzz nearby. We pause to bask momentarily in its glow and immediately we are fried. A sizzle signals that another one bites the dust, and Satan snickers in the wings.

THE ANSWER—JAMES 1:16-18

> Stop being deceived, my brethren, beloved ones. Every good gift and every perfect gift is from above, coming down from the Father of lights with whom there can be no change or shadow cast by variation. According to his will, he brought us into being through the word of truth, to the end that we might be a kind of first fruits of his creatures.

Sin and temptation are serious business. Make no mistake about it. James implored his readers to "Stop being deceived" (1:16). The warning is urgent. Turning from temptation is essential.

I tour extensively each year, teaching Bible classes wherever I'm invited, in homes, banks, offices, meeting rooms, restaurants, churches, college campuses. I have observed that somehow the young seem less able to hide their pain and regret than we older folks who have grown good at masking our true emotions. Each class I've taught for university students has contained some obviously heartbroken young men and women. The effects of sin are written all over their faces as they meet with me to ask if there is any hope for them. The pressure to go with the flow has just about drowned them.

"Mr. Anderson," began one lovely young woman from a large state university, "I see no use for living. I'll never enjoy a normal marriage. You see, I've been living with this guy. Nobody's going to want me. I won't have a future with a man who will love me and want to have a family. My life is based totally on the physical." She couldn't have been more than twenty years old, and she saw no future for herself.

There is a breaking of the will as we say yes to temptation. A bending of convictions occurs. Once we give in, it is easier to say yes the next time. And the next. And the next. Some of us repeatedly say no to the saving offer of Jesus Christ. Once we walk away from the gospel, the good news, it is easier to walk away again and again. We stride out the door full of pride and self-confidence and hardened of heart, eternally lost unless we finally say yes.

James begged us to beware the breaking of our wills. He urged us to be deceived no longer by the glitter and glitz of temptation; what is underneath the gilded exterior is foul and rotten. Instead of listening to the father of lies, we are to turn to the Father of lights.

TURNING TO THE FATHER

That Father of lights, James continued, is the giver of every "good and perfect gift" (1:17). What a wonderfully positive statement, offering a solution to handling temptation.

Resisting temptation involves praise and thanksgiving that Jesus Christ is truly adequate to meet our needs. God is the giver of every good and perfect gift. The Lord's objective for our lives is to bless us. He desires to do the best for us. Those are truths we should all hang onto.

Before my five kids left the nest, I recall having a certain conversation with each of them at least once. Those father-child talks happened in the teen years, and began with a comment which you too have probably heard if you have teenagers around the house. If you haven't heard it, you will. They each said, "I will be so glad when I am eighteen so I can get out of this house and be on my own."

My response was always the same. I simply reminded whichever dear child it was (looking him or her straight in the contact lenses, braces, and face redeemed from the dermatologist with a price) that my only purpose for the first eighteen years of his or her life was to bless him or her, to do everything possible to make life meaningful, and to prepare that son or daughter for their eighteenth birthday when they would be ready and able to go out on their own. Could anyone really argue with my intentions?

Like our teenagers, we often look at the restraints of a heavenly Father who loves us, who knows the end from the beginning, and we become bitter because of something God permits in our lives. We rationalize our resentment toward him because of the person He allowed us to marry, the financial crisis that wiped out our savings, the disease that riddles our bodies, the injustice of a court decision, the pain of a tragic loss. "Why did God do this to me?" we question in our anger. Somehow we feel we have legitimate reasons for rejecting him.

James comes across loud and clear against such conclusions. The gifts of God are good and perfect. They are designed for our ultimate good. The Lord desires to bless us, to make life meaningful for us, to prepare us to grow into his likeness. As we saw in the last chapter, even the tough times come to make us more Christ-like, just as the disciplines and restraints we place on the lives of our own children are designed to help them grow up into responsible adults.

When we yield to temptation, however, and unwanted fruit is born, we must not blame God, although that is sometimes easy to do. The fact is we are reaping what *we* have sown, nothing more or less.

Temptation comes from below. The bad comes from beneath, from the father of darkness.

AN ESCAPE HATCH

One of the Lord's perfect gifts is specifically designed to rescue us when we are tempted. With every temptation comes a God-given escape hatch. We are promised this in 1 Corinthians 10:13: "No temptation has overtaken you but such as is common to man; and God is faithful, who will not allow you to be tempted beyond what you are able, but with the temptation will provide the way of escape also, that you may be able to endure it" (NASB). God knows our limits. He knows what we can take at any particular time. He doesn't send the temptation, but He does control it by preventing it from becoming too much for us. He will not allow temptation to go beyond our capacity to bear it.

In the Old Testament, the story of Joseph illustrates this. Enslaved in the household of the Egyptian Potiphar, Joseph found himself the object of his master's wife's attentions. Mrs. Potiphar zoned in on Joseph like a heat-seeking missile. She set her sights on seducing him. One day when the house was deserted except for Joseph, she grabbed him by the coat and suggested that they become intimate. Such a conquest would have fueled Joseph's ego, appealed to his masculinity, given him bragging rights in the locker room, but he chose not to sin. His God-given escape hatch was the doorway through which he ran. Soon God used circumstances to remove him entirely from the house, making the escape permanent (see Genesis 39:6ff).

Think about the times when you have been tempted. Whether or not you succumbed, wasn't the potential there to say no? David could have pulled the windowshade instead of continuing to gaze at Bathsheba. A cold shower wouldn't have hurt either. The choices David had were to fight, to go with the flow, or to flee. Victory would have come with number three.

I heard the story of a little boy who was helping his attorney father move the contents of his library upstairs. His dad placed three volumes into the boy's outstretched arms. "I can take more, Daddy," the little boy insisted.

"Oh no, you can't, son. You've got enough," the father replied.

Walking up the stairs the child was heard to say, "My daddy knows how much I can carry."

Our loving heavenly Father knows how much temptation we can carry too. Each time, the escape hatch will be there for the using. God guarantees it.

The Greatest Gift

The Lord is changeless and constant (1:16). He is the Lord God and He changes not (see Malachi 3:6). "Jesus Christ is the same yesterday and today and forever" (Hebrews 13:8 NIV).

Yes, the gifts of God are perfect. The greatest of these is the gift of his Son, Jesus Christ. In the words of the apostle John, "For God so loved the world, that He gave His only begotten

Son, that whoever believes in Him should not perish, but have eternal life" (John 3:16 NASB).

Nearly two thousand years ago, nailed on a wooden cross on a little hill called Golgotha outside the city of Jerusalem, Jesus Christ, the God-man, was suspended one Friday. His trial had been a mockery of justice, his condemnation a political gesture. He had done nothing to deserve his sentence of death. His life was perfect, spent in service to others. He healed the lame and blind and raised the dead. He embraced sinners and sufferers—no one was exempted from his compassion except the religious hypocrites of the day who operated through pride and led others astray. Even some of them, like Saul of Tarsus, were eventually touched by his hand.

Christ was the seed promised to Eve in Genesis 3:15, come for the salvation of humankind. Hundreds of Old Testament prophecies were fulfilled literally in his birth, life, death, resurrection, and ascension.

More eyewitnesses saw Christ during the forty days following his resurrection and before He ascended into heaven than saw Michelangelo paint the Sistine Chapel, or saw the pilgrims who set sail on the *Mayflower*. How strange that people do not doubt the reality of what is written in history books, yet question the truth of the resurrection. Had He been tried on the charge of being resurrected from the dead, Jesus would be found guilty in any of our courts.

His mission was mighty. God's standard is perfection. In order to experience friendship with him and eventually to dwell eternally with him in heaven, we must be perfect. Not just nice people, good people, generous people, but *perfect* people. But we cannot be perfect people on our own.

Romans 3:23 tells us that all have sinned and fall short of the glory of God. Sometime, somewhere, there will be a wrong thought, a selfish act, a dirty deed. We will break one of God's laws. We may not commit murder, but we will become angry at a neighbor, and Jesus said that is sin (see Matthew 5:22). We may never commit adultery, but we will probably look on a member of the opposite sex with lust, and Jesus said that also is sin (see Matthew 5:27-28). We may not rob a bank, but we may keep silent when the storeclerk gives us too much change, and that is sin too. I hope you get the picture. None of us is perfect. You are not perfect. Neither am I. Jesus Christ came to take care of that imperfection.

We don't know the intimate details of his personal agony; we do know that along with unimaginable physical pain and deprivation, He also suffered spiritual separation from the heavenly Father. For the first time in his life, Jesus was utterly alone. "Eli, Eli, lama sabachthani" or "My God, My God, why hast Thou forsaken Me?" came his cry (Matthew 27:46 NASB). Then He bowed his head in death: "Tetelestai . . . It is finished!" was his statement of surrender and cry of victory (John 19:30 NASB).

What about us? We have but to accept the sacrifice. We have but to trust Christ as our Savior. We have to believe that it is finished, that Jesus did what He did—paid the penalty for our broken law—and by our faith in his finished work, we become righteous in God's sight. Ephesians 2:8-9 puts it this way: "For by grace you have been saved through faith; and that not of yourselves, it is the gift of God; not as a result of works, that no one should boast" (NASB).

We cannot work our way into heaven. In the end our deeds won't be weighed in the balances to see if we have done more good than bad. In the end, what will matter eternally is if we have trusted Christ as Savior. If so, God's Spirit, the helper promised in John 14:26, enters us and empowers us to begin doing what we ought to do, thinking what we ought to think, being what we ought to be—as we are submissive to his leading.

THE FIRST FRUIT

When we come to know Christ as Savior, we enter the family of God. We start a life-changing relationship with the Father. As James put it, "According to his will, He brought us into being through the word of truth . . . that we might be a kind of first fruits of his creatures" (1:18). Let's look more closely at that statement:

According to his will—It is God's will that we enter into a relationship with him through Christ Jesus (John 3:16; Ephesians 1:5). He also has plans for that relationship, as we will see.

He brought us into being—God is the giver of life. Unlike Satan, who is the author of death, the Lord gives us eternal life as we are born again in Christ. We become those who "were born not of blood, nor of the will of the flesh, nor of the will of man, but of God" (John 1:13 NASB; see also John 1:4; 1 John 5:11-12).

Through the word of truth—God's word, recorded in holy scripture and embodied in the person of Jesus Christ, is the tool by which the Lord gives us eternal life. We are "born again, not of corruptible seed, but of incorruptible, by the word of God, which liveth and abideth for ever" (1 Peter 1:23 KJV). We read of God's Son in scripture; we come to personally trust his Son by faith (Ephesians 2:8; 3:15,17).

That we might be a kind of first fruits of his creatures—What is God's purpose in giving us life? We are to be a "first fruits" of his creatures. One of the reasons God redeems us is so that, for the rest of our earthly lives, we can glorify him by becoming more Christ-like. He saves us so we will start acting like Christians. Then the watching world will see the miracle of extraordinary changes He can work in the lives of ordinary people. Ephesians 2:10 says that "we are His workmanship, created in Christ Jesus for good works, which God prepared beforehand, that we should walk in them" (NASB).

Another reason God reaches out to offer us his salvation is so we can glorify him eternally. He will be able to show us to the angels, fallen and faithful, and all will know that by his grace, mercy, and power, He was able to redeem such sinful individuals as we are (Ephesians 3:10; 1 Peter 1:12; Jude 24-25).

WAITING TO BLESS

God is waiting to bless us. I am not talking about television sets and VCRS motor homes and swimming pools, or other evidences of material wealth. If we have never come to his Son in faith, He is waiting to bless us with the person of Jesus Christ. Events in our lives are occurring which may draw us to him, if we respond properly. We hear the gospel in a church, from a friend, on a radio program. We run across an old family Bible, or maybe leaf through a booklet someone has left behind. Perhaps we face a personal crisis and seek help from God. Sometime, somewhere, somehow, we have the choice to respond to God or to reject him. He will reach down to pluck us from the ocean as we start to sink. "I love you," He will cry. "Let me rescue you," He will offer. We can grasp his hand or choose instead to drown. How we answer him is our responsibility, not his.

If we are Christians, He is waiting to bless us with whatever it will take to make us more Christ-like. He will test us. He will provide for us. He will supply us with escapes from temptation. But we must never forget the awful consequences of saying yes when we ought to say no.

In *Pilgrim at Tinker Creek*, Annie Dillard gave a graphic description of the fate of a tiny green frog. I can think of no more compelling way to illustrate what sin indulged does to us.

> At last I knelt on the island's winterkilled grass, lost, dumbstruck, staring at the frog in the creek just four feet away. He was a very small frog with wide, dull eyes. And just as I looked at him, he slowly crumpled and began to sag. The spirit vanished from his eyes as if snuffed. His skin emptied and drooped; his very skull seemed to collapse and settle like a kicked tent. He was shrinking before my eyes like a deflating football. I watched the taut, glistening skin on his shoulders ruck, and rumple, and fall. Soon, part of his skin, formless as a pricked balloon, lay in floating folds like bright scum on top of the water: it was a monstrous and terrifying thing. I gaped bewildered, appalled. An oval shadow hung in the water behind the drained frog; then the shadow glided away. The frog skin bag started to sink.
>
> I had read about the giant water bug, but never seen one. "Giant water bug" is really the name of the creature, which is an enormous, heavy-bodied brown beetle. It eats insects, tadpoles, fish, and frogs. Its grasping forelegs are mighty and hooked inward. It seizes a victim with these legs, hugs it tight, and paralyzes it with enzymes injected during a vicious bite. That one bite is the only bite it ever takes. Through the puncture wound shoot the poisons that dissolve the victim's muscles and bones and organs—all but the skin—and through it the giant water bug sucks out the victim's body, reduced to a juice. This

even is quite common in warm fresh water. The frog I
saw was being sucked by a giant water bug. I had been
kneeling on the island grass; when the unrecognizable
flap of frog skin settled on the creek bottom, swaying, I
stood up and brushed the knees of my pants. I couldn't
catch my breath (Dillard 5-6).

Each time I read that account, it takes me a moment to catch
my breath too. This is especially true as I imagine Satan and
sin to be the giant water bug, and then the deflation and
destruction of believers caught in his deadly life-sucking grip.

Too Late?

What if you have said yes when you should have said no?
You've gone with the flow. You've let desire dominate you and
you are hooked and hurting. Is it too late? The answer is no.
If you have trusted Christ as Savior, read this. There are steps
you can take to make things right again.

1. Confession—Agree with God that you have done wrong.
First John 1:9 is the guideline. Listen also to David in Psalm
51:1-13.

2. Repentance—This is a turning away from the sin. In brokenness you forsake the disobedient behavior.

3. Accountability—Come under the care of a trusted believer.
Seek to develop an open, honest, transparent relationship with
a mature Christian who will hold you accountable.

4. Sensitivity—Intensify your time in the scriptures and in
prayer. Be open and sensitive to the Lord. Memorize Psalm 1:1-
3 to get started.

5. Rejoice—Be thankful for the restoration of your fellowship,
your friendship, with the Lord. Read Psalm 32 for encouragement and reassurance.

6. Finish the race—Just because you've hit the wall and even
stopped, doesn't mean you can't get back into the marathon
of the Christian life. Heaven is a place for finishers. Take a look
at Hebrews 12:1-2 and Philippians 3:13-14 as you prepare to
re-enter the race.

If you have never come to Christ, it is not too late for you either. The cold truth is that you are dead in your trespasses and sins, because you have yet to avail yourself of the work accomplished at Calvary's cross.

As Satan blinds believers to the consequences of yielding to temptation, so he blinds those who do not know Christ: "The god of this age has blinded the minds of unbelievers, so that they cannot see the light of the gospel of the glory of Christ, who is the image of God" (2 Corinthians 4:4 NIV). One chapter later, the apostle Paul pleaded, "Therefore, we are ambassadors for Christ, as though God were entreating through us; we beg you on behalf of Christ, be reconciled to God. He made Him who knew no sin to be sin on our behalf, that we might become the righteousness of God in Him" (2 Corinthians 5:20-21 NASB).

How do you do it? "But as many as received Him, to them He gave the right to become children of God, even to those who believe in His name" (John 1:12 NASB). It's simple. You take the gift of eternal salvation. You receive Jesus Christ as Savior by trusting him alone for your salvation. Nothing you can do of your own will get you to heaven—only trusting Christ alone, as you would a lifeboat to save you. So you trust the Savior to take care of your sins and make you righteous in the sight of God the Father.

When? Why wait any longer? Right now, as you are reading these lines, this may be your last opportunity. Please hasten to make things right.

> And working together with Him, we also urge you not to receive the grace of God in vain—for He says,
> "At the acceptable time I listened to you,
> And on the day of salvation I helped you";
> behold, now is "the acceptable time," behold, now is "the day of salvation" (2 Corinthians 6:1-2 NASB).

Points to Ponder

1. Human nature tends to resist the test and to respond to the temptation. God desires the reverse. Can you think of a situation in your life where you have responded to temptation when you should have either resisted or fled it? What could you have done differently? What can you do to make things right with God and other persons now?

2. Who is the source of temptation? What are some of the results of saying yes when we ought to say no?

3. What are some of the reasons God offers us new life in Jesus Christ? Refer to 2:18 as you consider your answer.

3

Working Out in the Word

James 1:19-27

Mornings—it's a subject on which people are seldom neutral. We love them or we hate them.

I've come to the conclusion that most people aren't morning people. Erma Bombeck says when her kids were young, the only way she survived mornings was through self-hypnosis. Her basic a.m. vocabulary of seventeen words included "No. I don't care. It's in the dirty clothes hamper. Mustard or ketchup? In your father's billfold" (Bombeck 183). Sound familiar?

After doing a morning radio show for a year and rising every day at 4:30 a.m., Ludlow Porch came to "one inescapable conclusion" about mornings: "If a sunrise was so great, the Lord would have had it happen around 3:30 in the afternoon, so more folks could see it" (Porch 43). Many people are inclined to agree with him.

But mornings aren't all bad. In fact, getting up early each morning can be beneficial.

THE EARLY BIRD GETS THE WORD

Why rise early in the morning? What possible good can come from getting up at the crack of dawn? In the still quiet of a house, before the crush of the day begins and the clamor of kids, pets, or carpools erupts, early morning moments can give us solitude to spend time with the Lord. Early morning may well be the only time during the entire day when we are by ourselves.

No law says we must spend quality time in scripture and in prayer at the start of each new day, but it helps. Often, if we wait till later, we never get around to opening the Bible or bowing before God. We get busy. People make demands on us. Errands, phone calls, and crises at work interrupt us. Night falls, and we're so tired that all we want to do is collapse in bed. Twenty-four hours are gone, and we have never gotten around to opening up God's word.

One of the hardest things in my life has been to discipline myself to rise early enough to exercise and to meet with the Lord on a daily basis. Only recently have I been doing this consistently. What a difference it makes. The biographies of persons greatly used by God bear this out. C. T. Studd, a turn-of-the-century English missionary statesman who arose at 4:30 each morning to spend time with the Lord, said, "If you don't desire to meet the Devil during the day, meet Jesus before dawn" (Cosgrove 82).

Mornings are good times to set aside for spending time with God. But what is most vital is that we meet daily with the Lord, no matter when and where it is. We must consistently commune with him in prayer. And, if we are ever going to grow up in him, we must consistently study his word.

The Ultimate Workout

A word workout is what James recommended in the passage we are about to consider. What is a word workout? It means taking a passage of scripture and focusing on it for all it will reveal to you. Meditating on it. Uncovering the context. Finding out what God really means. Seeking to understand how the teachings can be applied to your own life. You can pore over commentaries and Bible handbooks if you like, but don't neglect the primary source.

Have you ever bought weights, exercycles, rowing machines, or aerobic videos and never used them? Unused exercise equipment does nothing to get us in shape. Study Bibles, modern translations, commentaries, and handbooks that lie untouched on dusty shelves are not going to help us shape up spiritually, either. To have a successful word workout, we have to use the tools.

THE PRIMARY TOOL: THE WORD

The Bible is our primary word-workout tool. It is more than a piece of equipment; it is a weapon. "For the word of God is living and active and sharper than any two-edged sword, and piercing as far as the division of soul and spirit, of both joints and marrow, and able to judge the thoughts and intentions of the heart" (Hebrews 4:12 NASB).

Written over a period of 1,600 years by forty-four human authors inspired by the Holy Spirit, scripture tells one story from Genesis to Revelation: the story of God's plan for humanity through the working of Jesus Christ. With perfect unity and consistency, the Bible instructs us in godly living. Used properly, holy scripture is the ultimate weapon in the hearts and hands of believers. Knowing and applying God's word is the basic equipment of any spiritual shape-up program. In the words of the psalmist:

> How can a young man keep his way pure?
>   By living according to your word.
> I seek you with all my heart;
>   do not let me stray from your commands.
> I have hidden your word in my heart
>   that I might not sin against you (Psalm
>   119:9-11 NIV; see also Jeremiah 15:16;
>   1 Peter 2:2).

Those to whom James originally wrote his letter did not have the advantage we do of possessing the entire canon of scripture. They did have God's principles and prophecies as recorded in the Old Testament. Some had access to the early New Testament letters too. All had news of the life, works, and words of Jesus Christ, who perfectly embodied every principle of scripture, and who showed us the mind and heart of God in the only way we could understand—by becoming one of us.

James did not know at the time, but the Holy Spirit prompting him to write knew, that his letter to the displaced Jewish Christians would one day be included in what we call the New

Testament. God knew that millions of believers would eventually read the words of the epistle, as well as the writings of Matthew, Mark, Luke, John, Paul, Peter, and others. The fact that we possess the entire revealed written word of God should excite us. It should make what we are about to read in the last part of James 1 even more real and relevant to us.

We have already seen two marks of maturity that should be manifesting themselves in the life of the growing-up Christian. The first is that believers making spiritual progress are growing taller through testing. There is genuine joy in their hearts as they encounter trials and tests, not because these things are enjoyable, but because they are producing Christ-like qualities in their lives.

We have also seen that growing Christians are facing and resisting temptation. Although tests come from the hand of a loving God to produce growth, temptation comes from the evil one and is designed to destroy us. If he cannot prevent us from receiving Christ as Savior and thus entering the family of God, Satan's second supreme desire is to stunt our spiritual progress. He likes us to remain childish in our faith so that even if we are not his, we won't be much of a threat to him. The growing-up Christian is saying no to Satan by saying no to temptation.

Notice, the biblical directive is to submit to the test and resist the temptation. Often we do just the reverse. We fight against the test, crying, "Why God? Why this? Why me? Why now?" We become angry at the Lord for not making the ride easy and the road smooth, instead of submitting to what He has allowed and trying to discover what He longs to teach us through what He has permitted. On the other hand, when temptation rears its seductive head, we sometimes too easily capitulate. We give in. We compromise when we ought to dig in our heels and stand firm. And when we are saying yes when we ought to be saying no, we are not going to grow spiritually. We will find failure and frustration even as we long to go forward.

We experience growth when we are victorious over temptation and we are submitting to the test. But how? How do we do it? In what practical ways can we handle tests and temptation?

Let us never forget the powerful weapon God has given us for the battle: his holy word. Letting scripture sink into our hearts is a key to winning victory in the Christian life. James wrote just that in the last part of chapter 1 of his letter. Let's see what he had to say.

THE THREEFOLD TASK—JAMES 1:19-20

> You know this, my beloved brethren, now let every man be quick to hear, slow to speak, slow to anger. For a man's wrath does not bring about the righteousness of God.

We have all seen the recruiting poster from which the face of a tough-as-nails drill sergeant peers at us. The caption beneath reads, "The Marines are looking for a few good men." God is doing some looking too. He is examining our hearts as we face tests and temptations like those James has mentioned so far in his book. And while He searches, God is also looking to develop certain qualities in us.

James 1:19 describes the kinds of people the Lord would have us be when facing trial and temptation. There we read a threefold job description for the growing Christian: Quick to hear. Slow to speak. Slow to anger. Why would James be concerned that we manifest those qualities? I believe it is because when we are confronting tough and tempting times, we tend to do just the reverse of those. Think about it.

1. *Quick to hear*—By nature we don't like to listen. We fuss and fume when hassled. Our impulse is to act. We want to do something about the situation. Satan knows this, so he uses temptation to sneak in and apply enough pressure so that we will act impulsively. He loves for us to jump into things prematurely.

Remember when the devil tempted Jesus? The first thing he did was to urge Christ to satisfy his hunger by turning some stones into bread. Jesus' greatest physical need at that moment was for food. He had been tested in the wilderness by having to go without food for forty days, and He was hungry. What a temptation it was to him to be encouraged to manufacture some food on his own. How easy it could have been for him to jump into action, turn a pile of rocks into loaves of bread, and yield to Satan's temptation.

But Jesus wasn't one to act prematurely. He didn't jump into the middle of things independent of the Father. Instead, He was quick to listen. Quick to pick up on Satan's motives. Quick to observe the scheming heart behind the seemingly innocent statements.

When we face tests and temptations, we too must be quick to hear. We have to stop and listen. We must seek advice from trustworthy, wise people around us. More important, we must seek advice from the Holy Spirit by searching God's word for answers. Our willingness to hear is a sign that we are becoming submissive to what God would have us learn through it all. We are growing when we are ready to pay attention to him.

2. *Slow to speak*—It is also natural for us, when facing a test, to blurt out things we shouldn't. "Boy, Lord, thanks a lot! You really gave me a raw deal. My situation stinks." We discuss our discontent with whoever will listen. We yield to the temptation to complain, gossip, spit out angry words.

When confronted by temptation, it is often our words that get us into trouble. We make promises we can't keep and say things we don't mean. If we are not slow to speak, we will probably be eating our words later. The parrot and the owl are good examples of the foolishness of chatter and the wisdom of silence. I'm not sure where this short poem comes from, but its message packs quite a punch:

> A wise ol' owl lived in an oak.
> The more he knew, the less he spoke.
> The less he spoke, the more he knew.
> And this same thing applies to you.

It may be significant that God created us with two ears and one mouth! Could He have been suggesting that we listen twice as much as we talk?

3. *Slow to anger*—Hand in hand with our inclination to react to tests, trials, and temptations with very little listening and a whole lot of talking, comes our tendency to become frustrated and angry when things don't seem to be going our way. It shows up in what we say. It shows up in what we do.

When a devastating trial came into my life several years ago, I remember how quick I was to tell God just how annoyed I was that He had placed me in that position. At such times, my mouth often runneth over. My ears closeth up. It was weeks before I became receptive to learning what God desired to teach me through it all.

My change of heart came about as I turned to God's word. "And your ears will hear a word behind you, 'This is the way, walk in it,' whenever you turn to the right or to the left" (Isaiah 30:21 NASB). The Bible is the key. It can clue us in to what God may be teaching us through the test. It gives us the wisdom and the words to help us say no to a particular temptation. As we see from the temptation of Jesus in the wilderness, in God's word is the most secure place to be when the winds howl and the waves rage round about us.

ANGER DOESN'T CUT IT

Turning to scripture is essential in becoming quick to hear, slow to speak, and slow to anger. What is the reason for James's threefold command? It is because, as he put it, the Lord will not accomplish his righteousness in us when we are angry (1:20). We are not going to become what and who He wants us to become while we are spitting and sputtering.

Scripture is full of examples of people who, ruled by their emotions, became sidetracked in their relationships with God. Their anger rendered them unresponsive to the Lord's leading, sometimes with awful results. Cain disobeyed simple instructions and came to the altar with an offering of the fruit of the ground instead of with an animal sacrifice. Angry because God rejected his offer, Cain sought out his brother Abel, who had done things according to the book. The first murder in human history soon followed as Cain killed Abel in a fit of rage.

Moses, too, succumbed to anger, striking the rock instead of speaking to it as he had been told. The consequence? Moses was never allowed to enter the promised land, much less to have the privilege of leading the children of Israel there.

And there was Naaman, the leprous king, who vehemently rejected the prophet's directions to immerse himself seven times in the Jordan river so that he would be cured of his leprosy. Angrily Naaman refused to comply, until his emotions subsided and his heart changed. On his seventh dunk in the Jordan, his body was made whole again.

Even Jonah, whom God gave a whale of a time till he agreed to go to Nineveh and preach judgment, became furious when things didn't turn out as he expected. The citizens of Nineveh listened to Jonah's warnings, and because of his preaching, a great revival swept the city. They repented. God told Jonah that judgment would not be necessary at that time because of their repentance. What was Jonah's reaction to this good news? He became angry. He pouted underneath a gourd, angry at God's change of heart. What kind of a prophet would people think he was anyway? Who did God think He was, giving success to Jonah's preaching? Sitting stewing under the tree, Jonah wasn't in a position to accomplish much for God. He was ineffective, just as we are when we allow hot tempers to rule us.

THE MILK AND THE MEAT—JAMES 1:21

> Wherefore having laid aside all moral uncleanness and wickedness, which is abounding, in meekness receive the implanted word which is able to save your souls.

When a test or temptation threatens to nail us, what must we do? James gave us instructions with a two-part command (1:21): Lay aside evil. Receive the word.

PRESCRIPTION: STOP!

A prescription that works when your world is falling apart begins with a four-letter word: *Stop.* Instead of becoming a victim of the circumstances, stop. Lay aside anger, bitterness, envy, desire, and open up your Bible. Ask the Lord to show you his wisdom for handling the situation. Carve out an extended period of time and pore over God's word. Read it intensely. You are looking for more than a ten- or fifteen-minute fix. You may have to stay up late or get up before dawn to squeeze in the time, but do it. Just do it.

Disciplined Bible reading is much like training for a marathon. On an average day, a runner in training will run for five or six miles. Six weeks before the big race, the entrant will increase his daily distance to eight to fifteen miles. Some days he'll begin loading up on carbohydrates. He works out more intensely as the test of endurance approaches. Similarly, we may find that the tough times in our lives demand we work out more vigorously in God's word.

If you are not sure where to begin, try consulting a concordance or, without revealing any more details about your circumstances than you want to, try asking a knowledgeable friend or pastor for passages dealing with the issues you are facing. The more you use the book, the better you will know it. Soon you will remember passages on your own which you can turn to for strength and comfort.

In *Essentials of Discipleship*, Francis M. Cosgrove, Jr., suggested that we ask ourselves these questions concerning whichever passage of scripture we're reading:

1. Is there an example for me to follow?
2. Is there a command for me to obey?
3. Is there any error for me to avoid?
4. Is there any sin for me to renounce?
5. Is there any promise for me to claim?
6. Is there any new thought about God?
7. Is there any new thought about Jesus Christ?
8. Is there any new thought about the Holy Spirit's ministry in my life? (Cosgrove 74).

Don't forget to pray, either. It's an essential part of the prescription. After an extended period of interaction with God through his word and prayer, you will come away refreshed, usually with clear instruction about the direction your life should go. At that point, victory begins, but you have to be willing to learn. The answers are there. They always have been for me.

God made clear his direction for my life some seventeen years ago. I couldn't understand why He was dramatically leading me away from a fulltime Christian camping ministry. In six weeks time He brought healing to my spirit and emotions through the Psalms, Proverbs, and Isaiah. When I was ready for him to lead, He provided people to set up our Ministries as a nonprofit corporation. The rest is now history.

Opening the Bible during the crunch can be difficult. The normal human impulse is to rush and hurry and try to plug the holes in the dam. On our own, we want to do anything we possibly can, except to wait and listen. We'd much rather act. Do something. Fix it ourselves. But James has told us that we grow spiritually as we partake of God's word (1:21). The scriptures should be an integral part of our lives. It is the ultimate how-to book. It contains the best advice columns. It is a manual on marriage, morality, worship, parenting, and relationships human and divine, all rolled into one.

DEVELOPING SOLID SPIRITUAL APPETITES

The intake of God's word is one sure way God grows us up as Christians. The apostle Peter wrote, "Therefore, putting aside all malice and all guile and hypocrisy and envy and all slander, like newborn babes, long for the pure milk of the word, that by it you may grow in respect to salvation" (1 Peter 2:1-2 NASB). That sounds like James 1:21, doesn't it?

If you have ever had a newborn baby around the house, you know that in the early hours of the morning when the little lungs start warming up and noises come from the nursery, you can quiet the baby with warm milk. The cries signify need. Baby is really saying, "I'm hungry! Feed me!" in the only way he or she knows how. Within many Christians the Holy Spirit is saying, "I'm hungry. Feed me." As young believers it is essential that we partake daily of the milk of the word. Drink it in.

When we do that we begin to develop an appetite for the word. The more we get, the more we want. Our spiritual taste buds awaken; we stop being satisfied with the sweets, the fluff, the superficial. Like athletes in training we begin getting a good, honest hunger to know more of God. We want to dig into his scripture ourselves, without relying solely on books, sermons, Sunday school lessons, or radio programs for our spiritual enlightenment. On our own we start to see just how the word of God relates to the daily dilemmas we face. If we miss an appointment with God in his word one morning, we begin to feel spiritually empty halfway through the day. Our increasing sensitivity to the power of scripture signifies that we are growing up in Jesus Christ.

Neither James nor Peter was telling us that we must become perfect before opening God's word. But we must be willing to get rid of the ugly things, the cheap substitutes, before we can expect to have solid spiritual appetites. The word of God becomes the bread on which we feed. As the word starts to work in our lives, the old things—bad habits, wrong emotions, thoughtless speech—pass away. New things take their place.

The process sometimes seems slow. In one of his books Keith Miller described the growth rate of the Chinese bamboo tree. Evidently, for the first four years of its life, the Chinese bamboo makes little if any visible growth. Suddenly, sometime during the fifth year, it shoots up ninety feet in sixty days. Is it correct to say that the bamboo tree grew in sixty days or in five years? (Miller 51). The same may be true of your spiritual life. If you are faithful, the word will do its work. Don't be disappointed if your growth isn't rocketlike, but don't be surprised either if later on a warpspeed spurt occurs in your spiritual maturity.

In Meekness Receiving the Implanted Word

"In meekness receive the implanted word" urged James (1:21). Meekness does not equal weakness. It signifies the inner strength to receive rather than to rebel.

Note also the phrase, "the implanted word." I am reminded of Matthew 13, where Jesus told the parable of the sower and the seed. Some of the seed fell beside the road, where the birds ate it. Some fell on rocks, where there was little soil; the plants that sprouted soon withered and died. Some of the seed landed among thorns, which choked out all growth. Some of the seed fell on good soil, yielding lovely fruit. Our lives as Christians can be like the picture in the parable. As the word of God comes into our hearts, will it find the stony, shallow, stubborn ground of rebellion, as we refuse to relate rightly to trials and tests? Will it find us resisting temptation or will we be telling ourselves, "Why not? Just once never hurt anyone, will it?" When we are submitting to the test, resisting temptation, and searching the scriptures, it is amazing how the word of God springs up and makes us fruitful.

At the Proper Time

Some stumbling blocks always exist to stop you before you even get started in seriously reading God's word. Let me warn you about a major one. Paul mentioned the "milk" and "meat" of the word (1 Corinthians 3:2 kjv). Traditionally, theologians define the "milk" as the simple basics of the faith, and the "meat" as the more difficult sections of scripture. Interpreted this way, we see that it is a mistake to try to bite into the meat when you haven't consumed enough of the milk.

"I read John and Revelation," a college student told me the other day. "I didn't get anything out of it." Talk about the milk and the meat! I wasn't surprised.

A human infant progresses from mother's milk or formula to cereal to strained vegetables, fruits, and meats. It takes time till the magic day arrives when only table food is consumed. Soon the baby can feed herself or himself, and a harried mom feels she is free at last. But no matter how busy Mom and Dad are, they would never feed chunks of table food to a newborn infant. They wouldn't rush the process, because the baby wouldn't be ready. The parallel to the spiritual life is evident.

Why should young believers wade into the most complex portions of scripture before they have been exposed to passages easier to understand? Why should any of us become anxious because we don't understand Ezekiel, the seventieth week of Daniel, the book of Revelation, premillennialism, post-tribulationism? We will grasp such teachings better some day, if we are faithful to study God's word. Let's start off with the milk.

My suggestions? I recommend the following reading schedule to new believers. It is by no means the only way to explore the word. Others have their own, very valid, ideas about what should be tackled first. But this is my two cents' worth on the issue. I generally advise new believers to start with the gospel of love, John. Then I suggest they progress to 1 John, Mark, Psalms, Proverbs, Matthew, and Luke. Getting hold of a *One Year Bible*, particularly in the Living Bible edition, is a great way to get the big picture too.

BE YE DOERS—JAMES 1:22-25

> But keep on becoming doers of the word and not hearers only, deceiving yourselves. Because if anyone is a hearer of the word and not a doer, this one is like a man looking at the face of his birth in the mirror. For he looked at himself, and he has gone off and immediately forgotten what sort of person he was. But he who has looked into the perfect law, the law of liberty, and has continued in it, not having been a hearer who forgets, but a doer who works, this man shall be blessed in what he does.

Where there's life, there's going to be a desire to grow, a hunger for something to feed the soul. The milk and the meat of the word can do it. We are what we eat. But the Christian life is more than just receiving the implanted word. There is also the vital matter of doing something about it. We are called to put scripture into practice. We are to be more than hearers of the word. We are to be doers.

Being doers of the word may signal that we are actually partaking of the meat of God's word. I'd like to credit Dr. Earl Radmacher with opening my eyes to an alternative explanation of what Paul called the "milk" and "meat" of the word. Jesus said, "My meat is to do the will of him that sent me, and to finish his work" (John 4:34 KJV). It is possible that a "milk drinker" is one who may know scripture, but does not practice or apply it. Conversely, a "meat eater" is one who practically applies the teachings of the Bible to his or her own life. What is clear is that scripture exhorts us to practice what we're taught.

In the Old Testament we meet Ezra, a hearer and a doer. Of him we read, "For Ezra had devoted himself to the study and observance of the Law of the Lord, and to teaching its decrees and laws in Israel" (Ezra 7:10 NIV). The King James version tells us that Ezra "prepared his heart." For what tasks did he prepare his heart? Ezra devoted himself to doing three things, the ingredients of spiritual richness:

1. *Seeking the law of the Lord*—Ezra studied scripture thoroughly, delving into it, reaching below the surface, knowing it intimately.

2. *Doing the law of the Lord*—Ezra implemented what he learned from scripture. He didn't just read about honoring God; he honored God. He didn't just read about moral purity; he kept himself morally pure. He didn't just read about sacrificially serving God; he did it by going back to Jerusalem to reinstate the worship of the Israelites and to instruct them in the scriptures.

3. *Teaching the law of the Lord*—Ezra did even more than hear and do the law of God. He taught it to others. He saw his knowledge and wisdom spiritually reproduced in the hearts and lives of other believers. What a source of satisfaction!

STUFFED SHEEP, STILL QUITE CARNAL

To receive God's word, to do it, to teach it to others—I know of no better recipe for spiritual growth. Each ingredient is an essential component of the process. Doing more than just hearing God's word is crucial. Far too many Christians today are stuffed with content but are still quite carnal (see Hebrews 5:11-14).

The fact is, according to James, if we cram ourselves with scripture without ever applying it to our lives and allowing it to change us, we will be sinning. "To the one knowing how to do good, and . . . not doing it, to him it is sin" (4:17). God doesn't want stuffed sheep grown fat and lazy because the pickings are easy. He wants tough, disciplined servants who are going to tell others about his kingdom, and who will instruct those who have entered his family about godly living.

People who only hear the word, and never do the word, are candidates for frustration. They are the smug saints who sit in the pews and criticize the preacher, programs, music, youth workers, Sunday school teachers. Their self-righteousness is a mask concealing angry hearts which haven't changed very much following their conversion. They have lost their first love.

An arrogant, unteachable spirit often develops in those who have a lot of Bible knowledge, yet do not apply it. How easy it can become to excuse such sins of the flesh as anger, envy, jealousy, strife, and bitterness. John wrote of such a man, "Diotrephes, who loves to be first among them, does not accept what we say" (3 John 9 NASB).

People who hear the word and do not implement it in their lives may also become depressed. I ought to know. The other day I sat in the frustration/depression seat. I was sharing with a friend some concerns for the future of the Ministries because of the U.S. economy and my physical condition. My friend responded, "Why don't you practice what you preach? Philippians 4:6-7 are the verses you gave me in a similar situation."

> Be anxious for nothing, but in everything by prayer and supplication with thanksgiving let your requests be made known to God. And the peace of God, which surpasses all comprehension, shall guard your hearts and your minds in Christ Jesus (NASB).

Bam! My friend got to me with the word. My frustration level sank. Now when I start to get depressed about circumstances, I reflect on that verse.

Don't think that refusal to do the word of God is anything new. Nearly six hundred years before Christ's birth, the prophet Ezekiel was preaching to the children of Israel. The audiences had been coming, sitting, soaking up his words. Then came a truth straight from God who read their hearts, "My people come to you, as they usually do, and sit before you to listen to your words, but they do not put them into practice. With their mouths they express devotion, but their hearts are greedy for unjust gain" (Ezekiel 33:31 NIV). What a frustration. The problem in Ezekiel's day was the problem in James's day and is the problem today. As Professor Howard Hendricks often reminded us at seminary: Impression without expression leads to depression. People get hungry for the word and they start consuming it but they fail to do it. Then they are just as depressed and frustrated as they were before they knew it. They are targets for temptation.

SECRETS OF SUCCESS

I remember one fireside at a high school camp when a student stood up and said, "I've been coming to camp for years, making promises and not going through with them. I'm going home this year and be obedient." What a joy it was to see him halfway through the school year, bearing witness to his commitment by saying, "Hey, it really works!" He was a three-dimensional testimony of the truth of 1 John 2:3-6:

> And by this we know that we have come to know Him, if we keep His commandments. The one who says, "I have come to know Him," and does not keep His commandments, is a liar, and the truth is not in him; but whoever keeps His word, in him the love of God has truly been perfected. By this we know that we are in Him: the one who says he abides in Him ought himself to walk in the same manner as He walked" (NASB).

Three often-quoted rules for hearing and doing the word are these which I recall from my first inductive Bible study class with Dr. Hendricks:

1. Observation—What do I see?
2. Interpretation—What does it mean?
3. Application—What does it mean to me? What must I do now to express my obedient heart?

When we hear and do the word, we are laying the right foundation for our lives. In the sermon on the mount, Jesus said of those who hear and do:

> Therefore everyone who hears these words of Mine, and acts upon them, may be compared to a wise man, who built his house upon the rock. And the rain descended, and the floods came, and the winds blew, and burst against that house; and yet it did not fall, for it had been founded upon the rock (Matthew 7:24-25 NASB).

And of those who hear, yet refuse to act upon his instructions:

> And everyone who hears these words of Mine, and does not act upon them, will be like a foolish man, who built his house upon the sand. And the rain descended, and the floods came, and the winds blew, and burst against that house; and it fell, and great was its fall (Matthew 7:26-27 NASB).

On that day, the people listening stood amazed at Christ's words. But the message should be loud and clear. We must obey the written word.

Spiritual blessing and spiritual success follow obedience. Moses knew that. We read his "swan song" in the last few chapters of the book of Deuteronomy. As he prepared to die, Moses reminded the children of Israel of all that God had done for them. "Take to heart all the words I have solemnly declared to you this day, so that you may command your children to obey carefully all the words of this law. They are not just idle words–they are your life. By them you will live long in the land you are crossing the Jordan to possess" (Deuteronomy 32:46-47 NIV). The patriarch died later that day.

When the time of mourning had passed, and Joshua, Moses' successor, prepared to lead the Israelites into the promised land, the Lord gave him this message, "Do not let this Book of the Law depart from your mouth; meditate on it day and night, so that you may be careful to do everything written in it. Then you will be prosperous and successful" (Joshua 1:8 NIV). Do you want to be spiritually blessed? Do you desire to be spiritually rich? Begin to implement in your life what you know of God's word, and you will be on your way.

IN THE MIRROR

Because growth can take place in our lives only as we see things as they really are, God has provided the mirror of the word to correct, instruct, and guide us. We deceive ourselves if we ignore its significance. James said as much (1:23-24). If we come, hear, listen, and then neglect to implement God's truth in our lives, we become like a man who looks in a mirror, notices that he needs a shave and haircut, and then walks off without taking care of his appearance. He neglects his responsibilities, and even forgets what they are, once he walks away from the mirror.

That hits home, doesn't it? How many times have you heard a message from a teacher or preacher or read a passage from the Bible, and been struck by the need to clear up some obvious sin in your life? Have you done anything about it?

Maybe you hear a message about the need for transparency and total honesty in the Christian life. You suddenly remember that you fudged on your last expense report, you blew your stack at the receptionist at work, you promised your son you'd toss the football around and then you forgot your promise. You did any number of things that were contrary to God's standards. You resolve to do something about it. You'll make amends to the boy. You'll clear up the discrepancy on your expense report. You'll apologize to the receptionist for getting out of line. You'll plan to clean up your mess—while you're still sitting down, that is. Come the next day or the day after, as you've distanced yourself from the convicting message of God's word, you slack off. You rationalize. You decide not to dredge up the past. Justifying your inaction will be as easy as it was originally to resolve to do the right thing. And you will be like a kid who has looked in the mirror, seen his dirty face, and promptly forgotten it. Not too appealing to the watching world. Certainly not transparent with humility and Christ-likeness.

It is bad enough when we don't clear up everyday sins. But when habit patterns of sin build, we are in even bigger trouble. The mirror of the word will always show us the truth, if we are willing to look inside and take it to heart.

One of the most frustrating facets of my counseling ministry is that often I encounter a Christian who is rationalizing away a habitual sin. "God wants me to be happy," said one fellow. "I'm not staying in a marriage I don't want. I'll take care of the kids financially. She can get a job. But there is no way I'm staying." He had made up his mind. After several sessions and hours of listening, I shared scriptures with him about the sanctity of marriage, the place of the family, God's will for him and his wife as a couple. But he wasn't receptive. I couldn't convince him to look, really look, in the mirror of God's word. Today a shattered family is the result of his selfishness.

THE BLESSINGS OF MIRROR VISION

The apostle Paul admonished the Colossian believers, "Let the word of Christ richly dwell within you, with all wisdom teaching and admonishing one another with psalms and hymns and spiritual songs, singing with thankfulness in your hearts to God" (Colossians 3:16 NASB). What rewards there are for people who look in the mirror and come away changed! James said, "But he who has looked into the perfect law ... and has continued in it ... this man shall be blessed in what he does"(1:25). If we are hearers and doers, we will be blessed in what we do. The growing Christian is one who is blessed.

What kind of blessings was James talking about? Here are a few ideas. We will have a sense of well-being; we will know the smile of God's approval; we will have fellowship with the Lord and with other believers; we will see his direction in circumstances and provision; we will change toward Christ-likeness; we will be given opportunities for ministry; we will be overwhelmed with his love, goodness, and faithfulness.

Does your spiritual life seem dry and dusty? Does the Bible appear irrelevant, though you know you're a Christian? Has the hope of heaven become distant and uncertain? Perhaps the blessings aren't there because you are not lining up to the plan of God as revealed in his word. When I come to the point where I can read the Bible, implement its messages, and deal with areas in my life that do not coordinate with God's standards and will, I'm on my way. I can expect blessing and growth.

Notice that James called God's principles and standards the "perfect law, the law of liberty" (1:25). The Old Testament law was a law of bondage and condemnation, impossible to keep. New Testament commands are laws of liberty, achievable because of the Spirit of God working in us (see Galatians 5:1; John 8:32; Romans 7:6).

"And ye shall know the truth, and the truth shall make you free," Jesus promises (John 8:32 KJV). Do you want freedom? Knowing God's will and plan for your life will not restrain you, but will give you the greatest liberty imaginable. It means you are placing your life into the hands of the one who created you the way you are.

Knowing the scriptures is part of the process of surrendering to him. The psalmist put it this way:

> Blessed is the man
>   who does not walk in the counsel of the wicked
> or stand in the way of sinners
>   or sit in the seat of mockers.
> But his delight is in the law of the Lord,
>   and on his law he meditates day and night
>   (Psalm 1:1-2 NIV).

The blessed man doesn't listen to ungodly men; he doesn't play around with temptation; he does not laugh at or make light of the things of God. This man is happy.

These days we spin our wheels in seventeen directions trying to find happiness and contentment. We try materialism, one more possession. If we only had that car, that boat, that condo, we would be happy. We try family, friends, social ladders, corporate ventures. But the truth is that only in God and through God can we be happy. "Delight yourself in the Lord and he will give you the desires of the heart" (Psalm 37:4 NIV; see also Matthew 6:33). Solomon put it this way, "A man can do nothing better than to eat and drink and find satisfaction in his work. This too, I see, is from the hand of God, for without him, who can eat or find enjoyment?" (Ecclesiastes 2:24-25 NIV).

I am a one hundred percent advertisement of God's ability

to change a life. And believe me, He is still working on me. Pruned branches produce fruit, and mine are constantly snipped. I thank God that through his infinite patience, He is making something out of me. He is making me someone He can use. He has given me, and is giving me, an intense hunger for his word, a deep desire to do with the rest of my life only what pleases him, the capacity to reflect Christ more and more brightly on a daily basis, the desire to learn to let him do things his way, and the ability to find joy and contentment whatever the circumstances.

A HEARER WHO DOES—JAMES 1:26-27

> If any man is thinking himself to be religious, not holding in check his tongue, but is deceiving his own heart, his religion is worthless. Religion which is pure and undefiled in the presence of our God and Father is this, to look after orphans and widows in their distress, to keep oneself unspotted by the world.

The Christian who is growing is the Christian who is changing. He or she is not perfect yet. As Paul described himself, "Not that I have already obtained it, or have already become perfect, but I press on in order that I may lay hold of that for which also I was laid hold of by Christ Jesus" (Philippians 3:12; see also 2:13-14 NASB). We are all somewhere along the way to glory. We are a jumble of positives and negatives. Yet some indicators that we are growing should become evident in our lives. James has given us a few of these qualities in the final verses of chapter 1. They are characteristics of a growing Christian. We do not earn our salvation by displaying these traits, but once saved, we receive the capacity to acquire them as we submit to the word and to the leading of the Holy Spirit.

THE GROWING CHRISTIAN IS . . .

The first characteristic of a growing Christian is tongue control (1:26). It is a topic that James later addressed at length (chapter 3). For now let's just see that the growing Christian is one who is manifesting self-discipline. An obvious way is through the control of one's tongue. We are to be slow to speak, and quick to hear—not the reverse.

Pearl once gave me a card that summed up James's sentiments here. "Be sure your brain is in gear before you put your
mouth in motion." Amen. When I think of tongue control, I
think of my good friend Tom. When he speaks, you listen,
because you know that what he says will be well thought-out,
positive, uplifting, and to the point.

Another quality of a growing Christian is compassion. As an
example James mentioned caring for the vulnerable of our
world, the widows and orphans (1:27). Compassion is love in
action. It is love with heart and hands and feet and talents and
resources. It means doing something for others. Maturing
believers love, care, and help. People come to them and know
they won't be turned away.

Our friend Nona is a genuine people lover. Tears fill her eyes
easily, and she is always ready to do whatever the moment
demands. She couldn't go on a recent Sunday school trip to San
Antonio because of her husband's emergency cancer surgery,
but she met the busload of us when we arrived home. Knowing that everyone was concerned about David and her, Nona
laid our worries to rest by reassuring us with her bright smile
and cheerful words. She even brought a red carnation for each
of the women, unselfishly thinking of ways to cheer others in
the midst of her own difficulties.

A third quality of a growing Christian is to be "unspotted by
the world" (1:27). Holiness and purity set these believers apart.
They have convictions, do not compromise, and do not conform to the standards of the world. Others may wonder why
they are different. My friend Dub is such a man. He literally
glows, and everyone who knows him realizes that his radiance
comes from spending time with the Lord. His sweet spirit has
been developed in the crucible of suffering. Uncompromising
where scripture is concerned, Dub does not hesitate to let people know tactfully what the Bible says about issues.

Are You or Aren't You?

Once you enter the family of God by faith, you have a choice:
to grow or not to grow, to stay a spiritual baby, or shed the dia-
pers, the bottle, the bib.

Are you growing up or not? Are you submitting to the test,
resisting temptation, perusing and practicing God's word? Can

your wife see a change in you? Your husband? Your kids? Your friends? Your co-workers? If they can't see any change, why not? The ball is in your court. Go for it.

Sara Boyd is one who is going for it. The wife of my good friend and (now former) running buddy, Doug, she is one of those people who will wear you out just watching her. The busy mother of three growing children, Sara finds time for Bible Study Fellowship, church work, and many other activities—including sponsoring the Ministries' Fort Worth class with Doug. Sara somehow manages to run a few miles each day, and she also always makes time to spend with God in his word. No skimming of Bible passages for her—Sara digs into scripture, relishing real workouts in the word. Her heart for God, love of his word, and spiritual growth are obvious to all. Her ministry has touched countless lives. Over the years I've watched Sara run uphill into the wind of adversity and keep going. Her tenacity is inspiring. Daily, it seems, God produces growth in her life. As Doug admits, he finds himself often just trying to keep pace. May her sphere of influence for God increase.

Points to Ponder

1. What three qualities does James encourage us to desire in 1:19? When in your own experience might it be beneficial to be quick to hear, slow to speak, and slow to anger? Think of specific situations you encounter as you consider your answer.

2. According to James 1:23-24, what sort of person do we become like when we hear the word of God and do not implement it in our lives? Have you ever been convicted by God's word of the need to change in a certain area, and then forgotten your resolve soon afterward? (If so, you're not alone.)

3. What, according to 1:25, is one result of being both a hearer and a doer of the word? Explain what sort of blessings James means, in your opinion.

4

Nobody Gets Cut from God's Team

James 2:1-13

T. Roland Philips recalls that as the Korean war escalated, a South Korean Christian civilian was arrested by communists and ordered to be shot. On learning that the prisoner was in charge of an orphanage caring for small children, the young communist leader who had condemned him decided to spare him. The decision was made to execute the man's son instead, and the believer was forced to watch as his nineteen-year-old boy was shot to death before his eyes.

In the course of the war, the young communist leader who had ordered the execution was himself captured by United Nations forces, tried, and condemned to death. But before the sentence could be carried out, the Christian whose son had been killed made a moving plea for the life of the communist. Declaring that the young man had not really known what he was doing, the Christian implored, "Give him to me, and I will train him." His request was granted; the murderer was released to live in the home of his victim's father. The believer fulfilled his pledge. Today, thanks to the compassion of a bereaved father who saw beyond his grief, the young man is no longer a communist. He is a Christian pastor (Tan 459).

NOT HIM!

Centuries before the Korean conflict, another unlovable man single-mindedly sought to crush anyone who claimed to know Christ as Savior. A man's man, traditionally believed to be small in frame but certainly powerful in leadership potential, Saul was born in the city of Tarsus and grew up in Jerusalem. A Roman citizen and full-blooded Jew of the tribe of Benjamin, he received his religious training from the most well-respected rabbi of the day, Gamaliel. Politically influential, Saul was a member of the Sanhedrin, the Jewish governing body.

Zealous for his ancestral traditions, Saul outstripped his contemporaries in keeping the law of Moses. When all the ruckus about the "dead heretic" Jesus erupted, Saul launched a personal vendetta, passionately pursuing the quest of wiping out the early church. He was avid in his persecution of anyone who followed the Way, as Christianity was called then (Acts 9:2). After witnessing the stoning of Stephen, Saul, armed with search, seizure, and arrest warrants, headed north toward Damascus to root out a pocket of believers. The firebrand never fulfilled his mission.

Just outside the city of Damascus, a piercing light from heaven flashed about him. Saul fell prostrate to the ground, the voice of the Lord Jesus confronting him with these words, "Saul, Saul, why are you persecuting Me?" (Acts 9:4 NASB).

"Who art Thou, Lord?" Saul gasped.

"I am Jesus whom you are persecuting, but rise, and enter the city, and it shall be told you what you must do," came the answer (see Acts 9:5-6 NASB).

Saul of Tarsus was led into the city by his companions. It was Saul, yet not Saul. A new man walked within the walls of Damascus, a man physically blinded yet spiritually illumined by his encounter with the resurrected Christ.

Three days passed. Then the Lord appeared in a vision to a Damascan believer named Ananias, instructing him to find Saul and lay hands on him so that his sight might be restored. Ananias hedged. "Lord, I have heard from many about this man, how much harm he did to Thy saints at Jerusalem; and here he has authority from the chief priests to bind all who call upon Thy name," he protested (Acts 9:13-14 NASB). In other words, he was saying, Lord, are You sure You know what You are asking me to do? This man Saul is nothing but trouble. He wants to arrest me, and he's got power to do it. God, I want nothing to do with him.

Despite his reservations, Ananias obeyed God anyway and went to Saul with this explanation: "Brother Saul, the Lord Jesus, who appeared to you on the road by which you were coming, has sent me so that you may regain your sight, and be filled with the Holy Spirit" (Acts 9:17 NASB). Scales fell from Saul's eyes, and his sight returned. He arose, ate, and was baptized. "He is the Son of God," the new convert now eagerly proclaimed of Jesus to his fellow Jews in the synagogues (Acts 9:20). Saul now spent many days in Damascus with disciples there who welcomed him in spite of their earlier reservations.

Returning to Jerusalem after narrowly escaping the Jewish authorities who had hatched a plot to kill him, Saul found himself greeted less warmly by the believers in that city. Luke records that "when he [Saul] had come to Jerusalem, he was trying to associate with the disciples; and they were all afraid of him, not believing that he was a disciple" (Acts 9:26 NASB). It was painful for those Christians to learn to love and to trust this once powerful persecutor. Only the kindness and compassion of a man named Barnabas convinced the apostles that Saul's conversion was real. It took a lot of teeth-gritting courage for the early Christians to accept this once unlovely man, later to be known as the apostle Paul. But accept him they did, because the God of love was reproducing his divine love within them. They knew that even Saul of Tarsus couldn't be excluded from the team, no matter what he had done.

Nobody who knows Christ gets cut from God's team.

LEARNING TO LOVE

Loving the unlovely doesn't come naturally. It is a learned response. James has shown us that growing Christians are those who are responding to tests, resisting temptation, and absorbing the word. An equally valid signpost of spiritual growth is that we are learning to love even those who are tough to love.

We grow as God's love grows in us, and we become his channels to show his love to others. We are spurred on to tell the unsaved world about the Lord Jesus Christ. We begin to want the best for other people, no matter who they are, how they dress, or what they do, because God's is a love without partiality. Hannah Hurnard wrote of divine love in her allegory, *Mountains of Spices*:

> "I am love," said the King very clearly. "If you want to see the pattern of true love, look at me, for I am the expression of the law of love on which the universe is founded. And the very first characteristic of true love, as I have manifested it, is willingness to accept all other human beings, just as they are, however blemished and marred by sin they may be, and to acknowledge oneness with them in their sin and need" (Hurnard 46).

As Hurnard suggested, no matter who we are, we are one in our need of the Savior. God is no respecter of persons. "For there is no partiality with God" (Romans 2:11 NASB). God longs for fellowship with *everyone*—the ugly and the beautiful, the cultured and the crude, the wealthy socialite and the welfare mother. We are all the same in significance to him.

Colonel Clarke of Chicago worked six days a week at his business, just so he might keep a relief mission going seven nights a week. Each evening a mixed bag of down-and-outers—thieves, pickpockets, alcoholics, hopeless men—gathered for supper and the colonel's sermons. Not a dynamic speaker, Clarke somehow kept the men spellbound with his ramblings. Some of the greatest preachers in Chicago visited the mission and spoke at times, but none ever commanded the men's intense attention the way the colonel did. Why? It was because Clarke's compassion and love for them were obvious. Tears often welled up in his eyes, and always seemed near the surface as he spoke. Men who had no hope in life found comfort in the words of one who cared deeply. Many of them found the Savior, thanks to the colonel's impartial love (Tan 1324).

It is one thing to learn to love unbelieving men like those at the Chicago relief mission, or even to love men like Saul who come into the Christian family carrying the baggage of a checkered past. It is something else entirely to reach out in compassion to those who have been Christians a while, but whose behavior does not reflect their relationship with the Lord. We tend to want to write them off, to drop them from the squad. Yet God calls us to love the unlovely, no matter who they are.

I was a Christian for many years before I discovered that I could grow spiritually through expressing my love to others. I can manifest God's love to other people by my willingness to be involved in their lives, in order to help them to grow. I've found I never give my time, talents, knowledge, or skills without coming away a richer person myself. Love in action is a means of maturing in the faith. Viewing the sometimes shattered lives of others gives me an appreciation of all that God has done for me. Helping someone else understand scripture often provides me with fresh insights into God's word.

The benefits of being available to love are tremendous. But how do we become channels of God's love? That is the subject James addressed in the verses that follow, as he took a practical look at dealing with discrimination.

A Discourse on Discrimination—James 2:1-7

> My brethren, be not holding the faith of our Lord Jesus Christ, the Lord of glory, while showing partiality. For if there comes into your synagogue a man with gold rings on his fingers in brightly shining clothing, and there comes in also a poor man in filthy rags, and you look upon the one wearing the clothing which is brightly shining and say, "You be seated here in a good place," and to the poor man you say, "Stand in that place or be sitting down beside my footstool," are you not divided in your own mind and have become judges with evil thoughts? Listen, my brethren, beloved ones, did not God choose out for himself those who are poor in the world to be rich in faith and heirs of the kingdom which He promised to those who love him? But you dishonored the poor man. Are not those who are wealthy exploiting you, and they themselves drag you into court? Are they not the ones who are defaming the good [beautiful] name by which you were called?

The Warning

James began chapter 2 with a call to arms for Christians, a command to lace up our boots and start slogging through the mud to reach the unreachable, to touch the untouchable, to love the unlovable. We must not hold "the faith of our Lord Jesus Christ, the Lord of glory, while showing partiality" (2:1).

Jesus is both "our Lord" and "the Lord of glory." The latter term indicates the presence of God. It was used in the Old Testament for the shekinah glory, when God appeared over the tabernacle and also in the wilderness during the exodus as a cloud by day and a fire by night to guide the children of Israel (see Exodus 13:21-22; 40:34). Here James was referring to Jesus Christ as the perfect, pure manifestation of God to humankind. As the apostle John put it, "And the Word became flesh, and dwelt [tabernacled] among us, and we beheld His glory, glory as of the only begotten from the Father, full of grace and truth" (John 1:14 NASB). There is no doubt about it. To James, Jesus Christ is God in visible flesh.

James's warning is basically this: Brothers and sisters, don't say you're believers and yet show partiality. Don't claim the cross and still be concerned with social climbing. Instead, remember that "the rich and the poor have a common bond, The Lord is the maker of them all" (Proverbs 22:2 NASB). We often make the mistake of bringing the standards of the world over into Christianity. At the cross of Jesus Christ the ground is level. Rich and poor are alike to him.

THE ILLUSTRATION

To prove that God hates partiality, James next provided a picture of preferential treatment within the church (2:2-4). The scene is sadly still too common in churches today. Imagine it. Into your church one Sunday strides a man with gold rings, a Rolex watch, Gucci loafers, Brooks Brothers shirt, suit, and silk tie. His nails are manicured, his hair shaped and styled. He carries an elegant Bible: full-grain leather, gilded pages, the right translation. He smells of expensive cologne, and he exudes confidence. His demeanor tells you he is successful, powerful, and used to commanding respect. The ushers promptly seat him as far to the front as he will let them.

Behind him comes a shabbily dressed man. His pants need ironing, and his shirt collar is frayed. There are stains on his tie, and his coat was tailored for someone two sizes larger. He could use a good shave, and it would take more than a shine to make his shoes presentable. He smells musty, stale, and sour. His Bible is well-worn and torn at the edges. The ushers see him and glance quickly at one another. One takes him by the arm and guides him to a seat at the back, unless there's a balcony where he would be even less conspicuous. He is not one we want others to notice, not one we would show off as a sheep representative of *our* flock.

If those men keep attending, and it is evident that they are both believers, soon one will probably be asked to serve on committees and councils. He will be voted into church leadership as soon as congregational rules allow. His opinion will count. The other man will remain in the back rows Sunday after Sunday. Guess which is which.

The pathetic truth is that we in the body of Christ tend to assume that worldly success equals Christian success. The well-to-do doctor, lawyer, or businessman who comes to Jesus is far more likely to find himself a leader of the local church than is a poor man, no matter how spiritually minded he might be.

Jerry and Bob started coming to one of our churches at approximately the same time. Jerry drove a Cadillac, lived in a large house, wore expensive well-tailored suits, and quickly let us know that he had been the chairman of the board at his last church. As for Bob, his clothes weren't as nice, and his retirement income modest, but he loved the Lord and desired to serve him in any way possible. Always the first to volunteer for the dirty work, church workdays found Bob with paintbrush, broom, and gardening tools, ready to get to it for the glory of God. Sunday school substitute needed? No problem. Bob could be counted on to fill the vacancy. Very few people knew of Bob's heartfelt desire to serve the Lord as a church officer, and he was never elected. Jerry, on the other hand, not nearly so enthusiastic in service as Bob, served several terms as an elder.

THE DOUBLE-MINDED DANGER

Human nature prefers the attractive to the unlovely. Each year at the Ministries it is a challenge to encourage our camp counselors to be sensitive to the needs of kids who are constant sources of irritation. Every year at least one of those children arrives at camp. He (or she) always has to be first in line, sparks cabin fights, breaks the rules. He is the only one who doesn't make his bed, and bellyaches about cabin clean-up. He pushes and kicks the girls, tells dirty stories, and uses profanity. At least twice a day he sneaks off into the woods to try to smoke the cigarettes he has smuggled in.

How tough it can be to convince our college-aged counselors that they can have an even greater ministry with the unlovable kid than they can with the kid who does everything right and knows all the answers. Invariably we are drawn to the beautiful ones. We leave out the ugly, the poor, the vulnerable, the hurting. We move with the people who appeal to us most. We single out the ones who already have all the advantages, because just knowing them feeds our egos. But the hard truth is that if our love for others is based on favoritism, it is a product of selfishness rather than of the Holy Spirit.

According to James, if we love with partiality, we are "divided" in our own minds (2:4). Remember, James said earlier that a "double-minded man" is "unstable in all his ways" (1:8). Showing partiality indicates that we are living by our old minds rather than by the new mind or new nature we received when we trusted Christ. We are not thinking with the mind of Jesus, but rather are spiritual schizophrenics on the issue of love.

James was direct in his assessment. When we judge people on the externals and do not seek the heart, we are "judges with evil thoughts" (2:4). The Lord once said as much to the prophet Samuel.

When instructing Samuel in the selection of the next king of the nation of Israel, the Lord told him, "Do not consider his appearance or his height, for I have rejected him. The Lord does not look at the things man looks at. Man looks at the outward appearance, but the Lord looks at the heart" (1 Samuel 16:7). Soon a mere shepherd boy named David, the youngest of Jesse's sons, was anointed king.

One of the challenges of parenting is not to show favoritism. Has a son or daughter ever accused you of something like "You don't love me as much as you love Johnny!" or "You love Mary more than you do me"? In essence, your child is telling you that to his way of thinking, you play favorites. As parents we must fight against the tendency to be partial. From my perspective as a father of five, let me admit that it is easier to show love to the kid who is submissive and cooperative than to the child who digs a rut with his feet resisting every attempt to lead him. Some kids fight you every step of the way. Yet often they are the ones who require a consistent demonstration of love most of all.

I love all my children. The fact is that some were easier to raise than others, but that is not an excuse to show favoritism. A difficult truth to swallow came the day I realized that the harder ones were just more like me than the others! How ironic that the things you like least in your kids are often reflections of your own weaknesses.

GOD CHOOSES THE LITTLE PEOPLE

As we must not show partiality in our families, we cannot afford to show partiality within the body of Christ. The principle is clear: God chooses the little people, those who are despised by the world, those who don't seem to count, and uses them for great things. "Listen . . . did not God choose out for himself those who are poor in the world to be rich in faith and heirs of the kingdom . . . ?" asked James (2:5). Paul agreed with that observation.

> For consider your calling, brethren, that there were not many wise according to the flesh, not many mighty, not many noble; but God has chosen the foolish things of the world to shame the wise, and God has chosen the weak things of the world to shame the things which are strong, and the base things of the world and the despised, God has chosen, the things that are not, that He might nullify the things that are, that no man should boast before God (1 Corinthians 1:26-29 NASB).

Those who seem insignificant are often the ones whom the Lord uses to topple the mighty and bring down the great. To God, the little people count.

It was a teenager named David who dropped the giant Goliath. Gideon took only three hundred men with him into a God-directed battle against a swarm of Midianites and Amalekites too numerous to count. Samson, empowered by the Lord, seized the jawbone of a donkey and single-handedly wiped out about a thousand Philistines. Queen Esther swayed a monarch's mind and saved the nation of Israel from destruction.

James feared that his readers would prefer outward show over inner spirituality. To do so is to make a tremendous mistake. Often those who are materially poor are spiritually rich. An impressive bank balance is not the litmus test of Christian character.

Several widows in our churches at Emerald Bay and Hide-A-Way Lake have few of the world's goods, but are rich spiritually. They are joint-heirs with Jesus Christ and they have a glorious inheritance reserved for them in heaven. They are "little people" used greatly by God.

Love People . . . Use Things

Treating the wealthy better insults the poor. "But you dishonored the poor man," James put it (2:6). He went on to point out a real and present danger of being rich: "Are not those who are wealthy exploiting you and they . . . drag you into court? Are they not the ones who are defaming the good name by which you were called?" (2:6-7).

When material wealth increases, it becomes easy to love things and use people. What a mistake that is. God would have it the other way round. Even today, it is not often the poor who are busy taking opponents to court. Grinding out a day-to-day, month-to-month existence consumes energy and leaves little time for fighting city hall or anybody else. Wealth brings leisure and the opportunity to use the legal system to one's own advantage.

God wants us to love people and use things, in that order. If he prospers and materially blesses us, we are free to make wise and disciplined use of the things money can buy. The key word is *use*, not *abuse*.

How do you know if you are abusing your wealth? It's when what you have begins to consume you. You worry about hanging onto it all. You get stingy about sharing it. You think you can't live without it. Those are danger signals. All about us we find people using people, within the legal system and outside it, just so they can pursue things.

The philosophy of the selfish heart generates favoritism. There is no place for it in the life of a growing Christian.

MOTIVATION TO LOVE THE UNLOVELY—JAMES 2:8-13

If indeed you are carrying out the demands of the royal law according to the scriptures, you shall love your neighbor as yourself. You are doing what is right [splendidly]. But if you are showing partiality, you are committing a sin, being convicted by the law as a transgressor. For whoever pays attention to the whole law and yet sins in one respect, he has become guilty of all. For He who said, "Do not commit adultery," also said, "Do not commit murder." Now, if you are not committing adultery, but you are committing murder, you have become a transgressor of the law. So be speaking and so be doing as those who are about to be judged by a law of liberty. For the judgment is merciless to the one who did not show mercy. Mercy triumphs over judgment.

How do we love the unlovely, avoid showing partiality, treat all people the same? It is a matter of motivation. "If indeed you are carrying out the demands of the royal law according to the scriptures, you shall love your neighbor as yourself," wrote James (2:8). The question for the Christian is, Whom do I desire to please?

One day a theological student, a legal authority, asked Jesus, "Teacher, what shall I do to inherit eternal life?" In reply, as He often did, the Lord countered with a question, "What is written in the Law? How does it read to you?" The fellow reeled off his answer without hesitation, "You shall love the Lord your God with all your heart, and with all your soul, and with all your strength, and with all your mind; and your neighbor as yourself." "You have answered correctly; do this, and you will live," replied Jesus (Luke 10:25-28 NASB). "But give me some definition, will you?" implored the theological student. "Just who is my neighbor?" (my paraphrase; see Luke 10:29). The Lord answered him with the parable of the good Samaritan (Luke 10:30-37).

In Jesus' parable, a traveler is beaten, robbed, stripped, and left for dead. Holy men, a priest and Levite, pass by and ignore the wounded man. Finally, a Samaritan happens along. The Samaritan treats and bandages the traveler's injuries, transports him to a nearby hotel, cares for him through the night, pays his bill, and leaves him in the care of the innkeeper with a promise to cover all additional expenses on his return trip. The Samaritan in the parable is the good neighbor.

To understand the impact Jesus' words must have had on the seminary student, we must understand what the mention of a Samaritan would have done to him. Samaritans were half-breed Jews at best. Jews had intermarried with foreigners to produce the race, and the Samaritans held to a mixed jumble of religion that resembled Judaism only to a point. Jews in general hated Samaritans. Samaritans embodied all that was unholy, impure, detestable, shameful. Why, if a Jew desired to travel from Jerusalem to Galilee in the north, he wouldn't even think of taking the most direct route, because that would lead him through Samaria. Instead he would cross the Jordan River, journey up through neutral territory, then cross over again to the north. He would go miles out of his way to avoid setting foot on Samaritan soil.

When Jesus started talking about showing compassion, fulfilling the law of liberty, loving the unlovely, he picked a Samaritan as the star of his story. Were He speaking to a modern Israeli, He might have used an Arab or even a Nazi soldier as his main character. It would have produced much the same effect. The Lord forced the student to admit that *yes*, a Samaritan was a good neighbor, the hero of the story. It was a lesson in freely accepting all persons as our neighbors. It was a lesson in loving without partiality.

God wants us to become channels of his love. Is that kind of love being produced in your life by the Holy Spirit? Do people feel loved by you? I will never forget one man who is now with the Lord. How I miss him. Whenever I went into his office, I was greeted by a radiant smile as though he had just finished talking with the Lord and was ready to talk to me. The quality of his life could be explained only by the presence of the Spirit. Never have I seen such tenderness and compassion. Seldom have I felt so completely accepted by another person. Is it any wonder that, even today, some fifteen years after his passing, I still feel his loss?

Are you that kind of channel of God's love to other people? You please God if you are loving your neighbor as yourself. That ought to be high motivation.

UNDERSTANDING THE *WHAT* OF LOVE

One Sunday in 1856, the congregation of Chicago's Plymouth Church had been ushered as usual to their rented pews. A sudden commotion at the door caused the elite churchgoers to turn their heads and behold a spectacle never before seen in that society church. A nineteen-year-old salesman walked in, followed by a large group of tramps, slum people, and alcoholics—the "dregs" of society. The young man led the motley group to the four pews he had personally rented for them. He continued doing that until he was called into a worldwide ministry. His name was Dwight L. Moody (Tan 1319).

Moody had it right, didn't he? Compassion, caring, and concern manifested without partiality is authentic Christianity. Loving others equally pleases God. The reverse is true too. Playing favorites is sin, James wrote (2:9). We are sinning, we are breaking the law, if we show partiality.

Perhaps you are thinking to yourself, okay, fine. I'll love my neighbor as myself. But I need to know how. Tell me how to love. Tell me how to avoid playing favorites. Central to understanding *how* is understanding *what*. Specifically, what sort of love was James talking about? What sort of love does it take to love our neighbors as ourselves?

In the Bible, three Greek words are used to convey the idea of love. The first is *eros*, meaning physical or sexual love; we get the word erotic from it. Second, there is human love, brotherly love, *phileo* in the Greek; the word signifies the human affection between friends. The third kind of love is *agape* love; it calls for the lover to set aside his or her own best interests for the sake of the one loved. It is God's kind of love for the world, because it involves sacrifice.

Agape love is not "I love you *because*." It is "I love you *despite*." It is not "I love you because you are so beautiful . . . because you are such a wonderful wife . . . because you make good grades . . . because you take care of me . . . because God made you mine." Agape love is the kind of love that says, "I love you even though there is nothing in you worthy of my love. But I love you anyway." It is the love of which Paul spoke in Romans 5:8, "But God demonstrates His own love toward us, in that while we were yet sinners, Christ died for us" (NASB). Agape love in action sent Jesus to the earth, and then to the cross. "For you know the grace of our Lord Jesus Christ, that though He was rich, yet for your sakes He became poor, so that you through His poverty might become rich" (2 Corinthians 8:9 NASB).

First Corinthians 13:4-7 is the beautiful description of agape love; there Paul listed fifteen characteristics of it. I often test my agape love quotient by replacing the word *love* in the passage with my own name. Instead of "Love is . . . ," I rephrase the verse to read: "Don Anderson is patient, is kind, is not jealous, does not brag, is not arrogant, does not act unbecomingly, does not seek his own, is not provoked, does not take into account a wrong suffered, does not rejoice in unrighteousness, rejoices with truth, bears all things, hopes all things, endures all things, never fails." You can't do that without being brought up short every time.

The story is told of an elderly black man who wanted to join a local church in the 1920's. The gentleman spoke to the pastor after the service and expressed his wish. The pastor replied, "Would you please go home and pray about this for a few weeks?"

The weeks passed, and one Sunday as the black gentleman was going out the door, the minister questioned him, "Sir, have you been praying about what we discussed, and have you received any guidance about the matter?"

"Yes, I surely have," answered the black man. "God told me that He himself had been trying to get into this church for the last fifteen years, and since He's been unable to up to this point, I might as well quit trying too."

As amusing as that anecdote may be, the truth is that the absence of agape love in our lives signals one of two things. Either we are not Christians in the first place, having never come to a saving knowledge of Jesus Christ, or we are not being submissive to the Spirit's instruction and leading. As Christians we can experience the reality of agape love. The love that levels all labels, breaks down all barriers, plays no favorites, knows only openness, honesty, and compassion, can be ours. Manifesting such love shows that we are growing up in Jesus Christ. It is a witness to the watching world that Christianity is real.

"By this all men will know that you are My disciples, if you have love for one another," Jesus said (John 13:35 NASB). One of the saddest rebukes to the churches in Revelation was given to Ephesus: "But I have this against you, that you have left your first love" (Revelation 2:4 NASB). The Ephesians were organized, busy doing good, but they had forgotten that the *why* behind it all must be their love of Jesus Christ.

If there is a continuous absence of agape love in your life, it's time for a spiritual checkup. Maybe you're not a believer at all. Maybe you've left your first love. Perhaps the Holy Spirit is grieved by some ongoing sin in your life, and He cannot produce agape love in you. Something is wrong between you and God. You're saying no, somewhere, somehow. You are putting out the fire that longs to burn through your life to reach and warm others. You are guilty as charged of lack of love. And this in one sense is as great a sin as murder, because it violates God's law.

GUILTY AS CHARGED—OF BREAKING GOD'S LAW

If we fail to love, we sin. If we play favorites, we sin. When we fail in even a small way, we become guilty of the entire law. "For whoever pays attention to the whole law and yet sins in one respect, he has become guilty of all" (2:10).

The law to which James referred is the mosaic law, given by God to his chosen people. The law was given to display God's righteous standard of holiness. It reveals our sin and transgressions, as Paul stated:

> Now we know that whatever the Law says, it speaks to those who are under the Law, that every mouth may be closed, and all the world may become accountable to God; because by works of the Law no flesh will be justified in His sight; for through the Law comes the knowledge of sin (Romans 3:19-20 NASB).

> Therefore the Law has become our tutor to lead us to Christ, that we may be justified by faith (Galatians 3:24 NASB).

It is interesting how the human heart grades sin. We think to ourselves, "Showing partiality? No problem. I can sweep that one under the rug. It is not an important sin." If we murder someone or if we commit adultery, those are biggies. Those are SINS. But from God's point of view in determining whether or not we have sinned, the law is like a big chain. When even the smallest link is broken, the entire chain breaks. Showing partiality is breaking a link. It is violating the law of God. If you have done it, you are guilty of the whole law. God doesn't grade on the curve. One strike, and you're out. One fall, and you're down for the count.

We may get hung up on comparing ourselves and our behavior to that of others. We think to ourselves, "I'm not perfect, but I'm better than that guy over there. At least I haven't done this or that." But in heaven, there will be no chance to say, "Lord, I wasn't as bad as old Joe. You ought to accept me, right?"

A comparison is not good enough. We are not good enough—not until we obtain the righteousness of Jesus Christ through faith in his finished work, that is. The law convinces us of our sin. It cannot make us acceptable to God. It can point up our need of the Savior. "Christ redeemed us from the curse of the Law, having become a curse for us—for it is written, 'Cursed is everyone who hangs on a tree,'" (Galatians 3:13 NASB; see also Galatians 3:22 and Romans 7:4). When Jesus died, He died for our broken law because He never broke the law of God himself. But we have.

Partiality, murder, adultery—whatever your failure, you have broken the royal law, just as any other violation of any of the commandments, in thought or deed, makes us wrongdoers (see Matthew 5:21-22).

Partiality degrades. Adultery negates the importance of another. Adultery says that my desires are more important than my wife's, or my husband's. Murder is the ultimate violation of the sanctity of human life. In each case, selfishness is present in some way. In each case, God's law is broken (2:11). And once is enough to indict us.

In Light of Grace

But we believers do not live under the law. The law does not make us perfect, and we cannot perfectly fulfill it. We live in the light of the resurrected Christ. God's grace makes the provision for our eternal salvation. We are judged not by a law of sin and death, but by a "law of liberty" (2:12). Let's start living like it!

We have the free gift of eternal life in the presence of the Lord. We have the hope of eternity and the presence of the Holy Spirit. We have freedom from having to strive to fulfill each jot and tittle of the law. Let's live like the freely forgiven people we are. Our speech and actions should be saturated with love. And they will be, if we are growing up in Jesus Christ.

What if our speech and actions are not saturated with love? What if we show partiality? What if we fail to forgive? What if we ignore the less fortunate in favor of the well-to-do? What if ulterior motives rule our emotions? There is an event in the future we won't be too excited about.

As Christians, our eternal salvation is secure. We will not be cast out of heaven if we fail to love. But at the judgment seat of Christ, where each person will "be recompensed for his deeds in the body, according to what he has done, whether good or bad," and will receive eternal rewards, we will not be as fulfilled as we might have been (2 Corinthians 5:10 NASB; see also 1 Corinthians 3:10-14). God's judgment there will be tough, according to James in 2:13. We will not be denied access to heaven, but we won't have any crowns to cast at the Lord's feet, either. We may be mourning what might have been, even as we enter into the dwelling place prepared for us. No wonder John urged us:

> And now, little children, abide in Him, so that when He appears, we may have confidence and not shrink away from Him in shame at His coming (1 John 2:28 NASB).

LOVE IN ACTION

Love. The world oversentimentalizes it. Movies romanticize it. People use it. Some abuse it. Some never see it. Others live it. We all need it. Even the atheist Bertrand Russell, who spent much of his public life criticizing religion, observed that what the world needed was Christian love. How right he was. And where will that love be shown, except in the hearts, hands, feet, lips, and lives of believers? You know you're making progress in your faith when your love begins to shine.

The supermarket was crowded one Christmas eve as we made our way to the produce section. This night, love in action meant doing a few last-minute errands with Pearl—no small feat since grocery shopping is way down on my list of fun. I rank it next to going to the dentist. But we needed a few items for the next day's family dinner, so here we were.

The couple in their early twenties was hard to miss. A young man with a scraggly beard, long matted hair, a half-torn T-shirt, and ragged jeans, walked alongside the grocery cart pushed by the girl in tight grubby shorts. (Yes. shorts in December.) In the basket sat two squalling kids. The oldest couldn't have been more than three; the other a year or so younger. Both were dirty, runny-nosed, and whining. We followed them up one aisle and down the other, and it broke my heart to watch the scene. Every time one of the children would express a desire for something, the mother would slap him and say, "Shut up! Keep still!

I knew that the young man and woman were tired, harried, and financially hard up, yet my heart went out to the children. I thought to myself, what a tragedy of American life it is that we bring children into the world, kids who need love, acceptance, guidance, consistency, maturity, and we slam them down and silence them. These parents weren't ready for the responsibility of love. I made a renewed commitment to be dedicated to my own children, to make sure they knew that whatever mistakes I make, I love them.

My heart still feels a tug when I think back to that Christmas eve. As a Christian, love in action that evening could have meant more. Maybe I could have slipped the couple a few dollars to buy something for the children for Christmas. The few words of counsel I could have shared would have been made more palatable by the gift. I might have asked for their names and address or phone number—just to follow up with an offer of the gift they really needed, the gift of Jesus Christ. I might have handed them a booklet explaining how to be saved, or even a New Testament with key passages underlined. The pair desperately needed God. I could have done more than just stare and judge.

Today I think I would.

How about you?

AT THE CAMPFIRE

During a recent trip to the Pacific Northwest where I was speaking at a youth conference, Pearl and I sat around the campfire one evening while a teenaged girl gave her testimony. As part of her talk, she shared the following story written by Dennis Reusser, a graduate of Colorado Christian College who played basketball with Athletes in Action. Think about this story, the next time you face off with one of the world's "least beautiful" people.

> One night I was walking down the street, when this man started to walk toward me. . . . [He] had an awful limp and he was dressed in rags. His face was dirty, and his hands had grease all over them. I thought to myself as he walked closer, "Please Mister, don't say anything to me." I even thought about turning around and walking away, but I didn't. As we got closer to each other, I noticed he was trying to focus in on me; his eyes were twisted and he couldn't even look me in the eye. I felt even more awkward. Then he said to me, "God loves you."
>
> I was so surprised, I said, "Excuse me?" He then started to quote John 3:16. As he got about halfway through, I joined in, quoting it with him. The moment we finished, his eyes became straight, he dropped his cane, and he was able to stand straight. His clothes all at once turned into a radiant white robe.
>
> I was so surprised and confused I didn't say a thing. He then disappeared.
>
> When I got home that night, I began to realize how I act and react to people every day. I often judge a person before I know him. I find that so unfair of me. It also makes me wonder how many times I have passed by Jesus and ignored him completely.

Points to Ponder

1. What is the command of James in 2:1? Can you think of ways in which you have shown partiality in the past? What about within your church? What can be done to correct situations in which partiality is shown?

2. Showing partiality is sin to God. What does 2:10 tell us about our guilt before God if we have violated any of his standards? Besides Jesus Christ, is there anyone who has not broken at least a part of God's law? Read Romans 3:23 before you answer.

3. What does James tell us about God's opinion of the poor of the world? Refer to 2:5 as you answer. Knowing this, how should Christians treat those who are economically underprivileged? Name at least one practical way in which you can show compassion to the poor.

5

The Bottom Line

James 2:14-26

On April 17, 1988, I was doing a scriptural exposition from Paul's second letter to the Corinthians at Hide-A-Way Lake Community Church. On that Sunday morning, Les was born again. He followed the Lord in the waters of baptism two weeks later, on May 1st. On June 1st, he celebrated his sixty-eighth birthday.

I have been discipling Les for more than a year now—we've been spending an hour a week together. His spiritual growth in eighteen months' time has been phenomenal. He has memorized nearly one hundred scripture verses, knows the names of the books of the Bible, and can reel off the names of the twelve apostles. He has worked through several topical Bible study booklets, and has also read through the entire Bible. Recently Les wrote:

> As a Christian, I can say I believe that Jesus will return to take us home, simply because He said He would. He cannot lie, so why doubt? But we must continue to do his work, to evangelize, spread his gospel, and recruit more souls to him.
>
> And on that glorious day when He does appear, we too will be glorious, and we will see his smile of approval,

and hear him say, "Well done, good and faithful servant."
My heart is fairly bursting with joy as I write!

Les is currently praying for two things: (1) he wants to find
someone he can lead to Christ, (2) he is longing to find someone he can disciple.

Then there is Gary, a successful lawyer. I had the privilege
of leading him to Christ last fall. I gave him a *One Year Bible*,
and started the follow-up process, but we haven't met together
since. Gary hasn't found time in his busy schedule to return to
Bible class when we've toured in his area. He has had numerous opportunities to get together with believers who care about
him, but has always found some excuse to decline. As far as I
know, all efforts to encourage him to visit one of the many
good local churches have failed, because he has been unresponsive.

Are both Gary and Les believers? We'll talk about that in a
minute.

What Is the Gospel?

Today a great deal of confusion exists about the gospel. Some
say that trusting Christ cannot be a gradual process, but must
happen in a specific moment in time. Some say that a change
of life must accompany faith. This change does not save the
person, but marks one's conversion as real. Some say that a
person is not saved by faith alone, but must rack up a sufficient
number of good deeds in order to qualify for heaven—sort of
a career ladder to the stars. Some say that praying a certain
prayer saves us. Some say that being baptized saves us.

What are we to believe and communicate? Whatever we
say, we must speak with care, "handling accurately the word
of truth," as Paul told Timothy (2 Timothy 2:15b NASB). The
consequences are awesome.

Here are the basics of the gospel:

1. Christ died for our sins according to the scriptures, was
buried, and arose again from the dead (1 Corinthians 15:3-4).

2. Faith involves knowledge of Jesus Christ: his deity, his
humanity, his death to pay for our sins, his resurrection.

3. Faith involves emotionally and intellectually accepting as

truth the gospel (good news) that Jesus Christ died for our sins and arose again.

4. Faith also involves a willful decision to trust Jesus Christ alone to save us. We recognize our sin and our need, and acknowledge that Christ alone is the answer.

We can understand all about Christ. We can intellectually accept as truth that He died for our sins and arose again. But we are not saved until we personally trust in Christ alone to save us (see John 5:24; Romans 1:16-17; 5:15; 1 Peter 1:23).

Don Anderson was not saved until Don Anderson personally trusted Christ alone. My wife Pearl was not saved until she did that. Neither were my children, our co-workers at the Ministries, our publishers, our supporters, the members of our congregations. Once we did trust Christ—some of us realizing the truth in a single dramatic moment, some coming to faith more gradually over a period of time—we were saved permanently. We entered God's family eternally. The words of Jesus assure us that this is so: "Truly, truly, I say to you, he who hears My word, and believes Him who sent Me, has eternal life, and does not come into judgment, but has passed out of death into life" (John 5:24 NASB). "He who has the Son has the life; he who does not have the Son of God does not have the life" wrote the apostle John (1 John 5:12 NASB; see also 5:11).

A GOSPEL TO GO BY AND GROW BY

Once we are saved, what is next?

God wants us to grow. In the book of James we have already looked at four measures of Christian maturity. Now we read a fifth: Faith is dead without deeds (James 2:14-26).

As we approach the passage, we must keep in mind the ground rules. James was writing to Christians. Some of what he wrote may seem to contradict our understanding of the gospel of Christ, but he was writing to people who had already received that gospel. They had already trusted Christ. They already were in God's "forever family." We must look at his statement, "Faith without works is dead" (2:26), in the proper context.

James's point must not be misunderstood. Good works flowing out of the life of a Christian indicate that the Christian is growing up in faith. Lack of good works may indicate that an individual has never truly trusted Christ and is not saved. As we will see, however, there may be other reasons why a believer fails to make spiritual progress after coming to faith. Never does James suggest that good works themselves bring salvation. We are not saved by what we do, but by whom we know. Our trust must be in Christ alone, not in Christ and works, or in works alone. Our faith in Jesus Christ guarantees our passage to heaven; the good we do as Christians glorifies God and tells others we are going there.

Remember Les and Gary? We have no doubt about the salvation of Les, do we? The evidence of a changed life is there. But what about Gary? He hasn't changed. He seemingly still has little desire to get to know God better. Who is to say he is really saved? Perhaps he is not. Yet there may be other reasons behind his lack of spiritual growth. Let us not be quick to judge the heart. Let us not set ourselves up as God's jury to bind him over for trial on the charge of unbelief.

Someone should make sure that Gary really understands what saving faith is all about. Believe me, if I get an opportunity, I am going to do just that. But let us never measure the validity of a conversion by the performance of the converted. God will read the heart. God sees the big picture, the opportunities to grow that lie ahead. It may be that good works are waiting to happen in the life of the one whose faith we question. Maybe the changes are incubating and will hatch later. (For a more complete look at the issue of the place of works in the believer's relationship with Christ, please refer to my book, *God Wants a Relationship Not a Performance*, Loizeaux Brothers, 1989.)

The good works of a Christian life signify that we are growing up in Jesus Christ. Authentic Christianity goes from head to heart to hand and foot. It is squeezed into shoe leather and pounds the pavement to show compassion to others. It shows up in a new quality of life, new direction, new motivations. That is the bottom line.

How Fruit Relates to Faith—James 2:14-17

> What good does it do, my brethren, if a person is saying, "I am having faith," and he is not having works? That

faith is not able to save him, is it? If a brother or a sister be poorly dressed and in need of daily food, and one of you says to him, "Be going in peace, dress warmly [keep warm], and feed yourselves," and you do not give them the things needful for the body, what good does it do? So also faith, if it is not having works, it is dead by itself.

Jesus said to his followers, "By this is My Father glorified, that you bear much fruit, and so prove to be My disciples" (John 15:8 NASB). One of the ways we know if we have the disease is by the symptoms. One of the ways we can tell if we are Christians is by the fruit that comes forth from our lives. People have a right to expect some changes in us after we trust Christ as Savior. Let me again stress the crucial point that these changes do not bring about our salvation. They result from our salvation (see also 2 Corinthians 5:17; John 15:16; Galatians 5:22-23).

CAN "DEAD" FAITH SAVE?

At the outset of his argument, James has posed two questions (2:14): (1) what good does it do for a person to say he has faith if he is not doing good works? (2) the kind of faith without any visible manifestation of good works is not able to save someone, is it?

If we have genuinely accepted Christ as Savior, some evidence should be showing up in our lives. Authentic faith will make a difference in us, somehow, somewhere, sometime. "For we are His workmanship, created in Christ Jesus for good works, which God prepared beforehand, that we should walk in them" (Ephesians 2:10 NASB).

God calls us for good works. In fact, He already has our assignments ready the moment we enter his family.

I run across many people each year who claim to be Christians, and whose lives reflect nothing of Christ. They tell me they believe in Jesus. Since childhood they have heard about his death on the cross. They know He is the Son of God. As I mentioned earlier, we must be careful to leave the judgment of their commitment to God. But I can't help wondering if some of those individuals possess only head knowledge of Jesus Christ. Intellectually they know He died for their sins. Intellectually they know He rose again. Intellectually they understand that only through faith in him can they be saved. Intellectually they comprehend the gospel.

It's as if they have seen the lifeboat, known it would sustain their weight, known it would keep them from sinking into the watery depths, yet they have never climbed aboard. They have never stepped inside to trust themselves totally to the care of the lifeboat. They have never cast themselves completely upon the Christ who is sufficient for salvation and adequate for all the circumstances of their daily lives. Officiating at the funerals of such "secret disciples" is among the most difficult duties of my ministry.

It is this intellectual "faith" to which I believe James was referring when he stated that such "faith is not able to save" (2:14). Merely knowing who Jesus is isn't enough. It isn't enough to walk down an aisle, pray a specific prayer, raise a hand in church. We must make the decision to trust Christ totally.

That is God's will for us. Faith that is merely intellectual assent cannot save us, because it involves only knowledge and not genuine trust. If we are trusting Jesus to save us, then some of our Christianity ought to be making its way into our behavior patterns.

WHY GOOD WORKS?

Why are good works such a critical part of the Christian life? Paul wrote to Titus, "Concerning these things I want you to speak confidently, so that those who have believed God may be careful to engage in good deeds. These things are good and profitable for men" (Titus 3:8 NASB). One of the means by which God brings others into his kingdom is through the changes He works in the lives of believers. Good works show unsaved people the wonder of the God who motivates the act, who catalyzes the positive change.

I remember a conversation with a young man in my North Dallas class when he discovered I was also teaching in Waco, a city some three hours away.

"I've got a friend in Waco. I sure wish I could get him to your study. He needs to hear this."

"What's his name?" I asked.

"Brad Jones. He works with the city."

"Brad Jones? There's a guy named Brad Jones who has been coming to class."

"Not Brad! In a Bible class? In flesh and blood? I can't believe it! That's a miracle!"

"Yes—and you know, he seems really interested in spiritual things. In fact, from talking to him, I'm convinced he has recently become a Christian. He sure asks me questions after class that tell me he's reading God's word."

"No kidding! That sure doesn't sound like the Brad I know. That's great!"

The description didn't match the Brad Jones my friend knew because Brad had changed through an encounter with Jesus Christ. He was a different person. And he is still different today. A changed life—what an argument for the gospel. What an encouragement to those looking on.

What good does it do to have faith but not works resulting from that faith? Commitment but no change? Profession but no progress? Faith without life-evidence is like an apple tree with no apples, a car without wheels, a watch that doesn't run. It profits no one. Nobody is brought into God's family from looking at an unchanged Christian. Many believers run cold in their Christian lives, but the greatest danger is that a person who professes to know Christ and yet remains totally unchanged may not have truly trusted Jesus at all.

OBJECT LESSON

By now you are probably wondering. Have I done enough? Do my works reflect Christ? Should I sign up to teach Sunday school? Volunteer for the blood drive? Send a check to a missionary?

Don't let me discourage you from doing any of those things. Sell all your possessions and donate the proceeds to the poor, if you believe that God is leading you to do it. But don't make the mistake of spinning your wheels in every semi-spiritual direction, trying to please God. Avoid the "churchianity" trap described by Calvin Miller in *Becoming: Yourself in the Making*:

> Most new converts in the church are not so much reno-
> vated by Christ as they are overhauled by Christian
> approval or disapproval. They speak of the "Lordship of

> Christ," yet they are more controlled by the masses than the Master. In but a little while they move from being controlled by divine command to the neurotic no-no's of the congregation. Made free in Christ, they all too soon become congregational captives (Miller 53-54).

The fact is, you don't need to look far to find ways to serve God. Above all, He desires a living, growing, vibrant relationship with you, not some kind of power performance from you.

If you don't think you've changed a bit since you came to know Christ, make sure you are really trusting Jesus to save you. Make sure you are not placing your confidence in Christ and good works, but in Christ alone. Ask yourself, whom am I trusting right now for my eternal destiny? You'll know. "The Spirit Himself bears witness *with our spirit* that we are children of God" (Romans 8:16 NASB, italics mine).

If you are certain of your salvation, look up and look around for the things God would have you to do to honor and glorify him. James 2:15-16 gives us an example of such an opportunity. It's an object lesson in our need to have open eyes and ready hearts.

> If a brother or a sister be poorly dressed and in need of daily food, and one of you says to him, "Be going in peace, dress warmly [keep warm], and feed yourselves," and you do not give him the things needful for the body, what good does it do? (2:15-16)

Suppose a fellow believer tells you that he is struggling financially. He has been laid off and can't find another job. Money has run out. His kids need shoes and medical care. He could use a decent suit for interviews. His family has been living on canned goods and even those are about gone now. What good does it do if you send the man on his way without doing anything tangible to help him?

If you hear of such a need, you don't have to second-guess what the Lord would have you to do. Help the man and his family as much as you are able. Take over some groceries. Arrange an interview. Give him money for a suit, or find one he can borrow. Do what you can with the resources God has given you. If your means are limited, you might even confidentially mention his needs to people who are in a better position to help. This still doesn't let you off the hook—you've got to give what you can. I am talking about more than a pat on the back and a promise to pray.

Several years ago a missionary couple visited one of our churches. When asked what urgent needs their ministry had, they replied that medical bills for the wife's emergency surgery had mounted and they were unable to pay. Could we, in good conscience, have heard that and smiled, saying, "Go, in peace and pay your bills, friends," and still claimed to be doing God's will? Of course not. We took up a collection to help them. What good is faith that is unwilling to care? Who would come to Christ if all Christians were compassionless, cold, and close-fisted?

WHEN CHRISTIANS CARE

First John 3:17 states, "But whoever has the world's goods, and beholds his brother in need and closes his heart against him, how does the love of God abide in him?" (NASB). "If I speak with the tongues of men and of angels, but do not have love, I have become a noisy gong or a clanging cymbal" (1 Corinthians 13:1 NASB). If you do nothing to assist the needy brother or sister, you are not showing love and compassion. You are demonstrating the absence of God's love in your life. You aren't proving to anybody that you are really a child of God and have experienced saving faith. You are waist-deep in hypocrisy and self-concern, when your Christian faith ought to be producing a compassionate, unselfish heart.

Read in scripture about the first Christians, the early church. "There was not a needy person among them, for all who were owners of land or houses would sell them and bring the proceeds of the sales, and lay them at the apostles' feet; and they would be distributed to each, as any had need" (Acts 4:34-35 NASB). Those early Christians shared their goods; they met one another's needs; they ministered to one another amazingly. And people noticed.

Beautiful things happen when Christians care. Paul commended the Christians at Thessalonica for, among other things, their tangible demonstration of love toward one another. "We ought always to give thanks to God for you, brethren, as it is only fitting, because your faith is greatly enlarged, and the love of each one of you toward one another grows ever greater" (2 Thessalonians 1:3 NASB).

It has been my joy to proclaim God's word for the past fourteen years to two congregations in recreational and retirement communities. Those two churches represent eighteen different denominations, yet the love of Jesus and of scripture pervades both congregations. It is fascinating to watch these people of different backgrounds minister to one another. At times of crisis there is an outpouring of prayerful concern. Men and women sacrifice themselves to do whatever needs to be done to help. Widows do not cry alone. Children are shielded by an umbrella of prayer. Sick persons are neither shunned nor forgotten. The churches aren't perfect. But it is clear that God is at work in them.

How Much Is Enough?

Perhaps you are wondering, how many good works must I do to prove my Christianity? How much is enough? A word of caution: Don't get hung up on quantity. Think about the quality of your life since coming to Christ. Galatians 5:22-23 lists the fruits of the Spirit as "love, joy, peace, patience, kindness, goodness, faithfulness, gentleness, self-control" (NASB). Those are the qualities of the new life in Christ. These characteristics are developing in you if you are a growing Christian. "But we all, with unveiled face beholding as in a mirror the glory of the Lord, are being transformed into the same image from glory to glory, just as from the Lord, the Spirit" wrote Paul (2 Corinthians 3:18 NASB; see also Romans 12:2).

Christlike qualities will show up in the things you do, but what is most important is the deeper motivation behind the activity. As a Christian, you are running spiritually on new fuel, and this more than anything proves that you are a child of God.

In Romans 5:5, Paul stated that "hope does not disappoint, because the love of God has been poured out within our hearts through the Holy Spirit who was given to us" (NASB). The Holy Spirit, who is given to each believer at the moment of salvation, enables us to manifest God's love in our lives. The Spirit is our seal, our badge.

If we are not showing love, it may be because the Spirit is

not there in the first place. Without love and compassion and fruit we are hearers of the word only, and not doers. Intellectually we know a lot about the Lord, but we don't really know him, because we haven't come to saving faith. As James put it, "So also faith, if it is not having works, it is dead by itself" (2:17). Again, the issue is one of motivation—of quality of life more than quantity of works—although changes in our hearts should manifest themselves in our behavior.

FAITH: WANTED ALIVE—JAMES 2:18-26

> But a man will say, "You are having faith and I am having works. Show me your faith without your works and I will show you my faith by my works." You are believing that God is one; you are doing well. The demons also are believing and are shuddering. But are you wishing to know, O! senseless man, that faith without deeds is useless. Was not our father, Abraham, vindicated by works in that he offered up his son Isaac upon the altar? You are seeing that faith was working with his good deeds, and faith was perfected in good deeds. And the scripture was fulfilled which said, "And Abraham believed God and it was credited to his account for righteousness and he was called a friend of God." You are seeing that a man by works is shown to be righteous and not by faith alone. Now in like manner was not Rahab the prostitute vindicated by works, in that she entertained as guests the messengers and sent them out another way? For just as the body without breath is dead, so also faith without works is dead (2:18-26).

Many times in classes or conferences people will express their frustration at the behavior of other believers. "How could Jill say she has faith, and start living with her boyfriend?" "How can Tom claim to be a Christian and yet always cheat on his taxes?" "Did you know that Mr. X says he believes in Christ? He is the most unscrupulous businessman in town. Nobody trusts him." The sometimes unspoken question on people's minds is this: How could God accept Jill, Tom, or Mr. X into his family? Maybe, just maybe, He never has. Maybe their lifestyles indicate they have never come into a saving relationship with Christ.

Maybe they are modernday Judases. Judas Iscariot, although he was with Christ and had every opportunity to know Christ's salvation, was never *in* Christ. Instead he wound up committing suicide, never appropriating God's forgiveness for himself personally. His was a tragic end to what might have been.

The heart-motivated works of a Christian life reflect the reality of the presence of Jesus Christ. They are the results of what we are, not what we are trying to perform.

So many of the men and women who come to the Ministries' Bible classes never experience the freedom of life in Christ. Often they are successful professionals, crowned with enough achievement to feel independent and self-satisfied. They enjoy corporate perks, high salaries, expensive homes, and sleek vehicles. They are confident that they are masters of their fate, captains of their own salvation. When someone comes to them as Jesus did to Nicodemus and says, "You must be born again," they find it hard to swallow (see John 3:7). To realize that salvation comes from relationship, not performance, is tough for these types, because it means that even those who are good enough for everything in our society can never be good enough to earn heaven by themselves. There must be an admission of need. It means telling themselves, "I can't do this alone." The idea ruffles the fur of the self-motivated achiever. It raises the hackles. But the truth of Ephesians 2:8-9 is undeniable. "For by grace you have been saved through faith; and that not of yourselves, it is the gift of God; not as a result of works, that no one should boast" (NASB).

James's words do not contradict Ephesians 2:8-9. He did not argue against the need for salvation by faith. He would be the first to admit that works without faith are worthless. But he dismissed as foolish those who say that one can come to faith and then legitimately continue to commit the same sins as before, displaying the same lifestyle as though nothing had changed. Salvation brings change, maybe slowly, maybe imperceptibly at times, but authentic trust will somehow manifest itself in good works and a different lifestyle. The changes in our lives, the good works we do in Christ's name because we love him, these mark our conversion as real. Good works are the proof of the pudding. James reiterated this point in 2:18: "But a man will say, 'You are having faith, and I am having works. Show me your faith without your works, and I will show you my faith by my works.'"

It is frightening to realize that it is possible to have an intellectual understanding of God and yet not experience saving faith.

Sid and Sue believe that God exists and that He has a plan for the universe. There must be a driving force, a unifying element behind creation, right? And yes, maybe this Jesus did live a wonderful life and die unjustly. Good for Sid and Sue—or is it? The problem is that the demons are in one hundred percent agreement with them. The demons, too, believe that there is a monotheistic God: "You are believing that God is one; you are doing well. The demons are also believing and are shuddering" (2:19).

Demons, too, believe in God. Yet the demons "shudder." Why? They are shuddering because they know that judgment is coming and they will not escape his justice. They know that "it is a terrifying thing to fall into the hands of the living God" (Hebrews 10:31 NASB). They know Romans 14:12. "So then each of us shall give account of himself to God" (NASB). They know 2 Thessalonians 1:7-9: "The Lord Jesus shall be revealed from heaven with His mighty angels in flaming fire, dealing out retribution to those who do not know God and to those who do not obey the gospel of our Lord Jesus. And these will pay the penalty of eternal destruction, away from the presence of the Lord and from the glory of His power" (NASB). Although demons believe in God, intellectual acknowledgment of him alone is not enough.

GOOD FOR NOTHING

"But are you wishing to know, O! senseless man, that faith without deeds is useless" (2:20). The Greek word for *useless* is translated elsewhere in scripture as "careless," "idle," "unemployed," or "lazy." It is the same word Jesus used to warn us about misusing words. "And I say to you, that every careless [useless] word that men shall speak, they shall render account for it in the day of judgment" (Matthew 12:36 NASB). Jesus also used the word twice to describe those who were idle or unemployed (Matthew 20:3,6).

Paul used the word in at least two passages, both times in negative contexts to describe individuals who were not fulfilling their functions. Speaking of younger widows he wrote, "And at the same time they also learn to be *idle*, as they go around from house to house; and not merely *idle*, but also gossips and busybodies, talking about things not proper to mention" (1 Timothy 5:13 NASB, italics mine). The apostle said of Cretans, "One of themselves, a prophet of their own, said, 'Cretans are always liars, evil beasts, *lazy* gluttons'" (Titus 1:12 NASB, italics mine). "Lazy gluttons" could even be translated "unemployed stomachs." This kind of gets to you, doesn't it?

Taken together, then, we can conclude that James was saying that faith without deeds is useless, is idle, unemployed, and lazy. Good for nothing.

Peter's use of the word in his second epistle in an instructive passage may help us understand further what James was driving at. Peter first spoke of the believer's salvation in Christ (2 Peter 1:3), then the promises of Christ (2 Peter 1:4), and then the procedure for becoming like Christ (2 Peter 1:5-8). He concluded, "For if these [Christlike] qualities are yours and are increasing, they render you neither *useless* nor unfruitful in the true knowledge of our Lord Jesus Christ" (2 Peter 1:8 NASB, italics mine).

If we don't want to be "unemployed stomachs" in the family of God, we had better be manifesting our faith with some fruit.

FAMILY LIKENESS

If we have trusted Christ and are growing up in him, we will begin to resemble him in some ways. There is a family likeness among brothers and sisters in Christ: joyful demeanor, peaceful countenance, submissive spirit. Often our faith is written all over our faces.

During a study series at the University of Texas I taught some years ago one young woman who introduced herself at the first class meeting seemed vaguely familiar. I gave it little thought because I was meeting so many young people. Weeks went by and although we didn't get a chance to talk, she somehow reminded me of someone. One afternoon after the study she had a little extra time and stayed after class to visit.

She gave me her name again and then explained whose daughter she was.

"Oh, sure, I know your mom and dad!" I exclaimed. "He works for General Dynamics and they live in Dallas."

"That's right!"

She was the daughter of a couple we had known and she and I had a wonderful visit that day. During our conversation I noticed expressions, mannerisms, gestures, and features that reminded me of her folks. The determined look, the easy smile, the bright eyes, the movement of her hands—I wondered why I hadn't seen the connection between the girl and her parents right away. It was obvious whose daughter she was.

Similarly, there is a family resemblance among Christians. We manifest our saving faith in certain ways, and people shouldn't have to be around us for long before they notice.

One Sunday afternoon I was jogging around the track at the local high school. Before my arthritic hip laid me up, this was standard practice. A young woman was walking around the track. She went at a fast clip, but on her face was an expression of peace and contentment. She made a comment about the beautiful day as I passed her, and her smile lit up her face. She's a Christian, I thought to myself, although I had never seen her before. On my next lap around the track I noticed that another woman, the wife of a Christian I knew, had joined the first woman and the two were walking together, talking.

"Two saints fellowshiping together, right?" I commented on my next pass.

"Right!" they replied with big smiles. It was obvious that they were children of God.

If we are believers, especially growing believers, it is going to show up on our faces, in our hearts, in our lives. It will show up in a life arranged in view of something more important than the temporary, materialistic world in which we live. It will be a life with proper priorities.

PROPER PRIORITIES

James next gave his readers two illustrations from the Old Testament of lives with proper priorities, lives that reflected faith in God, lives displaying works that stemmed from faith. The first was Abraham (2:21). Genesis 22 tells us that in asking

Abraham to sacrifice his much-loved son Isaac, the boy he had waited twenty-five years to have, God was testing Abraham's faith. Notice, the faith was already there to test. In asking Abraham to ascend Mount Moriah and there offer up Isaac as a sacrifice, God pushed Abraham's faith to the limit. That Abraham obeyed God indicated his total trust. In such a way, James said, faith was "working with his good deeds and faith was perfected in good deeds" (2:22).

The result of Abraham's faithful obedience? "And the scripture was fulfilled which said, 'And Abraham believed God and it was credited to his account for righteousness and he was called a friend of God'" (2:23). Let's recognize that Abraham's willingness to obey God did not save him. Rather, Abraham's faith in God made him willing to obey.

"You are seeing that a man by works is shown to be righteous and not by faith alone" (2:24). Essentially, James was telling us that if we desire to be known as believers in Christ, it is not enough merely to say we have faith. We must show it by what we do. A manifestation of saving faith is trust, surrender, commitment to God's way of doing things, no matter what that might be. I cannot accept Jesus on my own terms, in my own way, and continue to do my own thing. In my new orientation the questions have been forever settled as to who is in control and where the buck stops.

Notice, James does not say that works make us righteous. Works *show* us to be righteous. Works illustrate our faith. They visibly manifest to others what we believe. Belief is still the essential element.

As if to show that righteousness comes from faith and not works, James next picked an Old Testament illustration of an unquestionable sinner, a prostitute named Rahab. Talk about two different ends of the social pole. Each Jew could identify with Abraham, the father of the nation, the hero of every Hebrew boy and girl. From the patriarch, James turned to the example of a woman of ill repute, but one who came to faith in God and showed her change of heart by what she did.

You remember the account. After forty years of wandering in the wilderness, the children of Israel arrived at the gateway to the promised land, a town called Kadesh-barnea. "We're going in this time," the Lord said. "Joshua is going to lead you" (my paraphrase; see Joshua 1:2). In preparation for the attack, Joshua sent two spies into the land to the city of Jericho. Inside the city walls a woman who had come to faith in God hid them and enabled them to escape. She was promised that, because of the faith she had demonstrated, she and her family would be delivered from the devastation that was to occur. When the walls of Jericho came tumbling down days later, with a ferocity reminiscent of the San Francisco quake of '89, the house of Rahab remained intact and unscathed. She and her family escaped death because of what she had done *in faith*! In her dealings with the spies, she showed what she already believed. Were she judged on her works, her past sins would have condemned her. But Rahab earned a place in God's hall of fame because she came to know the Lord. The authenticity of her trust was proved by what she did.

God's hall of fame? It is found in Hebrews 11. Some call it the hall of faith, perhaps a better term. There we read of the kind of faith in God that manifests itself in works time and time again. By faith Abel obeyed God and brought an offering that pleased him; by faith Noah, who had never seen rain, built an ark; by faith Abraham believed God and went to a far country; by faith Moses believed God and left the land of Egypt; by faith the early martyrs suffered and bled and died for the cause of Christ. The works did not make any of those men and women righteous. Rather, they were tangible manifestations of their living faith.

FROM VIABLE TO VISIBLE

James concluded his argument by repeating his main point: "For just as the body without breath is dead, so also faith without works is dead" (2:26).

What good would it have done for Rahab to have believed and yet not assisted the spies? Her house would have crumbled with the rest of them.

What good would it have done for Noah to have believed God and not built the ark? He and his family would have perished in the flood.

What good would it have done for Abraham to say he believed in God and yet refuse to move from his home town? He would have never entered the promised land.

Viable faith becomes visible—and thus the reality of God is demonstrated to the watching world.

So what are you going to do about it? Are you now going to start frantically looking for things to do to show yourself and others that you know God? Wait! Don't panic! Do ask yourself, am I trusting Christ alone for salvation? Do get into a regular study of God's word. Do ask God, through his Spirit who resides in you, to sensitize you to the things He would have you do in carrying on his mission in the world. He uses people to feed the hungry, clothe the needy, tell others about him. Opportunities are there for you to serve. A little looking will help you know where you individually are to pick up the towel and start washing feet.

If positive changes and good works are not flowing from your Christian life, you are like the baseball player who slams a home run over the fence, and then stands still instead of running the bases. He lays the wood to it, but forgets to score. As you become sensitive to the opportunities God is giving you, you will start running the bases. It will be amazing!

How Do I Measure Up?

James has given us solid, hard-hitting, practical examples of the works of the Christian life. Acts of compassionate love mark us as believers. Yet let's not forget that less tangible qualities, which the Spirit works in us, motivate the tangible works. For example, as we grow in Christ, the Spirit produces kindness in us. Spirit-motivated kindness then causes us to invite a newcomer over for dinner, or to pick up the phone and check on an elderly widow, or to offer to babysit the children of a young mother so she can get some things done. It's a process.

A mistake that believers often make is to compare themselves to other believers. I've seen new Christians look at others who've been vibrant, committed Christians for thirty years and then become frustrated because they themselves don't measure up. God accepts us as we are, where we are. He starts living the new life in us from Day One of our conversion. It is wrong to compare ourselves to someone behind us, in front of us, or alongside us.

God made you a pilot, an editor, a veterinarian, a homemaker, a lab technician, a doctor . . . and He expects you to be faithful in that job (Colossians 3:23). He desires for you to be a good husband or wife, son or daughter. He wants you to be dedicated to learning more about him. He wants you to keep checking in with him for new assignments. He will show you what to do as long as you are willing to be submissive to his leading.

WHY PEOPLE DON'T GO ON

It would be unfair to discuss James 2 without dealing with the fact that some people come to know Christ and yet never seem to "go on" for him. They are the frustration of preachers, teachers, and believing friends. The ones who led them to Christ wonder if they have really understood the gospel. Like Gary at the beginning of this chapter, they just don't seem to change much. They don't seem to hang in there with the Lord.

We would be denying scripture if we didn't point out that many times in the New Testament, the apostle Paul and others addressed comments to Christians who were at a standstill in their spiritual lives. Diotrephes said yes to the flesh too many times and couldn't shake off a critical spirit (3 John 9). Demas fell in love with the "present world," and took off for Thessalonica, abandoning the work and leaving Paul in the lurch (2 Timothy 4:10). John Mark jumped ship at Pamphylia, deserting the work and heading home to Jerusalem (Acts 13:13; 15:37-38).

The three individuals mentioned above aren't the only spiritual defectives mentioned in scripture. Far from it. Don't forget that David took up with Bathsheba. Peter denied Christ when the going got tough.

Were these people saved? Yes. David, Peter, and John Mark had bad laps in good races. They lost a battle, but won the war. Diotrephes and Demas? Their races were shaky, but Paul never suggested that they were not believers. Deserters? Yes. Eternally damned? Evidently not.

The door is always open to the Father's heart. He waits for each of us, as the father of the prodigal son did—longing to place rings on our fingers, clean robes on our backs, new sandals on our feet, fresh hope in our hearts.

Perhaps you know people who do not seem to have progressed spiritually. They may have knowledge of Christ, a lot upstairs but little in the life. Maybe their faith is merely intellectual and does not involve trust.

Yet there are other reasons why genuine Christians do not make progress in the faith. Evangelist Larry Moyer gave a few suggestions why in an article entitled, "Why Don't Some People 'Go on for the Lord'?" I will paraphrase his conclusions here.

Lack of commitment pervades our entire society. We shouldn't be shocked when it also pervades the spiritual lives of people we know. If you are concerned about people who haven't "gone on" for God, think about these possibilities:

1. It may be that saving faith has never happened. There is only intellectual agreement, but not trust.

2. Lack of proper follow-up is another reason. When we lead a person to Christ, we have a responsibility to see that he or she gets into a routine of reading God's word and of attending a Bible-based church. New converts need personal attention in order to begin to grow. If they don't get it, they may flounder.

3. Finally, Christians are saved sinners, and some sin may be stunting spiritual growth (Moyer 1,3).

AT THE BEMA

There may be other reasons why people don't progress in the Christian life. The judgment seat of Christ won't be as rich and fulfilling for them as it will be for others. There at the *bema*, as the judgment seat is called, the squeakers-in may mourn when they are confronted with a virtual video, so to speak, of their works as believers. What they have done selfishly, for the wrong motives, will be burned up, although they will be saved (see 1 Corinthians 3:10-15). Frankly, when I get to glory, I hope I'm not smelling like a smokehouse.

In his book, *The House on the Rock*, Charles Sell described a "Peanuts" cartoon in which Charlie Brown sculpts a sandcastle at the beach. Standing back to admire his work, he is engulfed by a downpour that levels his castle. Standing beside the smooth place where the structure had once stood, Charlie Brown comments, "There must be a lesson here, but I don't know what it is." As Sell put it, "Such will be the case of many who stand before the smoldering ruins of everything they've lived for at the judgment seat of Christ and there is nothing left that is worthy of reward" (Sell 18).

In the meantime, let's also remember that we are seeing only a segment of an individual's life. The big picture, the long haul, is known only to God. He will bring circumstances into the lives of every Christian designed to promote growth. Let's not judge the whole package on the wasted years.

THE NEW LIFE

Several years ago when our oldest son, Bobby, was in high school, he built an incubator as a science project. He is an engineer now, so I guess this was good training. One of the families in our community gave him some freshly laid chicken eggs which he placed inside. The large glass front of the incubator offered a bird's eye view of the contents; a light bulb regulated the interior temperature by going on and off automatically.

Day after day we peeked inside for signs of life. One afternoon all five kids came running into the dining room at top speed. "Daddy, come quick!" they hollered. When I reached the incubator and looked inside, I could see a small membrane moving inside one of the eggs. The slight movement was a sign that life was in there. It was better than the movies to watch the tiny chick peck and wiggle and struggle out of his shell and to see that there was life where all had seemed dormant for so long.

It is even more exciting to our heavenly Father, who has given us everything we need for life in Jesus Christ, to watch as we reach out to him in faith and trust him as our Savior. He loves to see new life emerge and begin to manifest itself in us. It delights him to see our faith go from head to heart to hand.

> Breathe on me, Breath of God,
> Fill me with life anew,
> That I may love what Thou dost love,
> And do what Thou wouldst do.
>
> Breathe on me, Breath of God,
> Until my heart is pure,
> Until with Thee I will one will,
> To do and to endure.

Breathe on me, Breath of God,
Till I am wholly Thine,
Until this earthly part of me
Glows with Thy fire divine.

Breathe on me, Breath of God,
So shall I never die,
But live with Thee the perfect life
Of Thine eternity.

                    (Edwin Hatch).

Points to Ponder

1. As James shows us, living faith manifests itself in Spirit-produced fruit in our lives. Read again Galatians 5:22-23, where Paul listed the fruits of the Spirit. Are any of these qualities becoming real in your life? Are any of them motivating you to act in certain ways or do certain things to glorify God because you love him?

2. It is a mistake to compare ourselves with other believers. We are all at different points of progress spiritually. Take a moment now to thank God for your own uniqueness, and to ask him to show you the new assignments He would like you to tackle, with him.

3. Are you concerned that you haven't done enough to be accepted by God? Remember, saving faith involves trust in Christ alone, nothing else. If you are worried about doing enough to earn favor with God, do a spiritual checkup. Make sure you are trusting in Jesus Christ alone for salvation. Reread Ephesians 2:8-9 if you are not convinced.

6

Word Processing

James 3:1-12

When I was in seminary, Pearl's sister Ardith Black typed out my papers on an old IBM manual typewriter. Commentaries, projects, thesis—I never would have made it without her long hours of loving labor. What a difference it makes today, as I complete doctoral studies at Talbot Seminary, to have some hyper-speed word-processing software and computer equipment in our offices. Pages need no longer be painstakingly typed and retyped, nor mistakes globbed over with Liquid Paper. Little errors disappear with the press of a button; entire paragraphs are moved or wiped out in milliseconds. A laser printer spits out the revisions as fast as they are entered. It is nearly impossible to misuse words with this high-tech equipment.

Too bad we can't say the same thing about the other type of word processing we do. You know what I mean: the words we process with our mouths and minds.

Statisticians tell us that we spend at least one-fifth of our lives talking. That is approximately thirteen years of mouth motion. Psychologists estimate that each day the average adult utters between 12,000 and 25,000 words.

What should come through loud and clear is that every single day we shove our mouths in gear and release the clutch on thousands of statements. Regrettably, our brains are not always engaged in that process. We often do a whole lot of talking before we do very much thinking about what we are saying and its consequences. Suffering from chronic foot-in-mouth disease, we ignore the effect our verbal word processing has on others. Our insensitivity is captured in Paul Simon's lyrics to "Sounds of Silence":

> And in the naked night I saw
> Ten thousand people, maybe more,
> People talking without speaking,
> People hearing without listening
> People writing songs that voices
> Never shared. No one dared
> Disturb the sounds of silence.

LITTLE LEAGUE LIP

My son Andy played Little League baseball for a couple of seasons. Overall, the experience was good, but all too clear are my memories of adult men yelling and stomping up and down in the stands, swearing at the little boys on the field who were trying to do the best job they could. One of the worst displays of tongue control imaginable comes from the mouths of middle-aged men whose kids are in competition.

Something about athletics triggers the tongue. It's pitiful. Unrealized goals, unfulfilled dreams and ambitions erupt in sideline tantrums. Forty-year-old men blast away at ten-year-olds. "C'mon! Be a hitter! What's the matter with you? Watch the ball, will you? Can't you do anything right?" And I've heard much worse.

A former New York Yankee third baseman is one of the few men I've met who wasn't in some way pushing his expectations off onto his son. "The guys who are the hardest on their kids are the guys who didn't make it themselves," he explained to me one time. "They are the ones who are pushing, screaming, yelling bloody murder, and clawing for every advantage for their kid so he can make it in sports. Those of us who've made it aren't sweating it. We know what our kids have to look forward to. If they want to play sports, okay. If they don't, that's okay too. Our image is not at stake."

Whatever the reason behind the sideline antics of some Little League dads (and moms), the fact is that an uncontrolled tongue can do great damage. How thankful Pearl and I were that our youngest son's first baseball coach was a gentle man who loved the kids. Often we would see him wrap an arm around their shoulders. He never lost control. Whether they won or lost was insignificant, as long as they played their best.

When the final and biggest game of the season came around, our boys were charged up and ready. They took on the only undefeated team in the league, the team that had occupied first place for weeks. Refusing to bow to pressure, Coach Ryan let everyone play—from the most talented to the least. Guess what? Our guys won 2-0, capping off a perfect season to our way of thinking—and theirs. What a contrast Coach Ryan was to some of the other coaches and spectators we had seen. His quiet, calm, controlled example rubbed off on our team's parents and we didn't have the kind of ranting and raving typical elsewhere.

My friend Dave Simmons tells a different story. I got to know Dave as I helped a little in the development of King's Arrow Ranch, and I have heard him relate this incident several times in group situations. Dave played for the Dallas Cowboys. His father, Amos, was a man you could never really please. When Dave called his dad after the NFL draft with the news that he had been taken second behind Joe Namath, Amos's only words were, "How does it feel to be drafted *second*?"

Years passed, and eventually Dave's own son began playing football. Dave, his wife Sandy, and their daughter all went to the son's first game. It was a fiasco on the field, and on the way home Dave found himself locked into a critical mode, picking apart every play. Arriving home, the boy burst into tears and ran into the house. Sandy and their daughter followed silently. Dave sadly drove the car into the garage and made his way toward the house. Sandy met him at the door. One word got the job done: "Amos."

TONGUE TAMING

The tongue uncontrolled can slice up someone's self-image, destroy a dream, shatter a relationship. The ability to curb one's tongue is a mark of Christian maturity. That was James's main point in the first twelve verses of chapter 3. He already showed us several signs of spiritual growth. Now he turned to the potential monster within us all and deals with the devastation this tiny member can cause. As usual, he minced no words.

James prepared us for his message with two previous statements. In 1:19 he said, "You know this, my beloved brethren, now let every man be quick to hear, slow to speak, slow to anger." In 1:26 we read, "If any man is thinking himself to be religious, not holding in check his tongue, but is deceiving his own heart, his religion is worthless." Tongue control is vital to the growing Christian. Loose lips sink ships and also shipwreck lives. They end friendships, destroy marriages, and ruin relationships with children and between siblings. Too much idle talk tears down our ability to be good witnesses for Christ. It destroys our credibility and discredits the Savior. We show spiritual growth when we think before speaking. James exhorted us to do just that in 3:1-12.

Being of a temperament similar to the apostle Peter's, I confess I say a lot of things before I have really thought them through. I am getting better, but it's an uphill struggle (as my wife and kids can tell you). In this passage, James hit me pretty hard and pointed out my weaknesses.

A GREATER CONDEMNATION—JAMES 3:1-2

> Stop becoming many teachers, my brethren, knowing that we shall receive a greater condemnation. For we commit many sins. If anyone does not stumble in word, this one is a fully developed man able to hold in check also his entire body (James 3:1-2).

TO THE TEACHER

James began with a serious warning. It is a message of caution to all who teach God's word to others, for they "shall receive a greater condemnation" (3:1).

With greater knowledge comes greater responsibility. When we assume the position of teacher, we had better be careful. We must never go into a Bible-teaching situation without first spending time poring over the Bible. This is no place for haphazard study—we should know our stuff. Instead of formulating pat answers, we should grapple with scripture. We should never be afraid to say, "I don't know. I'll try to find out." It is far better to admit ignorance than to give out wrong information.

Before every Bible class I teach or sermon I preach, this prayer is on my lips and in my heart, because eternal destinies are hanging in the balance: "Lord, fill my mind and heart with the message that I should convey to these people. By your Spirit open me up so that I can communicate that message in an effective manner. Speak through me, and may your words prosper and bear fruit in the lives of these listeners." I will not teach any passage of scripture that I haven't first dug into at length to gain understanding and knowledge. God wants us to take his word seriously.

But don't let James's warning scare you from volunteering to assist with vacation Bible school or Sunday school or leading a Bible study. The fact is, formally or not, every Christian ought to be some kind of Bible teacher. We're all on the faculty, to some extent.

To believers, Christ's great commission, the last set of instructions He gave before ascending into heaven, was this: "Go therefore and make disciples of all the nations, baptizing them in the name of the Father and the Son and the Holy Spirit, teaching them to observe all that I commanded you; and lo, I am with you always, even to the end of the age" (Matthew 28:19-20 NASB). Part of making disciples requires that we tell others about Jesus Christ, his work on the cross, his forgiveness. It means we share the gospel, and also the principles of the Christian life.

Whether we take on a Sunday school class or not, we will be teaching somehow. We will be teaching our friends, our spouses, our neighbors, our kids as we answer questions and strive to mirror Christ. So we had better get our facts straight. We had better not mislead. We had better not give flip answers to crucial questions. Jesus said, "And I say to you, that every careless word that men shall speak, they shall render account for it in the day of judgment. For by your words you shall be justified, and by your words you shall be condemned" (Matthew 12:36-37 NASB). If we have truly trusted Christ, we will be in heaven, no matter what we have said. But our rewards won't be as rich if our tongues have constantly shifted carelessly into overspeak.

The key to good interpersonal relationships is learning how to encourage, exhort, and affirm with the tongue. Words play a powerful role in motivation, maturity, and ministry. I will never forget the tremendous encouragement of some kind words written in a book review. My editor at Loizeaux Brothers, Claudia Mooij, mailed me a copy of the review. All the tension and battle-weariness of a difficult day melted immediately as my secretary Jan opened the mail and read the article aloud in the workroom where we were all gathered. The warm glow has lasted for weeks, motivating me to keep cracking on this present book.

ECHOES ACROSS ETERNITY

With the psalmist, this prayer should be on our lips, "Set a guard over my mouth, O Lord; keep watch over the door of my lips" (Psalm 141:3 NIV). We might add, "Help me to say only the things you want me to say."

Do we realize that as Christians we are going to be held accountable for every word we have spoken? What we say in the privacy of our homes—wives to husbands, husbands to wives, parents to children, brothers to sisters—will not be forgotten. We will face the record of those words at the judgment seat of Christ.

Research tells us that no word once uttered ever dies, but can be found somewhere in the vibrations of the atmosphere. Those tiny syllables reverberate endlessly, undetected by the human ear. It may well be that at the *bema* we will miraculously hear every word we have uttered, the way we uttered it, again. I don't know about you, but I would just as soon forget many of the things I've said. "But there is nothing covered up that will not be revealed, and hidden that will not be known. Accordingly, whatever you have said in the dark shall be heard in the light, and what you have whispered in the inner rooms shall be proclaimed upon the housetops" (Luke 12:2-3 NASB). There are no closed doors with God. We will face the record of our words.

The damage done by careless chatter is appalling. David described the awful feeling of being shredded by the lips of others:

I am in the midst of lions;
    I lie among ravenous beasts—
men whose teeth are spears and arrows,
    whose tongues are sharp swords (Psalm 57:4
    NIV).

The wisdom of the Proverbs speaks against loose lips:

Reckless words pierce like a sword,
    but the tongue of the wise brings healing
    (Proverbs 12:18 NIV).

He who guards his mouth and his tongue
    keeps himself from calamity (Proverbs 21:23
    NIV; see also 12:19; 15:1,2,4; 16:1; 18:21).

The apostle Paul knew all about being victimized by the words of others too. "Alexander the coppersmith did me much harm; the Lord will repay him according to his deeds" (2 Timothy 4:14 NASB). There is no telling exactly what Alexander did or said. We can only imagine possible slander, ridicule, or angry outbursts. Hurt by words and actions, Paul left the matter in the Lord's hands. Sometimes we just have to let go of our hurts and resentments and lay them at the Lord's feet. He will settle accounts later, in his time and in his way.

TONGUES OF BLOOD

One way God distinguishes humankind from the rest of creation is through the ability He has given us to communicate in words. People can be distinguished from others by the good or evil they accomplish with their tongues. "For we commit many sins," James wrote (3:2a), referring to the evil we spread with what we say and how we say it. A sarcastic comment, an insinuating remark, a critical statement, a lie, an unfounded rumor, a piece of misinformation—each of these can destroy. But arguably the greatest damage, because its consequences can be eternal, is tongue abuse by a teacher of God's word.

Often the tongues and pens of those who speak and write on theological issues are turned to bloody swords slaying others. It has been said that the Christian army is the only one that attacks its own soldiers. Our ranks can be bloody, indeed.

The world was repulsed at the bloodshed in Beijing when Chinese soldiers used their guns and tanks to crush their countrymen. We often stand guilty too, of verbally murdering brothers and sisters in Christ. Satan and the demons of hell are giving us standing ovations for some of our twentieth-century battles in the church. Issues that should be lovingly and impartially hammered out in seminary classrooms are flaunted before the world, demonstrating how little real love exists among us. How tragic that we are so strong on basic doctrine, but so weak on charity.

TONGUE CONTROL: A SIGN OF SELF-CONTROL

Why is it that our ability to control our tongues marks our maturity in Christ? "If anyone does not stumble in word, this one is a fully developed man able to hold in check also his entire body" (3:2). The connection is clear: individuals who can control their tongues are also able to control the appetites and desires of their bodies.

It is probably harder to control what we say than to control any other inclination or desire, except perhaps our thought lives. Consider it. Few of us will purposely physically injure another person, but just about all of us will speak angry words to someone else. We would never strip anyone of his clothes in public, but we just might strip him of his dignity with a cutting remark or by spreading a rumor. We would never deliberately set out to ruin someone's ministry, but it happens over and over through innuendo. We would never clap our hands and rejoice publicly over someone's downfall, but in private we may often say, "He deserved it. I could see it coming." The question is, if we could see it coming, why didn't we do something to stop it?

It is so much easier to sin with our tongues than to sin just about any other way. No wonder James said that if we are able to control what we say, we will be able to exercise self-control elsewhere. If we are curbing our tongues, we have more than halfway licked the problem of controlling our minds and bodies.

HOW CAN WE CONQUER?

Let me caution you. Tongue control does not come automatically the moment we come to Christ. Neither does control over the rest of our desires and appetites. We don't conquer the flesh, the old nature, what we were before we accepted Christ, by merely saying, "I'm not going to gossip any more. I'm not going to say things I shouldn't ever again." Neither can an act of will make us immediately acquire any of the qualities of a spiritually mature person which James has already discussed in his letter.

It doesn't work to wake up one morning and say, "Starting today, I'll be a different person. I'm going to respond properly to tests. I'll be joyful in trials. I'm not going to sin anymore. I'm going to dive into serious, consistent Bible study. I'm going to love the unlovely. I'm going to do good works in the name of Christ." Will is involved, in that we must desire to become all that God would have us become. But we will be able to accomplish none of this on our own. It is through the work of the Holy Spirit that every good and perfect change comes in our lives as Christians.

Change can come only from inside out. It is what we *are* that is the problem. Our words reflect the real us. As Jesus said, "The good man out of the good treasure of his heart brings forth what is good; and the evil man out of the evil treasure brings forth what is evil; *for his mouth speaks from that which fills his heart*" (Luke 6:45 NASB, italics mine; see also Matthew 12:34).

So, in our struggle, we are brought back to the mind. And God has given us a method of mind control.

God's Spirit, dwelling within us, enables us to submit to the situations that slap us in the face. Naturally we want to fight the fire or run from the flames, escaping the situation. We don't want any part of the disease, the job hassle, the kid problems, the neighborhood headaches. Naturally, we say no. It is God's Spirit who enables us to say, "Yes, Lord, I'm ready to learn what You would have me learn through this."

It is also the Holy Spirit who empowers us to resist or flee temptation, when another "little voice" inside us is urging us to try it because we'll like it.

When it comes to reading the Bible, what is our natural desire? It is so easy to find excuses not to read the word. The Bible is hard to understand, we tell ourselves. It's not relevant. It's full of inaccuracies (which is a lie from the pit of hell itself). Yet what the Spirit desires is that we develop healthy, holy appetites for God's word. The Spirit knows that the more we read scripture, meditate on it, and learn to apply it to our lives, the more like Christ we become.

Does the Spirit desire us to love the unlovely? We know He does. It is the old human nature that rejects individuals. It is the old nature that craves retaliation. It is the old nature that tells us to do it unto others before they do it unto us. The Spirit wants us to open up and love everyone sincerely. And what about speaking up about our faith? The old nature says, "Why bother?" Yet the Spirit produces boldness and fruit in the willing heart.

It is through the work of the Spirit that we gain tongue control. As we allow the Spirit to control our tongues, the reality of James 1:19 comes to pass, and we do become quick to hear, slow to speak, and slow to anger. That philosophy is contrary to the mindset of the world. Daily we are urged to speak up, say our piece, show what we know. After all, everyone else is doing it. What is the Spirit's position? He puts the clamp on things. If we are submissive to his leading, we will know when He wants us to speak. We will wait until He is ready to use our tongues to say what He wants us to say in any given situation.

ON THE HOME FRONT

If only moms and dads would learn this lesson of tongue control, amazing transformations could take place in their relationships with their children. Kids will push you to the wall—and beyond. Our oldest three gave us the pleasure of being teenagers at the same time. No sooner did the first three ship off to college and beyond than the second wave crashed ashore and our two youngest, Andy and Julea, became teens. Pearl and I did well to survive. It did not take us long to discover that our teens would verbally bait us when given the chance. They would say something outrageous—guaranteed to make the hair on the back of our necks bristle. Some startling statement would pop out designed to send us into orbit.

I think I'll go to Dallas to spend the weekend with some friends. We'll stay at the Marriott.

I think I'll buy that motorcycle anyway, with my own money.

I think I'll quit school and get a job.

At such comments my fuse ignited, and I usually hit the roof with a loud, "Over my dead body!" Watching me crash made Pearl realize that hitting the roof was painful and impractical. She found that at the moment she wanted to blast off, it was better to say something like, "Oh, do you really think so?" or, "Hmm. That's interesting. We'll have to talk about that later." Although our vocal cords silently shouted within, walking off quietly usually seemed a good next step and defused the situation. She could respond so calmly only when she prayed that the Spirit would control her tongue.

If the statement made by one of the children revealed a genuine problem, we made a point to go back later and discuss it with him or her in a calm setting. Did we handle every disagreement so spiritually with our kids? Ha! As our five will tell you, Pearl succeeded more than I did, and both of us failed on many, many occasions. Yet we learned that when we were willing to let the Spirit control our words, relationships were better and the family ran more smoothly.

Early in our marriage, Pearl and I committed ourselves to seeking the Spirit's control when we spoke to each other too, especially about differences of opinion. We tried not to argue in front of the kids. They knew we didn't always agree, but they also knew that we worked it out.

When breaks in communication did come—and they did, and still do—we would get into the car and go somewhere to hash things out. Now our nest is empty, so we don't have to put so much mileage on the Mercury. But the principle is intact. Dirty laundry doesn't need to be a family affair. We never wanted to give our kids the image of a mother and father fighting and fussing all the time. We never wanted our children to doubt our commitment to the marriage and to staying together as a family. I don't think they ever worried that we would become a divorce statistic, although I do believe they knew we had honest differences and resolved them. Often it takes a great deal of reliance on the strength of the Holy Spirit to keep silent until the appropriate time to discuss things. And even in the discussion, the Spirit is needed to keep things from heating up.

I also thank God for enabling our kids to grow up genuinely loving and liking one another. Unrestrained rivalry rips apart many families, producing adults who are hardly on speaking terms with their siblings. Many times the fault lies with parents who allow their kids verbally to bite and devour one another. We made it a rule at our house never to permit our children to insult or to degrade the worth of one another. Remarks like, "You're so stupid," "Where'd you get that pizza face?" and, "You eat like a pig, fatso," were strictly taboo.

This may sound like our family was the Brady Bunch. It wasn't. There were plenty of feuds at our house, but an undercurrent of loyalty bound our five together. When one would hear something negative said about a brother or sister in public, it was like a bull seeing red. All of our children can be fairly outspoken, and the outsider criticizing an Anderson was in for it.

I thank God that Pearl and I, our children, and their spouses and families, are close today. Our times together, rarer now because geography separates us, bring us all great joy. We are not perfect, but we have a lot of fun together. We credit Christ for allowing us to remain the best of friends through it all. We all know him and are walking together in him, and it makes a difference. Kids do not have to grow up carrying into adulthood the emotional baggage of childhood: rivalry and resentment. Consistent tongue control is a factor in any such success.

OF BRIDLES, BOATS, AND UNQUENCHABLE FIRES—JAMES 3:3-5

> Now if we are putting bridles in the mouths of the horses, in order that they may be obeying us, we are also guiding their whole body. Behold, also the ships, though they are so large and are driven by strong winds, are being guided by a very small rudder wherever the impulse of the steersman leads him. So also the tongue is a small member, and it is boasting of great things. Behold how large a forest a little fire sets ablaze. And the tongue is a fire; the sum total of iniquity. The tongue so presents itself in our members, staining the whole body and is setting on fire the course of existence and is being set on fire by hell.

When we begin to realize the serious ramifications of our words and the struggle going on over the control of our tongues, we are tempted to resign ourselves to such weak statements as, "Well, God, You made me this way." What an easy way out. Since our thoughts are not his thoughts, and our ways not his ways—and, we might add, our words are not his words—we have got a problem. The answer lies in the power of the Spirit activating our new divine nature to speak words that edify and encourage.

Realizing that right words will come as we learn the lesson of dependence on the Spirit, we ought to be sure we are in what I call the "Moses mode" before we speak. Remember, it was Moses whom God told, "Now go; I will help you speak and will teach you what to say" (Exodus 4:12 NIV).

The apostle Paul was in the Moses mode as he stood in a storm-tossed boat and spoke to 275 sick, starving passengers. As the waves crashed over the decks, Paul proclaimed, "Therefore, keep up your courage, men, for I believe God, that it will turn out exactly as I have been told" (Acts 27:25 NASB).

Spirit control of the tongue is not just a nicety for the growing Christian; it is a necessity. It is serious business. Tongue-taming is vital for spiritual progress. James hammered home his point with three illustrations of the power of the tongue. Each is an example of a small item capable of enormous effect.

THE BRIDLE

James first compared the tongue to a bridle (3:4). A small contraption of leather and brass, when strapped in place and held by a rider, the bridle is capable of guiding the entire body of a horse. It tells him to turn or stop, to trot or gallop. Similarly, a tongue under the control of the Holy Spirit is able to guide a person. It actually seals—confirms or marks—that person's destiny.

What we say reveals what we are, and where we are heading. Look at how the destinies of the following were sealed with their tongues: *The thief on the cross:* "Jesus, remember me when You come in Your kingdom!" (Luke 23:42 NASB). *The father of a boy possessed by an unclean spirit:* "I do believe; help my unbelief" (Mark 9:24 NASB). *The woman with the hemorrhage:* "If I only touch His garment, I shall get well" (Matthew 9:20 NASB).

In each case, living faith in the living Lord issued from the lips, the spokespeople of the heart. Scripture contains just as many examples of others whose words indicate missed chances, failed opportunities, refusals to bow before God's throne of grace, like the responses of the three men below who were evangelized by none other than the apostle Paul: *Felix*: "Go away for the present, and when I find time, I will summon you" (Acts 24:25 NASB). *Festus*: "Paul, you are out of your mind! Your great learning is driving you mad" (Acts 26:24 NASB). *Agrippa*: "In a short time you will persuade me to become a Christian" (Acts 26:28 NASB).

"Almost persuaded" is still *almost.* "Not quite" equals *never.*

The Rudder

I can't help but think of the kids who attend our camps each summer. Constantly I am amazed at the language that some of them use. Where do they get it? It comes from a father who explodes, a coach who cusses on the ball field, a TV cop who talks tough to look tough. Junior comes to camp and figures he's got to be Joe Cool, dragging the sacred name of Jesus into the dirt, swearing so he'll look important to the other kids. Kids have a way of preaching back to us what they pick up from us. If we are not controlling our tongues, we will soon have a houseful of mimics who duplicate our actions, attitudes, and vocabulary.

We must, as James urged us, give our tongues over to the right steersman. To illustrate this concept, he made reference to a ship's rudder (3:4). This thin blade controls the direction of the smallest sailboat to the largest ocean liner. Of course, the rudder does not operate independently, but is "guided . . . wherever the impulse of the steersman leads it." The parallel to our lives is clear.

If the Holy Spirit is that steersman, if He is controlling our tongues, we are in good shape. But if the rudder is manipulated by our own selfishness, watch out! The ship is off course and the rocks and ice are just below the surface. We may soon find ourselves rearranging the deck chairs on the *Titanic.*

A psychiatrist recently observed something very interesting about a dear Christian lady afflicted with Alzheimer's disease: "The fact that Mrs. R. never curses and has such a sweet disposition is a real testimony to her and to the Holy Spirit's work in her life through the years. So many of my patients with a form of senile dementia, their natural inhibitions gone, become ill-tempered, verbally abrasive, and hard to handle. Mrs. R's personality really reflects the work of the Spirit and her own character." What an accurate observation, I thought. Even in the tragic midst of a debilitating disease, it is possible for a Christian's changed heart and sweet speech to be manifested. They are tangible results of long guidance by the right steersman.

A Spark

"So also the tongue is a small member, and it is boasting of great things. Behold how large a forest fire a little fire sets ablaze," continued James, giving us a third illustration of the tongue's power (3:5). It takes only a spark, a match strike, to get a fire going. Just as Mrs. O'Leary's cow kicked over a lantern and burned Chicago, so can our tongues start an inferno of trouble.

I am originally from the Pacific Northwest, the land of lakes, trees, mountains, and snow. It's not heaven, but they say you can see it from there. Even though I am now a confirmed Texan, I still love to return to the Northwest to hike and climb in the mountains. (I'm told that Texas is where God works, and the Northwest is where He takes his vacations.) Looking out over the majestic landscape surely makes me feel close to God. His presence is unmistakable in the spectacular beauty of his creation.

Each year, however, thousands of acres of this spectacular beauty are incinerated because of tourists who are careless with fire. Some of my most vivid memories from childhood are of my father throwing on his canvas coat and boots and answering the alarms sounding for the volunteer firemen to battle forest fires threatening our city.

Have you ever witnessed the devastation of a forest fire? Several years ago, as a friend and I were hiking in the Northwest, we spotted a huge stretch of some fifty to seventy-five thousand acres of blackened terrain. Scarred, covered by charred matchstick trees, the land had been leveled—the result of a campfire left unattended. Even a thrown-away cigarette can smolder, burn, and destroy whole counties. Like the blazing forest fire, the tongue wreaks havoc too. The carnage is of a different sort, but the damage is also deadly and scarring.

In the Old Testament, David's son Absalom should have

succeeded his father to the throne. Their relationship damaged because of his murder of Amnon in retaliation for the rape of Tamar, Absalom sought to wrest the reins of the kingdom from David's hands. He began his quest for power with his tongue.

Accosting men in the city of Jerusalem, Absalom's insinuations, snide remarks, and subtle promises soon stole the hearts of the people away from David. David was forced to flee his own capital city. Eventually he regained his kingdom, but at a tragic cost. Absalom's rebellion resulted in a bloody civil war. Thousands of Israelites died. Absalom himself was murdered by David's lieutenant Joab and his men, who stabbed him repeatedly as he dangled from a tree, his thick flowing hair caught in the branches. It was the horrifying end of a fiery carnage that started with a spark from the lips.

THE TONGUE AFLAME

The tongue burns, no doubt about it. James continued his metaphor. "And the tongue is a fire; the sum total of iniquity. The tongue so presents itself in our members, staining the whole body and is setting on fire the course of existence and is being set on fire by hell" (3:6). As usual, James's words cut quickly to the heart of the matter.

A tongue that is uncontrolled and destructive is not set afire by the power of God. It is a product of Satan, an issue of hell. The implication is that Christians who are not in the process of taming their tongues are allowing themselves to be used by the devil.

A tragedy befell a church and its young pastor in our town. One man on the elder board took a disliking to the minister, and voiced his displeasure to all in the congregation who would listen. "I can't take it any more," confided the embattled pastor. "It's too tough on my wife and kids. I've got to think of them. I'm resigning." And he did, leaving his first pastorate sadder, wiser, and very much aware of the searing pain a scorching tongue can bring.

FIVE TONGUE BURNERS

How does the tongue burn? Here are five ways in which the tongue can be set afire, along with some scriptural suggestions for putting out the blaze:

1. *The tongue burns by speaking idle words.* Maybe we don't know all the details, and surely we wouldn't want to be quoted, but we'll put in our two bits anyway. We heard it this way, which may not be the right way, but who cares? We've got to have something to talk about, don't we? A good combat weapon for the counterattack is Proverbs 4:24, "Put away perversity from your mouth; keep corrupt talk far from your lips" (NIV).

2. *The tongue burns by uttering profanity.* James later condemned the hypocrisy of tongues that praise God, then curse men who are made in his image (3:9). How it grieves God that so many of his children seldom think twice about using his name as an exclamation. Many of us figure that if we don't stick a word of condemnation at the end, we're okay. We blurt out Christ's sacred name, or else we ask God to damn others—a sad irony, since He is in the business of saving them. We may feel provoked at times, but cursing reveals hearts of rebellion, ingratitude, and pride. Remember this passage, next time someone cuts in front of you on the freeway and you're tempted to punctuate the air with a few choice expletives:

> Let no unwholesome word proceed from your mouth, but only such a word as is good for edification according to the need of the moment, that it may give grace to those who hear (Ephesians 4:29 NASB).

3. *The tongue burns by insinuating evil.* This is not just spreading idle words, but spreading idle words with a purpose—perhaps to start a fight or to fan a fight. Communication with improper motivation brews discontent. Psalm 52:2 speaks sharply to this kind of talking:

> Your tongue plots destruction;
> it is like a sharpened razor,
> you who practice deceit (NIV).

Proverbs 16:28 also deals with the issue:

> A perverse man stirs up dissension,
> and a gossip separates close friends (NIV).

4. *A tongue also burns by magnifying the faults of others.* This

reflects negatively on the character of another person and may or may not be done face to face. It can take the form of telling a wife she's incompetent, a husband he's inept or inconsiderate, a child he's no good. It belittles. It also happens when Mom tells the neighbors about Junior's disobedience and never mentions his good points. Whether or not Junior is listening, he knows. Such talk criticizes, embroiders, wounds.

> They sharpen their tongues like swords
> and aim their words like deadly arrows (Psalm 64:3 NIV).

5. *A tongue burns not only by what it says, but by the way in which it says it.* Even the most innocuous of statements can become poison as it reaches the ears because of the way in which it is said.

"That is absolutely the best sermon I have ever heard!" gushed someone at a church where I was an invited speaker. "I haven't heard such a good sermon in a long, long time! I am sorry you won't be here longer." I was a little surprised at such excessive praise, until I realized that I hadn't been the only intended hearer. The pastor of the church stood well within earshot, and the person had obviously meant those comments (veiled criticism) to be noticed by him. May we remember, each time we speak, the words of Psalm 34:12-13:

> Whoever of you loves life
> and desires to see many good days,
> keep your tongue from evil
> and your lips from speaking lies (NIV).

THE SUM OF ALL INIQUITY

Notice that James called the tongue not only a fire, but also "the sum total of iniquity" (3:6a). What does this mean? James was telling us three things:

1. The tongue suggests the sin.
2. The tongue commits the sin.
3. The tongue defends the sin.

This is oftentimes the process. A sin is suggested: "Why don't we knock off a few minutes early and just ask Sara to punch us out at five?" A sin is committed: "No, Mommy, I didn't break that vase." "Sir, I know nothing about any congressional kickbacks." The sin is defended: "But everyone was doing it, Dad!" "I didn't consider the money a bribe."

The Senselessness of an Untamed Tongue—James 3:7-12

> For every creature, wild animals and birds, reptiles and sea creatures, is being tamed and has been tamed by humankind. But the tongue no one, in the human race, is able to tame; a restless evil, full of death-bringing poison. With it, we are praising the Lord and Father, and with it, we are cursing men who have been made in the likeness of God. Out of the same mouth are proceeding blessings and cursings. My brethren, it is not necessary that these things keep on happening. The spring is not pouring forth out of the same opening, the sweet and the bitter [water], is it? A fig tree, my brethren, is not able to produce olives, or a vine, figs, is it? Neither can a salt spring give sweet water (James 3:7-12).

Nobody ever said that tongue-taming was easy. How ironic that we can master most of the species on this planet, but not our own small tongues (3:7). Go to one of the Sea World theme parks and you'll view megaton killer whales leaping out of the water, speeding, splashing, diving—all at the command of a trainer. Those brave men and women even ride on the backs of Shamu and his friends, letting the mammoth creatures carry them underwater. A wet suit and whistle don't sound like much insurance to me, yet the trainers are unafraid. They are confident in the tameness of their big salt-water buddies.

If we can train such an immense creature as a killer whale, we can surely train just about anything on earth. Lions and tigers and bears—circuses overflow with examples of how such beasts have been "civilized."

The tongue, however, is another matter entirely. No human can tame his or her own tongue (3:8). But the Holy Spirit can.

The Spirit is capable of controlling that little member behind our teeth, that "restless evil, full of death-bringing poison" (3:8). Here James was comparing the tongue to a venomous snake, perhaps a cobra or copperhead ready to strike without warning. Paul described our natural state like this: "Their throat is an open grave, With their tongues they keep deceiving" (Romans 3:13 NASB). Christ came to change that.

DOUBLE-MINDED AND DOUBLE-TONGUED

James mentioned the double-minded man in chapter 1. Now we meet those who are double-tongued, alternately "praising the Lord and Father, and . . . cursing men who have been made in the likeness of God" (3:9). This is the picture of a person who vacillates between the control of the flesh and the control of the Spirit (3:9-10a).

This person is evidently a Christian—one moment under the control of the Spirit, with lips that praise the Lord; the next moment under the control of the flesh, and cursing others. It is a double standard that to some extent we will probably all experience as believers.

Is the situation hopeless? As Christians are we doomed to lives of hypocrisy? Not at all! "My brethren," wrote James, "it is not necessary that these things keep on happening" (3:10b). As we grow up in Christ, the periods of Spirit-control should be more frequent, and longer, as long as we consciously rely on him. The times of flesh-control should be fewer, farther between, and shorter. This is true as long as we're growing.

SWEET SPEECH

It is "spiritually unnatural" for Christians to misuse their tongues. They are going against the grain of their new natures when they do. They are rebelling against the work of the Holy Spirit.

James ended his discourse about word processing on this note. From a bubbling spring comes water of only one sort. The spring will not produce both bitter water and sweet water. Neither does an olive tree grow figs, or fig vines produce olives (3:11-12). The challenge is clear. We are to be springs pouring forth streams of living, sweet water.

A calm, quiet word. A timely silence. A kind remark. Such sweet speech can be balm to a wounded soul.

Some years ago a Christian brother confronted me in a fit of rage and anger. When his tirade was over, I felt the joy of the Spirit flood my heart as I sat in silent reflection, weighing his words. My normal response would have been to retaliate. Only the Spirit could have restrained me. I was able, in the power of the Spirit, to see beyond those words to his deeper needs, which helped me understand his actions. It takes two to tangle, and when we use 1 Peter 3:8-12 as our game plan, things really will begin to turn around for us:

> To sum up, let all be harmonious, sympathetic, brotherly, kindhearted, and humble in spirit; not returning evil for evil, or insult for insult, but giving a blessing instead; for you were called for the very purpose that you might inherit a blessing. For,
>
> "Let him who means to love life and see good days
> Refrain his tongue from evil and his lips from
> speaking guile.
> And let him turn away from evil and do good;
> Let him seek peace and pursue it.
> For the eyes of the Lord are upon the righteous,
> And His ears attend to their prayer,
> But the face of the Lord is against those who do
> evil" (1 Peter 3:8-12 NASB).

The tongue is a fire, true. But we have the foam and the water, the salt and the soda of the Holy Spirit, to cause the flame to fizzle. In Christ we don't have to be flame-throwers.

Points to Ponder

1. What does James tell us in this passage about the importance of teaching God's word with accuracy and care? Refer to 3:1 as you answer.

2. In 3:2, James stated, "If anyone does not stumble in word, this one is a fully developed man able to hold in check also his entire body." Restate his message in your own words and explain his meaning. Do you agree or disagree with him? Why or why not?

3. Think of an example in your own life when you spoke when you perhaps shouldn't have. What were the results of the statements you made? Would it have been better to have kept silent or to have spoken differently? The next time you are in a situation demanding tact and tongue control, purpose to ask God to direct his Spirit to direct your words.

7

Christ-minded Christianity

James 3:13-18

Humorist Tom Bodett reflected on the frustrations of life with a mentally deficient black Labrador retriever:

> The situation might not bother me so much if it wasn't compounded by the dog. I'm using the term "dog" pretty loosely. A wheelbarrow full of common garden vegetables would offer just as much companionship on a walk.
>
> He's three years old and a beautiful specimen of a black Lab. All except for one thing. He was born with a head of solid bone. You could say he's a good-natured animal, but that's what they always say about stupid dogs. We have to keep him tied up all the time because he'll follow anything that moves. He's never been in much trouble with the neighbor's chickens or anything, but that's because the chickens can outsmart him. The trouble is that he's big and scary-looking, and nobody wants a big scary-looking dog running around without a brain in its head. So he stays tied up, and we give him huge amounts of food for the pleasure of watching him lie in the sun and bark at clouds.
>
> It's driving me crazy. When a terminal patient stops producing brain waves, he's declared legally dead. My

dog's EEG is flatter than Kansas, but he's healthy as a horse and happy as a clam. We had him fixed a couple years back to see if he'd calm down. Now we have a cabbage on a chain in the front yard that eats its weight in Purina every month. Again, I don't know what to do about it. I harbored some hope for a while that he might redeem himself by eating the cat, but gave that up when I noticed the cat kicks him out of the doghouse whenever he feels like it (Bodett 51-52).

Having had a few dogs over the years—some about as bright as Tom Bodett's Lab, and others sharp enough to get into canine MENSA—I can say that the smart ones are much more fun to have around than the dumb ones. There is just something annoying about an animal that chews up the newspaper instead of fetching it.

We humans appreciate plain old common horse sense in our animals. We also admire it in the people we know.

GOOD JUDGMENT—WHAT'S IT WORTH?

Many years ago I had the privilege of meeting with Miss A. Wetherell Johnson, founder of Bible Study Fellowship. "How do you pick your leaders?" I asked. Her reply was, "I look for people who have others following them." People generally follow people they trust, men and women who exercise good judgment. The worth of wisdom cannot be overestimated. Good judgment, sound thinking, the stick-to-it-iveness to abide by solid, thoughtful decisions—these are the attributes we search for when seeking to fill leadership positions.

"We make our decisions, and then our decisions turn around and make us," Frank W. Boreham once observed. "Our best friends and our worst enemies are our thoughts. A thought can do us more good than a doctor or a banker or a faithful friend. It can also do us more harm than a brick," said Frank Crane. "The average man's judgment is so poor, he runs a risk every time he uses it," warned Edgar Howe.

Each statement reflects the same truth: Good judgment, the ability to make sound decisions, is of great value. The consequences of a bad decision can stick to us like gum on the underside of a school desk. Companies and colleges recognize this.

As a pastor I have often been asked to supply references for individuals seeking employment or for young people applying for college admission and scholarships. Invariably one question I am asked concerns the person's judgment. Here are some samples: (1) On a scale of one to ten, how would you rate this candidate's ability to make sound decisions? (2) How would you characterize this applicant's judgment? (3) In your opinion, is the subject able to evaluate facts and make responsible choices based on these facts?

In the corporate board room and college classroom, the ability to discern facts and make intelligent decisions is important. It is important to our heavenly Father too.

SOLOMON'S WISE CHOICE

God values wisdom. After Solomon was made king of Israel, God appeared to him in a dream and instructed him to ask for whatever he wanted. Solomon could have requested money, world power, personal safety. Instead, his reply to God's offer was this:

> Now, O Lord my God, you have made your servant king in place of my father David. But I am only a little child and do not know how to carry out my duties. Your servant is here among the people you have chosen, a great people, too numerous to count or number. So give your servant a discerning heart to govern your people and to distinguish between right and wrong. For who is able to govern this great people of yours? (1 Kings 3:7-9 NIV).

Solomon asked for wisdom. He recognized his insignificance and need. He knew the source of true wisdom: God almighty. God was so pleased by his request that He said to Solomon, "Since you have asked for this and not for long life or wealth for yourself, nor have asked for the death of your enemies but for discernment in administering justice, I will do what you have asked. I will give you a wise and discerning heart, so that there will never have been anyone like you, nor will there ever be. Moreover, I will give you what you have not asked for—both riches and honor—so that in your lifetime you will have no equal among kings" (1 Kings 3:11-13 NIV). By asking only for the most essential, Solomon got everything.

Believe me, Solomon needed every ounce of wisdom he asked for. When he assumed the throne, the past track record of the nation Israel was nothing to brag about. They had a history of biting the hand that was feeding them. The final phrase in the final verse of the book of Judges sums up the national picture well, "Everyone did as he saw fit" (Judges 21:25b NIV).

When Moses ascended Mount Sinai to receive the ten commandments, the children of Israel promptly forgot God's goodness and erected a golden calf. They chose not to go into the promised land at the first opportunity, a mistake that cost them forty years. Later, although God set up judges to rule over them, they wanted a king. No wonder Solomon begged for wisdom.

GROWING IN GOOD JUDGMENT

Why is wisdom so valuable to us today? A mature person in the natural, physical world who exercises good judgment is prone to success. He makes sound decisions in his business. She makes sound decisions in the home. He utilizes the wisdom of others, realizing that there is "safety in a multitude of counselors" (Proverbs 11:14; 24:6). She doesn't characteristically make snap decisions or split-second choices, but is careful, cautious, and calm. He doesn't allow circumstances to dictate his responses, but instead considers the whole picture. She is the type of person you would want to invest your money. You would buy his used car. You would ask her to be a reference.

As James has already shown us, Christians who are maturing spiritually are allowing the Holy Spirit to control them. When tough times come into their lives, when temptations hit, through the work of the Spirit, they often experience victory, not defeat. They have a healthy appreciation of the need to read God's word and to learn more of God's will for their lives. They understand about compassion. They are learning to respond to situations instead of reacting to them and saying things that shouldn't be said. The fruit of the Spirit is showing up in their lives.

In the passage we are about to consider, we will see that the growing-up Christian is, in addition to all of the above, exercising sound judgment. Right thinking, as much as any other quality we have discussed, is a mark of Christian maturity.

What is good judgment? F. B. Meyer once said, "Satan rushes

men, but God leads them." Often the key to sound spiritual judgment lies in our willingness to wait on God. Growing-up Christians are learning to do just that. When faced with decisions, they don't allow others to dictate to them. They aren't concerned with impressing the pack. They don't yield to pressure. They don't panic. Instead, they retreat to a quiet place to pray and reflect on God's word. They talk to their wives or husbands. They talk to spiritually minded counselors. They wait for God's will to become clear. The choices they make are the results of what I like to call Christ-minded Christianity. Proverbs 3:5-6 is more than just a nice verse to them; it is a living reality.

Hurry Up and Wait . . . for God's Will

Our society runs in the fast lane, so waiting on God's will can be contrary to every natural inclination we know. People urge us to be decisive. To quit wasting time. To seize and squeeze the moment. We are desperately afraid of missing out on anything we think might bring us personal or professional fulfillment. God comes along and says, "Wait," and we squirm with frustration.

Nobody ever said that waiting on God was easy. We want to jump ahead of him in choosing a college, selecting a husband or wife, taking a job, making a move, accepting an offer, tackling an assignment. Very often, to teach us to trust, God makes waiting our only option.

I remember counseling a young man whose position had been eliminated in corporate restructuring. After a few weeks of unemployment, he had received several offers, but nothing seemed right. He had just about decided to accept the most financially remunerative position, although he didn't feel confident in his ability or desire to do the job. He had some savings and a few months' severance pay due him, so I cautioned him to wait a while before making his decision. Some of his friends told him I was crazy.

I was able to tell that young man that I too had faced unemployment and a stalled career. Immediately after resigning as director of a large conference center, I was tempted to pursue several avenues of employment, some in the ministry and some in the business world. I very nearly signed on to sell insurance, since it wouldn't involve relocating and promised a quick income. With a wife and five mouths under the age of twenty-one to feed, that part of the prospect was most appealing. Then I realized that I had not adequately prayed about the situation. I had not consulted the scriptures to search for answers. I had not discussed the decision with spiritually minded friends. I was ready to jump into another situation without waiting on God. I was ready to fly without a flight plan. So I chose instead to wait.

Within a few weeks, a Christian brother had drawn up the papers for forming our ministry, a nonprofit organization dedicated to teaching the scriptures and offering quality Christian camps, conferences, and counseling. With a group of committed believers behind us, we launched out, and for over seventeen years we have been able to fulfill that original vision. Our staff has increased. We have served at two East Texas churches. We have conducted Bible classes in cities across the southwest. God has blessed us greatly. If I had rushed into another career, I would have missed out on all of that. I am convinced I wouldn't have been doing what God wanted me to do.

My unemployed friend listened carefully, and chose also to wait on God to provide him with an opportunity. Three months passed. During that time he tried many doors, but he was also faithful to read God's word and pray consistently for God's will. After three months it all came together. A new opportunity arose in a different city, a job that would use his talents and provide a challenge, and he accepted. It was a beautiful situation, uniquely suited to him, even providing a pay increase. He would have missed out on it by rushing headlong into second best.

THE JONAH SYNDROME

Finding the will of God and staying there rarely involves snap judgments. There are seldom fast answers. Yet perhaps because we live in a society where we want things accomplished overnight, even yesterday, we make the mistake of running ahead of the will of God, much like the Old Testament character Jonah. Jonah ran toward God, ran away from God, stood up to God, and submitted to God. He was inside and outside God's game plan.

You remember the story. God spoke to Jonah, commanding him to head for Nineveh, the sin city of the day, and "preach against it," because of its great wickedness (Jonah 1:1 NIV). "Not I," Jonah thought. "I am not going to make a fool of myself like that." The assignment was too tough. Instead, he ran straight out of the will of God, and booked passage on a ship bound for Tarshish. Jonah even told the ship's crew that he was running away from the Lord. When God's wrath was poured out on the boat in the form of a raging storm, the sailors hesitated, but eventually threw Jonah overboard. A suddenly calm sea signaled that they had done the right thing.

In Chapter 2 of the book of Jonah our hero was in the belly of a whale—not a pleasant experience. But inside the great fish Jonah was praying, on his way back to the will of God. Jonah's words from the depths finally indicated his readiness to do what the Lord wanted him to do. The whale vomited him up, and he hit the beach prepared for action.

In Jonah 3, the prophet had learned a great deal. The command of the Lord to go to Nineveh came again, and this time Jonah obeyed. He discovered the blessings of obedience to God. "Forty more days and Nineveh will be overturned," Jonah proclaimed, just as God had directed him (3:4b NIV). An amazing thing happened. The citizens of the city listened. They repented, fasted, donned sackcloths. The local king even complied. When God saw that they had turned from their evil ways, He decided to spare Nineveh and its inhabitants.

By chapter 4, was Jonah happy that his message had been heard and heeded? No, instead he was angry because he figured that, in choosing to spare the city, God had made him look stupid. The prophet had run so far ahead of God, second-guessing him, that when things didn't turn out as Jonah expected, he pouted. Again he was unhappy, this time because he had run mentally and emotionally ahead of the will of God.

You may well be in one of the following four positions regarding the will of God for your life. Here they are, the four facets of the "Jonah syndrome," descriptions of the ways you might be relating to God right now:

One—You could be Jonah in Jonah 1, running away from the will of God. Perhaps you have never come to Christ in faith, preferring to go it alone. Or perhaps you are a believer, but you are not willing to let God take charge of your life. God has a plan and purpose for your life, but you have your own ideas, and you are headed in the direction of your own design. Maybe your own idea is to become successful and materially prosperous. You want it all: the fancy house, the Rolls, the Fortune 500 presidency. You are literally living for such temporal goals as those. Making it to the top of the corporate ladder is the chief focus of your existence. God is saying, "Go to Nineveh." You are saying, "Not until I do what I want to do."

Two—Maybe you are Jonah in chapter 2, floundering in the belly of the whale. Things are incredibly tough. You are suffering and the walls are closing in. Perhaps God is dealing with you providentially. He is turning the screws on all sides so that you will be forced to look up. God is in the habit of getting his man, and He will do what He has to do to bring you back to his will because He longs for a growing relationship with you. You are somewhere in the process of coming back.

Three—It could be that you are Jonah in chapter 3, in Nineveh, doing exactly what God wants you to do. This is the place to be. You are finding the blessing and prosperity of an abundant life in the center of God's will.

Four—Or, you might be frustrated, like Jonah in chapter 4 after God chose to spare Nineveh, because you are either physically or mentally trying to run ahead of God. You are not trying to avoid him, as in number one, but you figure that you know him pretty well and that you can predict his plans for you. So you have kicked it into overdrive and are burdened by speeding about in a hundred different directions. Many of the assignments you are undertaking aren't things He had in mind for you to do in the first place. You are so busy second-guessing God that you have forgotten to wait on him to show you what He really wants you to do.

Where are you in relation to the will of God right now? Do you care what He wants and how He wants it to happen? Are you stuck in a difficult situation of your own making, as God tries desperately to get your attention? Are you in the center of his will? Are you running out in front of him, making his decisions for him, filled with expectations and anticipations that are not from him?

Take a reading on your life before any more time elapses. One way that you will know you are in his will is if you are running your life according to the wisdom that is from above. That is sound judgment of the best kind—authentic Christ-minded Christianity.

LIFE OVER LIP—JAMES 3:13

> Who is wise and learned among you? Let him show by his praiseworthy way of life, his works with humility of wisdom.

Learning to be dependent on the wisdom from above means following the admonition of Psalm 27:14, "Wait on the Lord: be of good courage, and he shall strengthen thine heart: wait, I say, on the Lord" (KJV). A major reason we have so many frustrated Christians and fear-crippled saints is because, like Jonah, they are chugging way out in front of God. They are running errands and going on missions to which they were never sent. They are doing things that God did not intend, but instead are rushing here, there, and everywhere, mirror images of our high-pressure society. Or, like Jonah, they are avoiding God in some way. Whatever the case, they are failing to be leadable.

"Who is wise and learned among you?" James began his comments on wisdom in 3:13, referring again to teachers of God's word. Remember, teachers have a "greater responsibility" to use words carefully and accurately (3:1). The principle stressed, as in James 2:18, is that of life over lip. If one claims to be wise and learned, then "Let him show by his praiseworthy way of life, his works with humility of wisdom" (3:13). To put it simply: The lives of teachers should reflect the principles they are teaching.

If a teacher's lifestyle does not measure up, God will see to it that numerous opportunities are provided for learning to embody the right stuff. We have seen examples of that in the scandals that have rocked Christianity in the '80s. Men who haven't practiced morally what they've preached publicly have been exposed and thus given a chance to repent, get back on track, and grow.

James was not interested in empty words or shallow gestures. People's lives must back up what comes from their lips. We are to do the right thing at the right time in the right way.

Satan loves to subvert things. He likes us to do the wrong thing, or even the right thing at the wrong time, so we'll fail. For example, playing racquetball is a good thing, a great way to relate to others one-on-one and earn the credibility to talk to them about Christ. But scheduling a racquetball game on the evening of your wedding anniversary or your wife's birthday is not a good idea. Right thing; wrong time. Eating a big dinner is good, but not when you are on a diet. Guarding church funds is good, but not when a pressing need within the body of Christ demands a quick financial fix.

I have seen missionaries in dire straits turned away by church boards because one dissenting voice says, "We can't be all things to all people. Remember the building fund. We've got to take care of our own needs first." Cautious stewardship; lousy timing. Satan accomplishes his objectives when things are out of sync.

The Wisdom from Below—James 3:14-16

> But if you are having bitter jealousy and selfish ambition in your heart, stop boasting and lying against the truth. This wisdom is not the wisdom coming down from above but is earthly, unspiritual, demonic. For where jealousy and selfish ambition are, there is disorder and every evil thing.

Can Christians operate their lives on Satan's wisdom? Unfortunately, yes. Remember, the first part of James is about teachers of the Bible. It is also about sin. When believers are sucked into the wisdom from below, the results can be horrendous. Although James was cautioning teachers whose hearts were not focused on the things of the Lord, his words apply to us all as members of God's family (3:14).

His reasoning is simple. When our hearts are filled with "bitter jealousy and selfish ambition" our judgment is impaired. We cannot be relied on. We cannot be objective. Our motives color our responses.

Jealousy and selfish ambition are bad enough in the secular

world. When they run rampant within the church, tragedies are born.

THE ROOT OF BITTERNESS

What brings about bitter jealousy? Many times it comes from a feeling of being used by other people. We may become jealous for other reasons, but when we are walked over by someone else, we become bitter. A wife who feels she is no more than an object to her husband becomes bitter. She envies the men and women he seems to respect. She loses confidence in herself and in her ability to make decisions. She is overwhelmed with resentment and it becomes tough for her even to function.

Maureen felt so bitter and resentful toward her husband Jim that she could hardly speak about him without barbs. Her voice was laced with sarcasm and veiled hurt as she told me she was tired of staying home, bearing children, cooking meals, washing clothes, cleaning house, driving car pools, and attending countless soccer practices. All Jim wanted to do when he came home was eat, read the paper, watch TV, and find Maureen fresh and available when they went to bed. Saturday mornings meant golf with the boys; Sundays, church with the family. "We never talk above the cliche level," Maureen complained bitterly. "I haven't had a card, flowers, or a new dress in several years. We haven't been away by ourselves since the honeymoon. *I want out.*"

An employee who feels used by his employer, a child who is abused by a parent or is somehow used to fill unmet emotional needs, a pastor who believes that his congregation expects too much from him—these too can become filled with bitterness and jealousy. When this happens, their judgment is severely impaired.

THE RAVAGES OF AMBITION

What about selfish ambition? Why would someone become filled with that? It happens when we consciously or subconsciously tell ourselves, "What I want is more important than anything else in the world. I want to attain what I want to attain in the way I want to attain it!" Selfish ambition uses and abuses others. Selfish ambition makes us take our toys and go home. Selfish ambition clouds our judgment.

Others suffer in its wake. Selfish ambition has wrecked many a family vacation. Two couples plan to pack up the kids and take a joint trip. But something happens between Mom and Dad Smith and Mom and Dad Jones. A silly argument, perhaps. A difference of opinion about the route to be followed, sights to be seen, places to stop. Soon the Smiths refuse to vacation with the Joneses. Two families of disappointed kids are the losers.

When selfish ambition worms its way into a marriage relationship, the consequences can be appalling. Often one partner seeks fulfillment in somebody else—a better time, a more meaningful relationship, better sex, less stress, fewer demands, more excitement. This self-centered marriage-massacring mindset is summed up succinctly in the lyrics to John Denver's song, "Seasons of the Heart": "Love is why I came here in the first place / Love is now the reason I must go." This is an invalid viewpoint, since genuine love hangs in there for the duration.

What are the dangers of selfish ambition in the church? Have you ever served on a church committee with a person who is suspicious of others and overly protective of his own position? You never know if his statements are made with the church's best interests in mind, or simply to protect himself. Personal ambition is perhaps at its ugliest when it cloaks itself in the guise of serving God.

Bitter jealousy and selfish ambition short-circuit good judgment. Each results in mind-clouding anger. When they infiltrate a church, power struggles ensue. Gossip burns up the phone lines. Leaders are toppled and ridiculed. Congregations are split apart. Children view the display of lack of respect and become disillusioned. No wonder James strongly cautioned Bible teachers to avoid those negative qualities.

THE WORLDLY, UNSPIRITUAL, AND DEMONIC

The outlook of one consumed with jealousy or ambition is "not the wisdom coming down from above but is earthly, unspiritual, demonic" (3:15). It does not come from the Father of lights, in whom there is no shadow of turning.

Earthly. Such twisted wisdom is "earthly," a product of the world system in which we live. Earthly wisdom limits its vision to this world. The here and now is all it knows or cares about. Earthly wisdom tells us that the world evolved, that man controls his own destiny, that there is no afterlife, that there is no God. Love and happiness are all that matter.

Of such "wisdom," Paul wrote, "For the wisdom of this world is foolishness before God. For it is written, 'He is the one who catches the wise in their craftiness'" (1 Corinthians 3:19 NASB). The wisdom of the world takes only the horizontal into account. There is nothing of the vertical in it, nothing of God.

Unspiritual. Selfish, jealous wisdom is also "unspiritual." It does not come from the Holy Spirit. It is the wisdom of the natural man, the person without Christ. Unspiritual wisdom tells us that we are our own masters. It says that we are okay, adequate in and of ourselves to function without God's help. It assures us that we know what's best for us. "But a natural man does not accept the things of the Spirit of God; for they are foolishness to him, and he cannot understand them, because they are spiritually appraised" (1 Corinthians 2:14 NASB).

Unspiritual wisdom many times makes people pour themselves into projects instead of people. Even Solomon wrestled with this problem of misplaced priorities. Ecclesiastes 2:1-11 tells of the massive undertakings of the king in his search for satisfaction. Solomon built mansions, constructed parks, became a gentleman farmer, dabbled in ranching, played around in the precious metals and commodities markets, patronized the arts, surrounded himself with beautiful women—all in an effort to find meaning in life. The result of his unspiritual search? In Solomon's words:

> Yet when I surveyed all that my hands had done
>   and what I had toiled to achieve,
> everything was meaningless, a chasing after the wind;
>   nothing was gained under the sun (Ecclesiastes
>   2:11 NIV).

What he did on his own—under the sun instead of empowered by the Son—was sound and fury, signifying nothing.

Demonic. Finally, selfish, ambitious wisdom is also "demonic"—of the devil and leading ultimately to division, destruction, and defeat. Satan is its source, thriving on its consequences. Such wisdom tempted Eve and Adam, and the human race fell.

Paul spelled out the results of Satan's wisdom. "Therefore, just as through one man sin entered into the world; and death through sin, and so death spread to all men, because all sinned" (Romans 5:12 NASB). Every time we pay our respects at a funeral home and view an open casket, we ought to realize that Satan's wisdom was wrong. The fact that there is physical death among us proves that Adam was gullible enough in the garden to follow the devil's wisdom. If we want to live by Satan's wisdom, we will not have good judgment in this life. Demonic wisdom appeals to the old nature. It encourages us to "do what comes naturally." It keeps us from coming to know Christ as Savior. Or if we slip through the cracks and become Christians, it stunts our spiritual growth.

DISORDER AND EVERY EVIL THING

There is nothing good about the wisdom from below. According to James, "For where jealousy and selfish ambition are, there is every evil thing" (3:16). The Corinthian church graphically illustrated this.

Like all Greeks, the Corinthians prided themselves on the wisdom of their culture, yet the wisdom of the world and the wisdom of God were then, as now, irrevocably in conflict. Disorder resulted. Paul spoke of quarrels among church members (1 Corinthians 1:11-13; 3:3; 6:1-8). The Corinthians argued about which teacher was best; they dragged one another to court. That kind of chaos created a climate in which "every evil thing" could thrive: immorality, improper behavior, false teaching. One believer was sleeping with his father's wife, his own stepmother (1 Corinthians 5:1). People became drunk at the communion table (1 Corinthians 11:20-21). Members even argued that there was no resurrection (1 Corinthians 15:12). What a sorry scene.

Even thinking about the wisdom that comes from below can be depressing. But God saves the best for the last in James's passage. The good stuff, the wisdom from above, is yet to come. How wonderful it is when this wisdom characterizes a Christian. It is a surefire sign that growth is taking place.

THE WISDOM FROM ABOVE—JAMES 3:17-18

> But the wisdom which is from above is first pure, then peaceable, kind, obedient, full of mercy, and good fruits, impartial, free from insincerity. And the fruit of righteousness is being sown in peace for those who are making peace (James 3:17-18).

Stop to reread the description of godly wisdom from the preceding passage (3:17). How different it is from the wisdom from below. The wisdom from above brings about consistent good judgment. It refreshes. It is like breathing the fresh air of heaven down here.

Think for a minute. If you are operating on the wisdom from below and you hit the test, what happens? You become bitter, don't you? You get angry at God for what He has permitted in your life. What happens when you hit temptation? You yield to it. Selfish gratification is, after all, your forte. You also tell yourself, "I don't need to be in God's word. It's a waste of time. I'll get my religion on Sunday, thank you." When it comes to the matter of love, you determine to love those whom you like. That's it. No one else is worth the effort. What about the tongue? If you are operating on the wisdom from below, you will say what you think, period. Let the chips fall where they may. Good works? If you are a believer following Satan's wisdom, you will convince yourself that bearing fruit is a waste of time. If you are not a Christian, you aim to rack up a few good deeds so your performance will get you into heaven.

What a contrast your life is when you operate on the wisdom from above. Notice, it is the Lord who produces these qualities in you. You can't do it on your own. As we read in the book of Job:

> Where then does wisdom come from?
>   Where does understanding dwell? . . .
> God understands the way to it
>   and he alone knows where it dwells,
> for he views the ends of the earth
>   and sees everything under the heavens.
> When he established the force of the wind
>   and measured out the waters,

when he made a decree for the rain
and a path for the thunderstorm,
then he looked at wisdom and appraised it;
he confirmed it and tested it.
And he said to man,
"The fear of the Lord—that is wisdom,
and to shun evil is understanding" (Job 28:20,
23-28 NIV).

EIGHT QUALITIES OF GODLY WISDOM

God is the creator of wisdom, and He is able to produce it in us. When we are living wisely, then at least some of the eight qualities James mentioned in 3:17 will be present in us.

Purity—"Blessed are the pure in heart, for they shall see God" (Matthew 5:8 NASB). Purity signifies freedom from ulterior motives. It isn't secretive. It means living in light of the fact that God is looking down, and that "all things are open and laid bare to the eyes of Him with whom we have to do" (Hebrews 4:13b NASB). Pure people do not try to play hide and seek with the Lord. It is no accident that my wife's name, Pearl, means "pure." She personifies the open unselfish heart, unashamed to come before the throne.

Peaceableness—Life lived according to the wisdom from above is a peaceable existence. The wisdom of God brings people closer together in the bond of peace.

You are at peace with God because of the reconciling work of Jesus Christ. You are also at peace horizontally with the people around you. In a Christian marriage both parties are drawn closer to the Lord and thus to each other.

Living by godly wisdom brings assurance, the knowledge that you are in his will. "The fruit of righteousness will be peace; the effect of righteousness will be quietness and confidence forever" (Isaiah 32:17 NIV). "Blessed are the peacemakers, for they shall be called sons of God," Jesus said (Matthew 5:9 NASB). "Great peace have they who love your law, and nothing can make them stumble" (Psalm 119:165 NIV; see also Romans 12:18). It is no surprise that at the deathbeds of those who have committed their lives to Christ, these words are often uttered, "I am at peace. It is well with my soul."

Kindness—Kindness characterizes the lives of those who operate by the wisdom from above. Kind persons have a sense of sweet reasonableness about them. Kindness is a characteristic of love (1 Corinthians 13). Kind persons know how to forgive. Kind persons don't stand up for their rights, but yield them for the benefit of others. Kind spouses are sensitive to each other. Kind parents are sensitive to the needs of their children. Kind Christians think of others.

Don Westra, past president of the Christian Medical Society, and his wife Mae are believers committed to acts of kindness. These precious servants of our Lord never forget a birthday, and always give themselves to hospitality. I think Jesus had people like Don and Mae in mind when He said, "Blessed are the gentle, for they shall inherit the earth" (Matthew 5:5 NASB).

Obedience—Every Bible I read, the word *obedient* crops up with disconcerting regularity. God wants obedient Christians. Then He blesses and prospers. The essence of the life lived by the wisdom from above is obedience, submission to authority, living by the principles of scripture. Often the Christians who seem to desire most to be obedient are new believers, enthusiastic, longing to implement principles they are learning. Sometimes those of us who have been in the fold a while find it easy to rationalize our faults. Let us not forget that the Lord said, "Blessed are those who hunger and thirst for righteousness, for they shall be satisfied" (Matthew 5:6 NASB).

Mercy—"Blessed are the merciful," the Lord said in the sermon on the mount, "for they shall receive mercy" (Matthew 5:7 NASB). Merciful people dole out kindness and acceptance in the face of criticism, adversity, and other ill treatment (see 1 Peter 2:20-21). Mercy runs contrary to human nature. Mercy made Jesus submit to the agonies of Calvary. Mercy made him cry, "Father forgive them," as the soldiers pounded in the nails and hoisted the cross in place.

Fruitfulness—Living by godly wisdom means that the fruit of the Spirit (Galatians 5:22-23) is being produced in us. This fruit is the result of our union with Christ. Jesus said, "You did not choose Me, but I chose you, and appointed you, that you should go and bear fruit, and that your fruit should remain, that whatever you ask of the Father in My name, He may give to you" (John 15:16 NASB). Fruit in the life of a believer is also the result of discipline: "All discipline for the moment seems not to be joyful, but sorrowful; yet to those who have been trained by it, afterwards it yields the peaceful fruit of righteousness" (Hebrews 12:11 NASB).

Impartiality—The wisdom from above is impartial; it does not make decisions on the basis of prejudice. It is single-minded. It has conviction and purpose. It is unaffected by emotions, unswayed by social currents. It loves the unlovely.

Freedom from insincerity—Like Nathanael, an "Israelite in whom there is no guile" (John 1:47), openness, sincerity, honesty, and freedom from hypocrisy characterize those who live by God's wisdom. There are no double standards in the wisdom from above. "Therefore, since we have this ministry, as we received mercy, we do not lose heart, but we have renounced the things hidden because of shame, not walking in craftiness or adulterating the word of God, but by the manifestation of truth commending ourselves to every man's conscience in the sight of God" (2 Corinthians 4:1-2 NASB; see also 2:17).

If you are growing up in Jesus Christ and growing in good judgment, your decisions will reflect those eight characteristics. Wisdom from above can be yours only when you are humble enough to receive it and patient enough to wait on God to reveal his will. Don't forget James's exhortation, "And if any of you is deficient in wisdom, let him keep on asking from God, who is giving to all generously [without reserve], and who does not reproach, and it shall be given him" (1:5). Asking for wisdom was Solomon's secret to success. It can be ours too.

Many of us become candidates for good judgment after we fail miserably in life. We grow, as a humorist has said, "too soon old and too late schmart." Bumps can be what we build on. Abraham had his Egypt; Jacob, his deceit; David, his adultery; Peter, his triple denial; John Mark, his turning back. Each man, like so many others, used the failures to grow on. Even when we fail, it is not too late to start seeking Christ-minded Christianity.

A PEACEFUL RESULT

The results of growing in good judgment? "And the fruit of righteousness is being sown in peace for those who are making peace" (3:18).

Psalm 1 describes the man at peace with God and living according to his will:

> Blessed is the man
>   who does not walk in the counsel of the wicked
> or stand in the way of sinners
>   or sit in the seat of mockers.
> But his delight is in the law of the Lord,
>   and on his law he meditates day and night.
> He is like a tree planted by streams of water,
>   which yields its fruit in season
> and whose leaf does not wither.
>   Whatever he does prospers (Psalm 1:1-3 NIV).

Bitterness and strife produce barren soil in which the seeds of righteousness do not grow and out of which no reward can come. Sometimes people cut themselves off from rewards by their refusal to pay attention to God's instructions in his word. Their steps are strewn with the wreckage of ruined relationships. My 1988 verse for the year was Hosea 10:12 in *The Living Bible*: "Plant the good seeds of righteousness and you will reap a crop of my love; plow the hard ground of your hearts, for now is the time to seek the Lord, that he may come and shower salvation upon you."

God is searching for the man or woman who is willing to say, "Lord Jesus, I live, yet not I." He is looking for people to live for him. To crucify their prejudices. To humble their pride. To show good judgment, a reflection of spiritual maturity.

God ought to be in the process of making you more like himself, and He will if you are willing. Don't be discouraged if you are not all you think you should be. God wants you just the way you are, because He knows just what you can become. He wanted Thomas with his doubts, Peter with his big mouth, Paul with his ambition, Nathanael with his prejudices, Judas with his greed. He wanted them all. Only one refused him, and great was his fall.

Don't be in the Judas league. Sign on to serve the Savior—on his terms. He knows what is necessary to bring into your life to develop wisdom. Give him a chance, and watch the wonder of work done his way, in his time—a wonder captured in "The Prayer" by Ruth Harms Calkin:

> For so many anguished months
> I've been waiting for You to answer
> The one longing desire of my heart.
> I've begged, pleaded, agonized.
> I've prayed at times fumblingly
> At other times intensely.
> I've knelt and prayed.
> I've buried my head in my pillow and prayed.
> I've prayed before breakfast
> And after lunch.
> I've prayed before dawn
> And after dark.
> I've prayed with spontaneous outbursts
> While tears washed my face.
> I've prayed over our kitchen sink
> And as I've shopped for groceries.
> I've prayed amid screeching traffic.
> At times I've prayed with such confidence
> At other times with fear.
> And yet, Lord, though I have waited
> Though I have strained to listen
> There is no answer.
> I hear nothing . . . just nothing.
> O God, I am so puzzled, so bewildered.
> A frightening thought haunts me.
> Could it be true, Lord?
> Don't You love me anymore?
>
> *My child*
> *Because I love you so much*
> *I wait for you to let Me*
> *Remove the harmful desire.*

Points to Ponder

1. Describe the wisdom from below in your own words, referring to 3:14-16. Why could this wisdom be especially harmful when present in a group of Christians?

2. What eight qualities characterize the wisdom from above? Refer to 3:17 as you answer. If these qualities were reflected in your decisions, would your relationships with other people be improved in any way? How so? Think of how you relate to your spouse, children, relatives, co-workers, neighbors, etc., as you answer. Would you be more careful with your words? Different in your actions or attitudes?

3. Living by the wisdom from above means waiting on God. Is there an area in your life right now in which you are waiting on the Lord? Share your answer, if you wish, with another believer who will pray for you in this situation.

8

Hold the Fort!

James 4:1-12

Philip P. Bliss composed some of the best-loved hymns of the church. "Jesus Loves Even Me," "I Gave My Life for Thee," "My Redeemer," and "It Is Well with My Soul" are among his contributions to the music of the gospel. Many of Bliss's songs were inspired by real-life events. His hymn, "Hold the Fort," reprinted at the close of this chapter, was no exception.

Bliss based his lyrics on an illustration given by Major Whittle, an officer in the Civil War. It seems a small company of Union soldiers was in charge of guarding a great quantity of supplies. Holed up in a fort, the Yanks were besieged on all sides by a much larger Confederate force. The Confederate commander, General French, demanded the surrender of the Federal troops. Vastly outnumbered, there seemed little choice but to raise the white flag. Then, unbelievably, on the distant horizon, the Union troops under assault detected a signal from General Sherman and his men: "Hold the fort. I am coming. Sherman." The message of imminent rescue pierced the battlefield haze. And the soldiers hung on till the cavalry came (Osbeck 92-93).

For the Christian embroiled in warfare today, the signal might read: "Hold the fort. I am coming. Jesus."

James 4 points to another sign of progress: Growing-up

Christians are engaged in a battle of epic proportions, a war on three fronts. They are struggling against the "big three": the world, the flesh, and the devil.

BATTLING THE BIG THREE

The Christian life is a warfare, a fight all the way home. Imagine our pre-Christ selves as enemy-held territories. Satan teases us, the world lures us, the flesh says, "Why not?" We are dead in our sins and trespasses, completely under the control of the sinful nature we were born with. Along comes news of Jesus Christ. We respond to the gospel and trust him as Savior. We eternally enter his family. Now a new nature lives within us, and God's own Spirit also indwells us (Romans 8:9,14,16; Galatians 5:17). Hold the fort! Help has come.

Now we have a choice. Do we respond to the old or respond to the new? Make no mistake, the old nature will remain with us till the day we die. We can let it rule us, or we can progressively submit areas of our lives to the leading of the Holy Spirit, allowing the Spirit to control us, to energize the new nature in these areas. The process is slow. In fact, it is lifelong, often a mix of three steps forward and two back. From the moment of our salvation, the battle begins. Spiritual growth is a gradual conquering of enemy-held territory—our minds, wills, emotions, desires—by the omnipotent king.

HE NEVER PROMISED ROSE GARDENS

I did not always think that the spiritual life was a warfare. To the contrary, I once naively assumed that all committed (emphasis on the word *committed*) Christians had a great time. Life was free and easy for these folks. Problems magically and mystically disappeared when one prayed a prayer to accept Jesus. Sins vanished.

Soon I discovered that many Christians I knew still struggled. They continued to face tough situations. They fought to overcome depression, bitterness, insecurity. They saw their kids go bad, their businesses fail, their loved ones suffer, their parents age ungracefully. They were no strangers to high blood pressure, pressure-cooker stress, or unemployment lines.

In my youth and inexperience I assumed that some of these people were finding things rough because they weren't very spiritual. I jumped to the false conclusion that embattled believers just didn't know Christ the way I knew Christ. I had the world by the tail on a downhill pull; my life was running smoothly. Everything was coming up roses—job, family, education. I arrogantly and ignorantly assumed that this was so because I was spiritual. God was blessing me and prospering me. The fact is, I was equating spirituality with calmness. The fact also is, God does not promise us a rose garden, at least not till we get to glory.

Much to my surprise, through the study of God's word and my own experiences, I have since discovered that my spirituality takes the greatest strides when I am undergoing the worst situations. The hours of difficulty, the days when the enemy seems at his height, are the times I grow the most as a Christian. Some of the advanced lessons in Christ-like character development can be taught only in the crucible. Cleansing and shaping take place as the Father uses the fire, file, hammer, and saw.

The start of Christian growth comes with a decision to trust Christ. Then comes commitment: the decision to grow spiritually, to learn more of the Lord, to become more like him. As soon as we determine to progress, Satan will come along with the intention of doing everything possible to keep us from effectively moving on toward spiritual maturity. He lost the first battle when he lost us to Jesus Christ and God's family. He doesn't intend to lose the second battle by letting us achieve spiritual maturity without a fight. He longs to keep us babies in God's family, content with the milk instead of the meat of God's word (see 1 Corinthians 3:1-3).

METHODS OF MADNESS

Satan will employ any means he can to prevent us from growing. He appeals to our flesh. He uses the world.

Think about how tough it is sometimes just to spend time in God's word. We decide to set aside some minutes in the morning to read scripture, and what happens? We shut off the alarm clock and roll over, squandering precious minutes by staying in the sack. Once awake, we get distracted by breakfast preparations, dirty dishes, the dog food, thoughts about morning appointments. We remember we've got to wash our hair, wash the car, walk the dog, mail a letter, watch the news, read the paper. Somehow the minutes we have promised to God slip away.

Much the same thing happens when we sit down to pray. I know people who have resolved to spend several minutes with God in prayer each morning. Yet as soon as they pause to pray, their hands almost involuntarily reach for a notepad. It's a reflex. They start to talk to God, and then seventeen different thoughts pop into their minds. Prayer is interrupted as they scribble on the paper so they won't forget.

Do you think it is any accident that "brilliant" insights often come at the threshold of prayer? Remember, Satan is notorious for suggesting the right thing at the wrong time. Satan harasses potential pray-ers with business pressures, phone calls, financial worries, interruptions from children, spouses, pets, and pocket pagers. Sometimes improper thoughts enter in to interfere with a few moments in God's presence. Anger, desire, envy, ambition—somehow the gates open for these nearly the second we quiet down and try to look up. Satan's strategy is simple. He launches a continual onslaught to catch us and keep us in our weakness. He pulls out all the stops to hinder our spiritual growth. It becomes a warfare just to spend time with God in his word and in prayer.

The world, the flesh, and the devil feed on one another in a concerted effort to keep us spiritual infants. We discover that our fleshly desires haven't left us at conversion. We are tempted to indulge; the old nature or the flesh is activated, and Satan comes along to cry foul. He pummels us with doubt. "Look at you! You call yourself a Christian? You're not one bit different than you were before. You'll never amount to anything."

Soon the pressure of the world starts moving in, and we cave in. We start conforming to its patterns. It becomes easier to cheat on our taxes or to pocket the change that was mistakenly given. We justify and rationalize, and all the while the evil one is assuring us that this is the wisdom we really ought to live by. Because he can be so subtle, he is never to be written off as a completely vanquished foe. We had better take him seriously until the day we die.

Do you want to grow up as a Christian? Be prepared to fight. Your maturity will be reflected in how successful you are in the threefold warfare you will face.

WARRING AGAINST THE FLESH—JAMES 4:1-3

> From what source do conflicts and quarrels among you come? Do they not come from this, namely your passions which are struggling in your members? You are desiring and not having. You are murdering and envying and not able to obtain. You are quarreling and fighting. You are not having because you are not asking. You are asking and you are not receiving because you are asking with wrong motives, in order that you might spend it on your pleasures.

Enemy number one is our *passions* (4:1). The term refers to the flesh or the old nature, the inclination or capacity to sin still within each of us. It is our inheritance from our ancestor Adam, whose disobedience in the garden stretched across time to infect each of his descendants. Nobody is perfect. Everybody sins, somehow, some way, at some time (Romans 5:12; 3:23).

LIFE ON A NEW LEVEL

After we become Christians, God expects life on a new level. We read of this in Colossians 3:1-2: "If then you have been raised up with Christ, keep seeking the things above, where Christ is, seated at the right hand of God. Set your mind on the things above, not on the things that are on earth" (NASB).

Once we trust Christ, a brand-new nature comes to dwell within us. But, as we have also discussed, our old nature doesn't go away. It will remain a constant, unwelcome companion, ever ready to rise up and sin the second we give it a chance or throw it a bone. Right now, as you are reading this, if you are a Christian, one of these is true of you: you are either responding to your old nature or to your new nature. You are reading this under the control of the flesh, or else the Spirit of God is leading you. Right now, this very minute. Which is it?

What should be encouraging to us as Christians is that the old nature, the passions of which James spoke, is really a deposed dictator. We can choose to yield to it, or we can choose to live in the freedom of the democracy of God and respond to the new nature through the power of the Holy Spirit. The old nature will produce the same old way of life we were used to before coming to Christ. It will generate the same insecurities, selfishness, and stubbornness—to name a few. But the option will remain to lean on the Holy Spirit and allow him to energize our new nature, producing the quality of spiritual life we long for.

The Jewish Christians to whom James was writing weren't there yet. They were wallowing in the trenches—quarreling, bickering, and just about raising the white flag of surrender to the old (4:1). But there was hope. If they were to go on to spiritual maturity, war must be declared against the old nature. The flesh must be a targeted enemy, and a constant struggle ensued to get and keep the old under control.

FROM COMPLACENCY TO CONTROL

I would go so far as to caution Christians who don't face some struggles to have spiritual checkups. It could be that they are super comfortable and spiritually complacent because they are actually living in the flesh rather than in the Spirit. It is possible to be a believer and yet rarely respond to the Spirit. There will be little growth, but there may be a sense of calm; that is, until God permits the rug to be pulled out from under us to get our attention.

Living in carnality—under the control of the old nature—can be sweet, smooth, and easy for a time, but then watch out! "For the lips of an adulteress drip honey, and her speech is smoother than oil; but in the end she is bitter as gall, sharp as a double-edged sword" (Proverbs 5:3-5 NIV). Sexual immorality, for example, may bring momentary pleasure. But the double-edged sword of disease, unplanned pregnancy, or divorce is poised to strike.

When we begin to move out from complacency and allow the Spirit of God to activate the new nature, that's when the warfare begins. Paul described his own struggle against the flesh like this:

> For that which I am doing, I do not understand; for I am not practicing what I would like to do, but I am doing the very thing I hate. . . . For the good that I wish, I do not do; but I practice the very evil that I do not wish. But if I am doing the very thing I do not wish, I am no longer the one doing it, but sin which dwells in me" (Romans 7:15,19-

20 NASB).

Substitute the term *old nature* or *sin nature* for the word *sin* in the verses above, and you will get the picture. Paul admitted that his behavior fell short of what he desired it to be. He freely admitted to battling with his old nature. He was experiencing growing pains while striving for spiritual maturity.

No Quick Fixes

Physical fitness doesn't happen overnight. It takes months of working out to start looking good. Rowing machines, treadmills, Nordic tracks, life cycles, push-ups, aerobics, bench presses, crunches—name your method, there is no gain without some pain (or at least some exertion). There are no fast fixes to fat bodies and flabby muscles. As we cannot physically shape up overnight, we don't become totally spiritually fit immediately either.

Physical fitness demands disciplined choices. Spiritual fitness demands discipline too. We shape up spiritually as we diligently spend time with the Lord. Working up holy sweats for the purpose of sustaining our energies to minister to others is also part of the process. Paul wrote, "But I buffet my body and make it my slave, lest possibly, after I have preached to others, I myself should be disqualified" (1 Corinthians 9:27 NASB). Paul was a tough individual, inside and out. Even his physical discipline was spiritually motivated. Here was sweat-shop Christianity with the goal of godliness.

Is spiritual maturity worth it? Oh, yes. "For bodily discipline is only of little profit, but godliness is profitable for all things, since it holds promise for the present life and also for the life to come" (1 Timothy 4:8 NASB).

How to Know Which Nature Is in Control

By now you may be wondering how you can tell if the pattern of your life is responding to the old nature or to the new. In James 4:2-3 we see five manifestations that the old nature is at the helm.

1. *Desiring and not having* are manifestation number one. This occurs when our desires are not God's desires. The wants of the old nature are not what the Lord wants for us. We feel frustrat-

ed. It seems we are always stuck with the short end of the stick. The truth is we are just not getting what is not good for us.

Like kids who are denied that extra piece of candy because it will bring on a stomachache, we are often denied what we think is right for us. Why? God knows the big picture. He knows what we need. He knows what is necessary to bring into our lives to make us more like Christ. If you are constantly desiring something and not having it, examine the desire. Maybe that new job, promotion, pay increase, RV, car, girlfriend, boyfriend, lakehouse, boat, plane, Porsche, or pickup is not what God wants for you at all. If you are growing desperate, bitter, angry, or anxious because you are not getting what you want, you may well be living under the control of the old nature.

The solution? "But seek first His kingdom and His righteousness; and all these things shall be added to you" (Matthew 6:33 NASB). Drop your desires at the feet of the master. Seek God first. Ask him to take away your longings and to replace them with his. Through the strength of the Spirit, become willing to give up the goals you have set for yourself. Wait on God for indications of his wise plan and desires for you. Remember, learning to wait is often the cornerstone of wisdom. If you are making serving the Lord the chief goal of your life and the center of your heart, you will receive the desires of your heart because you will be wanting the proper things. The ultimate choice each must make is to serve himself or herself, or to serve God.

2. *Murdering and envying* are a second manifestation of life under the old nature. Unsatisfied desire leads to unholy action. James was not necessarily referring to physical murder either. Let me explain. Jesus said, "You have heard that it was said to the people long ago, 'Do not murder, and anyone who murders will be subject to judgment.' But I tell you that anyone who is angry with his brother will be subject to judgment. Again, anyone who says to his brother, 'Raca,' is answerable to the Sanhedrin. But anyone who says, 'You fool!' will be in danger of the fire of hell" (Matthew 5:21-22 NIV).

As Jesus pointed out, there is more than one way to kill. We murder another's character through slander, rumor, and innuendo. We slay a spirit by criticism, harshness, and excessive expectations. Many a parent has destroyed the confidence of a child through constant criticism. We harp. We hate. We vent our spleens. We envy others who seem to get what they want. We run home because we don't get our way. We separate from others, forgetting friendships, forsaking fellowships, cutting loose from churches, when things don't go the way we want them to. We hope to make others pay the price for what we think they have or have not done. Unholy action. Wrong action. Products of unsatisfied desire, they are signs of living by the old nature.

3. *Quarreling and fighting* are another manifestation of the old nature. Disappointed ambition just about always leads to quarreling and fighting, doesn't it? That's why fistfights often break out after ball games, or toward their end. One team isn't going to win, so they'll mash the guys who are. Vindictiveness is the bedfellow of bitterness. When our hopes are dashed, it is natural to rail against those who are successful. But when we engage in quarreling and fighting, it is because we are responding to the old nature.

4. *Not having because we are not asking* is a fourth sign of life under the control of the old. It indicates an absence of communication with God. It means we don't pray. We don't seek him. We don't ask him for anything. We are trying instead to satisfy our own desires ourselves. We're doing it our way. We figure God won't give us what we want anyway. Why bother? So we never ask.

5. *Asking and not receiving* are a fifth manifestation of the old nature that reveals itself when we do ask. We may well be operating in the flesh if we are asking God for things that never come to pass. The key is *what* we are asking for. If we are living in the flesh, we cannot expect God to answer our prayers in the affirmative. The old nature's desires are the wrong motives for prayer. My thoughts are not your thoughts, says the Lord (see Isaiah 55:8-9). When we pray, we must honestly be able to close our prayers with "Thy will be done," not "My will be done."

Are you habitually living in the flesh? You are if your life is characterized by wrong desires, wrong actions, wrong thoughts, wrong requests. "For the flesh sets its desires against the Spirit, and the Spirit against the flesh; for these are in opposition to one another, so that you may not do the things that you please" (Galatians 5:17 NASB).

Although Paul also exhorted Christians to "walk by the Spirit" (Galatians 5:16), we shouldn't agonize about momentary lapses into the old. Part of growing up in Christ means achieving victory over these lapses. Pick yourself up; confess the problem to God and thank him for his forgiveness; make restitution and amends where humanly possible.

What ought to concern you particularly is a life pattern of answering the old. Be sure you don't make a habit of saying yes to the deposed dictator. And remember, success is not permanent, nor is failure fatal. It is courage that counts. Keep hanging in there.

AGAINST THE WORLD—JAMES 4:4-6

> Adulteresses, are you not knowing that your friendship with the world is enmity with God? Whosoever, therefore, would desire to be a friend of the world is being made an enemy of God. Or, are you supposing the scripture is saying to no purpose that He is yearning jealously over the Spirit which He has caused to dwell in us? And He is giving greater grace. For this reason, He is saying, "God is resisting the proud, but is giving grace to the humble."

The second of the "big three" enemies we will face as we strive to grow up in our faith is the world. When James used the term *the world* (4:4), he was not referring to the great outdoors. We can love nature; we can love where we live; we can love life! It is biblically okay to like your neighborhood, your job, your home town, your state, your country.

Biblically speaking, *the world* refers to the world system that rejected Jesus Christ. It is the world system made up of people whose god, whether they know it or not, is Satan. Paul gave Satan the label "god of this world" (2 Corinthians 4:4), and Satan is indeed that. Much of our world system exists without consciousness of God. Governments, moral standards, social practices, corporate creeds—the world's way isn't usually

God's way at all. The world says, "Cheat, compete, demonstrate, stand up for your rights, march for the option to kill unborn babies, conquer, control, be aggressive, indulge." When the world envelops us, we Christians become so saturated with inconsistencies that we become ineffective for the Lord. We win no one to Christ. Like beached whales, we are stuck in the harbor sludge instead of riding the currents of God's grace and favor.

James called believers who love the world "adulteresses." They are unfaithful to the one who should have their undivided loyalty: the Lord himself. We legitimately can't have two lovers at the same time. We can't serve two masters simultaneously. Around us will always be believers who are lured away by the world. There will always be Demases, the man who succumbed to the lure of the world and deserted Paul and the work of the ministry (2 Timothy 4:10). By the skin of their teeth the Demases will make it to heaven, if they have truly trusted Christ. But their lives are not going to give the Lord any glory down here.

Throughout his word, God begs believers not to become bogged down in the world system so contrary to him. Just look at this sampling of verses if you are not convinced.

> And do not be conformed to this world, but be transformed by the renewing of your mind, that you may prove what the will of God is, that which is good and acceptable and perfect (Romans 12:2 NASB).

> Do not love the world, nor the things in the world. If anyone loves the world, the love of the Father is not in him. For all that is in the world, the lust of the flesh and the lust of the eyes and the boastful pride of life, is not from the Father, but is from the world (1 John 2:15-16 NASB).

> For many walk, of whom I often told you, and now tell you even weeping, that they are enemies of the cross of Christ, whose end is destruction, whose god is their appetite, and whose glory is in their shame, who set their minds on earthly things. For our citizenship is in heaven, from which also we eagerly wait for a Savior, the Lord Jesus Christ (Philippians 3:18-20 NASB).

A Jealous God

Is this world the limit of our vision? As we have said, our natural inclination is to satisfy our own desires. Many live life as if this life were the end, as if there were no eternity. They are proud of what they have been able to accomplish independently of God's interaction and intervention. They take pride in what they really should find shameful: an enormous house with far more rooms and many more personal comforts than they need, luxury cars, ten-thousand-dollar watches, twenty-carat diamond rings. Pride in what we have done or acquired apart from God should not be part of a Christian's makeup.

We serve a jealous God. He is "yearning jealously over the Spirit which He has caused to live in us" (4:5). When we trusted Christ, the Lord gave us his own Spirit. He longs to possess us totally. He does not want the world to be a rival lover. He does not want our desires to have first place. Instead, He wants his desires to be paramount.

The Lord wants to settle in our hearts by faith and take total possession of us as individuals. He wants to bless us with what He can do in our lives when He is in control. Eating, drinking, and being merry for tomorrow we die, soaking up the best this world has to offer—such mindsets profit us little. So many Christians are caught up in grabbing for the gusto that they are missing the grace and the game plan. Jesus paid it all. Now He wants us all. Why don't we pray, as the popular song goes, "Why not take all of me?" We are no good without him.

Marvelous Grace

The challenge is to crown Jesus Lord of all in our lives, turn ourselves over to him, and see what He can make of us. In 4:6 we find a promise we can cling to as we surrender all. "And He is giving greater grace. For this reason, He is saying, 'God is resisting the proud, but is giving grace to the humble.'"

God's grace is his undeserved favor. His smile. His friendship. His benevolence. His kindness. His protection. His adequacy in tough times, so we have assurance of ultimate victory. We need his grace to face each circumstance when our desires are in conflict with his desires. We need his grace in order not to submit to the allure of the world but to his allure. We need grace for every need we have. God freely gives his grace to those who humbly seek it, but to the proud He withholds his favor. He resists the proud person who is living in the flesh; He gives grace to the one who lives in the Spirit.

My dear friend Tom Paulk, father of my secretary Jan, is a man who lives in the Spirit and knows God's favor. Tom came out of a liberal church background into a beautiful relationship with the Lord Jesus some years ago. I have had the pleasure of watching him grow in his faith and have seen him respond under the control of the Spirit even when opportunities to do otherwise loomed within easy reach. I have been in Tom's presence when a Christian brother publicly, openly, and viciously attacked him with unfair criticism. And like a sheep before his shearers is mute, Tom opened not his mouth. If anything, only quiet, cool, calm, collected comments issue from Tom, no matter what is said to him or how it is said. He does not burst into tirades. He rarely raises his voice. Each day, it seems, he reflects Jesus more and more intensely.

THE DEVIL—JAMES 4:7-10

> Be subject, therefore, to God, but resist the devil and he will flee from you. Draw near to God and He will draw near to you. Cleanse your hands, sinners, and purify your hearts, double-minded. Lament and mourn and weep; let your laughter be turned to mourning and your joy into gloominess. Humble yourselves before the Lord and He will exalt you.

The third enemy we will face as growing-up Christians is Satan. He uses the other two enemies and any other artillery he can find to try to keep us immature. But we don't have to give in to him. James told us to resist him (4:7). Satan need not have a seventy-year field day with our lives. This commandment is just one of ten that James gave (4:7-10). Not the original ten given to Moses on Sinai, these guidelines tell us how to experience the victorious Christian life. We might call them ten steps to success or ten guidelines for growth.

JAMES'S TEN COMMANDMENTS TO GROW BY

Commandment 1: *Be subject, therefore, to God.* Turn the controls over to him. This is crucial. It is one of the first things you must do if you desire God to bless you. You must be submissive. You must come to God with such sentiments as these: "Lord, my life is yours. I'm turning it over to you. I've made a mess of it by myself. I'm giving it to you."

I am not trained to fly an airplane. If I tried to take a pilot's place, I would make headlines. If I got off the ground at all, I would probably kill someone on the way back down. In the same way, I am not properly trained to run my own life. I have not been created to live independently of God. There is a vacuum in my heart that can be filled only by the presence of the Spirit. When the master pilot grabs the stick, only then does my life get off the ground properly.

We Christians must get through with arranging compromises and start caring about obeying commands. To be ready to move, we must be ready to let God move in us. "Be subject to God," James urged, giving us an essential ingredient of the victorious life. "Humble yourselves, therefore, under the mighty hand of God, that He may exalt you at the proper time" (1 Peter 5:6 NASB).

Commandment 2: *Resist the devil.* The world's idea is to do just the opposite of submitting to God and resisting the devil. Many persons resist God and cooperate with the devil. No wonder there is confusion and frustration. No wonder so many miss out on the life abundant. They are being led by Satan, and he is using their desires to accomplish his objectives.

Many Christians never have victory in their lives because they never take a stand against the devil. Instead they remain vulnerable. They toy with temptation. They consistently get into trouble. Why, many Christians do not even believe that Satan exists. "Who has to resist something that doesn't exist?" they ask themselves. Satan is delighted by such flawed logic; he loves to be underestimated. The Bible makes it clear that Satan is alive and well and doing great damage in the day in which we live. Walk around any high school or university campus, and you will see his influence: sexual immorality and even perversion and violence, drug and alcohol abuse, music with lyrics composed by the father of lies.

The sobering account of an eight-year-old boy's encounter

with the devil, included at the conclusion of this chapter, should convince you of Satan's reality if nothing else does. How sad that we evangelical Christians often remain ignorant on the subject of our greatest enemy.

As we make any strides spiritually, we can be assured that Satan is waiting in the wings to try to nail us. He is the number-one enemy in the warfare we face as believers. He wants to make it tough. He wants to make it tempting. He wants us to say yes when we ought to say no.

Just who is Satan? He is no red-suited critter with a forked tail, pitchfork, and pointy ears. He is no mythical creature, no sci-fi writer's fantasy.

Once Satan occupied a place in the heavenlies. He was an angelic being of unusual beauty and, regrettably, with unusual ambition and pride as well. When he rebelled against God and fell from favor, the book of Revelation indicates that as many as a third of the angels may have sided with him and fallen too (see Revelation 12:4, 9). The prophets Ezekiel and Isaiah wrote of this crash (see Ezekiel 28:12-19; Isaiah 14:12-17). Doomed to be the god of this present world, Satan currently roams the earth, assisted by the fallen angels in the mission of swaying people's minds away from Christ.

In Ephesians 6:10-12 we read:

> Finally, be strong in the Lord, and in the strength of His might. Put on the full armor of God, that you may be able to stand firm against the schemes of the devil. For our struggle is not against flesh and blood, but against the rulers, against the powers, against the world forces of this darkness, against the spiritual forces of wickedness in the heavenly places (NASB).

The devil shoots fiery darts at us. Wanting to accomplish his objectives, he constantly assaults every side to get it done. The Ephesians passage is also a picture of a Christian taking a stand, lacing up combat boots and donning the armor of God to resist the evil one (see Ephesians 6:13ff). Notice, when God says, "resist," He gives us the means to resist. He expects us to stand on the basis and power of his holy word to rebuff Satan. We cannot run, because there is no armor for the back!

Peter warned, "Be of sober spirit, be on the alert. Your

adversary, the devil, prowls about like a roaring lion, seeking someone to devour" (1 Peter 5:8 NASB). When does a lion roar? It is often after he sneaks through the grass. Silently, not disturbing a blade, the huge cat looks out from the cover to spy his prey. Then, just before he strikes, he lets out an enormous roar as he lunges. His noise stakes his claim and tells everyone else in the jungle to stay clear while he chows down. The devil too sneaks up on our backside. Using a chance meeting, a cancelled flight, a change in plans, a weak moment, a fleeting thought, he will pin us to the mat—sometimes before we can find out what's happened. With a wink at God, he says, "See, I got another one of 'em!"

Graphically described in Amos is the poor shepherd who runs out and is able only to retrieve two leg bones and a piece of an ear from the lion's mouth (see Amos 3:12). Satan can wreak that kind of devastation too. Putting up with him is a dangerous matter. The time is *now* to take a stand against him.

Satan has a plan for your life, and it is ugly. He wants to destroy you. He hopes to wreck your marriage, ruin your confidence to be a good parent, plague you with doubts about God, worry you with financial concerns, debilitate your physical body, distort your values, fill you with such despair and depression that you can see no future.

Satan must not be ignored. He must be resisted. You have a choice. Stand up to the creature. Satan cannot force you to do anything—the decision is ultimately yours. You have more going for you than he does: "You are from God, little children, and have overcome them; because greater is He who is in you than he who is in the world" (1 John 4:4 NASB). According to scripture, if you have trusted Christ, Satan is already a defeated foe. Tell him, the next time you are faced with a difficult choice, "In the name of Jesus Christ, I am taking my stand against all of this. I am not going to do it." Resisting may feel frightening, but God promises ultimate success.

What is the best way to resist Satan? Look in scripture and you will find the answers. Remember that when our Lord was led out into the wilderness and tempted by Satan, He answered with scripture. He resisted the devil by going straight to the Bible. We can do that too. When Satan plants such thoughts in our minds as the following, we can defeat him with scripture.

You aren't really a Christian; give him 1 John 5:11-12. *Your sins are too great for God*; try 1 John 1:7,9. *God doesn't love you*; level Romans 5:8; John 3:16; or 1 John 4:7-11 at him. *God doesn't answer prayers*; read John 16:24 or Jeremiah 33:3. *Why are you suffering?* Second Corinthians 12:7-9 gives an answer to that one. *God won't really guide you*; look at Proverbs 3:5-6; Psalm 37:23-24 and 31:3. *God doesn't keep his promises*; see Romans 4:20-21.

When any of the above satanically inspired doubts assail you, you can bet that the devil is attacking. Scripture will contradict him. Search the Bible for the right answers. Read the rebuking verse(s) out loud if you want to.

Commandment 3: *Draw near to God, and He will draw near to you.* Perhaps the biggest reason people do not draw near to God is because of guilt in their lives. Let me give you an example. Surely this scene is familiar to you if you have a house pet. Think of the family dog who has disobeyed. You walk into the kitchen to see that the leftover pot roast, mashed potatoes, and chocolate cake which had been sitting on the table have mysteriously disappeared. Actually, there is no mystery, because gravy and chocolate icing are splattered everywhere. Dishes lie in pieces on the floor, proving once again that glass doesn't bounce. It looks like the work of Flash, your 100-pound black Lab, whose name is more suggestive of his eating habits than his running ability.

Probably related to Tom Bodett's dog, Flash has a heart of gold, a stomach of epic proportions, and the intelligence of a sea slug. You call him once or twice. "Flash!" No response. Your voice edges up a few decibels. "Flash! Come!" Finally he comes. But how does he come? Bounding toward you, eyes gleaming, mouth panting eagerly? No. He slithers in on his belly, waiting for a whack with the newspaper, because he knows he's been bad. Often Christians act like Flash when they have disobeyed God.

The believer who has failed feels awkward about approaching the Lord. Our normal desire is to run. It is tough to 'fess up to the things that have gone wrong. Like the psalmist in Psalm 139:7, we ask, "Whither shall I flee from thy presence?" (KJV). We want to escape. We want to get away from the promptings of his Spirit. But if we are going to grow up, we cannot run away.

James's command is: "Draw near to God and He will draw near to you" (4:8). It is not, "Draw near to God if you are perfect." Nor is it, "Draw near to God and He might spare you a few minutes." Nor is it, "Draw near to God when you feel like it." God is waiting to get his arms of love around you. He has forgiven you. He is waiting to restore you to fellowship, waiting to show you just what He can do when you are obedient. The question is, what are you waiting for? Draw near to him through the word, through prayer, through meditation. Be still, and know that He is God.

Commandments 4 and 5: *Cleanse your hands, sinners; Purify your hearts, double-minded.* Commandments 4 and 5 go together. *Sinners* refers to the believers to whom James was writing. Like all of us in the family of Christ, they were not perfect—just forgiven. Our hands and hearts are cleansed as we confess our sins to God, agreeing with him that we have done wrong (1 John 1:9). Confession means thinking and saying the same thing about sin that God thinks and says. We ask him to do the work of creating clean hearts and hands in us (Psalm 51). Cleaning us up, from the inside out, is a project for our willingness and his work (see Isaiah 1:18).

Double-minded persons, as we saw in James 1, have faith one minute and doubt the next. They totally trust God when the road is smooth and straight; they panic when they are thrown a curve. One minute they are living for the Lord; the next they are doing the will of the devil.

The fact is, we are all double-minded to some extent, because of the two natures we possess as believers. The key to victory, fellowship, and abundant living is to remain under the control of the Holy Spirit, allowing him to energize the new nature toward Christ-likeness. He is the energy source. We, like streetcars connected to the cable, thrive from constant contact with him and his enabling power. We lose the ability to run when we are disconnected from the power source, or when the stream of current is interrupted as we respond to the old nature.

Commandment 6: *Lament.* The sixth commandment is a

tough one. It is to lament. This means to experience sorrow for sin, to experience a sense of wretchedness and of unworthiness. It indicates a sensitivity to the burden of sin. It means realizing how sin grieves our loving Father when we persist in it.

Commandment 7: *Mourn.* Not only should we lament, we should mourn deeply the reality of our sin. We should feel the sense of loss—of lost fellowship, failed chances, missed opportunities. We should also appropriate the comfort of Matthew 5:4: "Blessed are those who mourn, for they shall be comforted" (NASB).

Commandment 8: *Weep.* We are also to weep because of our sinful condition. Tears signify brokenness. They are a mark of repentance, an evidence of submission, a candid admission of helplessness and need. When a person begins to weep about his or her own shortcomings and sin, the Spirit of God is generally beginning to do something in that person's life. Self-sufficiency goes out the window. The human will is broken. The shades of the soul are thrown open and become receptive to the light.

Commandment 9: *Let your laughter be turned to mourning.* Solomon wrote:

> It is better to go to a house of mourning
>   than to go to a house of feasting,
> for death is the destiny of every man;
>   the living should take this to heart.
> Sorrow is better than laughter,
>   because a sad face is good for the heart.
> The heart of the wise is in the house of mourning,
>   but the heart of fools is in the house of
>   pleasure (Ecclesiastes 7:2-4 NIV).

Displayed in our brokenness is a soft, sweet, submissive spirit. We demonstrate that we care when we begin to hurt and are concerned about our lukewarmness, wayward lifestyles, and lack of vision and effectiveness in the Lord's service.

Commandment 10: *Humble yourself before the Lord, and He will exalt you.* This tenth commandment is closely tied to the first. We submit ourselves to God. Then we humble ourselves before him and allow him to do what He wants to do in us. We recognize our own limitations and his limitless ability. We give up on impressing the world for the sake of pleasing him. Literally, we permit ourselves to be humble.

Permitting ourselves to be humble—what a concept! "I am the Lord's servant . . . May it be to me as you have said," said a young girl named Mary to the angel who appeared to her (Luke 1:38 NIV). Sometime after this the Holy Spirit miraculously came upon her and she became pregnant with the Son of God. A virgin, she was shunned for her disgrace. She bore the stigma of a suspect pregnancy. She very nearly lost her fiance. She became the subject of idle talk and speculation. She said goodbye to whatever plans she had made for a big wedding and honeymoon and settled for a quick marriage to Joseph. She knew humility. She lived it.

God promises to exalt the humble. Was Mary ever exalted? Oh, yes! She became the honored earthly mother of the Lord. Today we marvel at her example of trust and purity. In her own age, however, few understood her sacrifice, just as relatively few appreciated her Son.

Mary's availability, not her ability, was the secret of her life. The Christchild was literally formed within her. This is a picture of what goes on in us as we continue to grow spiritually. "I have been crucified with Christ," wrote Paul, "and it is no longer I who live, but Christ lives in me; and the life which I now live in the flesh I live by faith in the Son of God, who loved me, and delivered Himself up for me" (Galatians 2:20 NASB; see also 4:19; 2 Corinthians 3:18).

The Final Caution—James 4:11-12

> Stop speaking evil of one another, brethren. The one who is speaking evil of his brother, or finding fault with his brother, is speaking evil of the law and finding fault with the law. Now if you are finding fault with the law, you are not a doer of the law, but a judge. One only is a lawgiver and a judge, He who is able to save and to destroy; but as for you, who are you to be the one finding fault with your fellowman?

James closed this passage with a warning. It is a final caution about a tremendous obstacle in making it to spiritual maturity. We receive a concluding condemnation of a huge roadblock to growth: criticism.

James urged, "Stop speaking evil of one another, brethren." Criticizing someone else is a subtle form of self-exaltation. We criticize to make ourselves look better. We often pass judgment without realizing or wanting to know the truth. Critical people are not humble people. When we are critical, we are failing to realize that God is the judge, not us.

The best cure for criticism I know of is to remember that each of us is eventually going to stand before Christ. The Lord is the judge. He is the one who is going to decide how well we have run the race, fought the good fight, finished the course. He is the one who will give out the rewards. I don't have any business judging you, and you don't have any business judging me. Our responsibility before the Lord is to let him do that.

Perhaps you are wondering how these final verses fit in with the rest of the passage. A student of mine once asked if these two verses show that criticism, bickering, and quarreling are results of losing the battle against the "big three." Perhaps they are. Maybe, too, we are warned against dishing out criticism because when we are critical of each other, particularly within the church, we forget about taking on Satan. We lose the battle on three fronts before it really starts, because we forget who the real enemy is.

THE DEBO

The world, the flesh, and the devil are not ever to be taken lightly. I am still amazed at the level of ignorance Christians have concerning Satan, the number-one enemy of the faith. We ought to be better informed about our greatest foe. Ask any group of believers the question, "Who is Satan?" and you will get such answers as these: He is a figment of the imagination. He is like Santa Claus and the Easter bunny. He is a force representing evil (the Darth Vader theory). He is the one who makes me act bad.

Make no mistake. Satan is no imaginary being. He is terribly alive and well. He is active in the universe. He is hard at work to snatch susceptible minds for himself. He is busy trying to keep human beings out of God's kingdom.

People across the nation and the world were horrified at the discovery of fifteen mutilated bodies, including that of a clean-cut University of Texas pre-med student named Mark Kilroy, in shallow graves outside Matamoros, Mexico, a popular border town. The victims of a weird satanic cult could tell you of the real and present danger of the devil. So could the volunteers in the San Antonio, Texas, Child Evangelism Fellowship Children's Enrichment Program.

In this pioneering project, trained Christian volunteers from various churches travel weekly to one of the toughest public housing projects in the city, the Menchaca Courts. There they conduct a Bible club for some sixty children, and they also offer tutoring in reading. The purpose is to meet the needs of the children at all levels, especially the spiritual, by telling them about Jesus Christ. The urban missions team faces tremendous obstacles, not the least of which is the devil himself. Following is an excerpt from an article by Jerry Zapata, the program director. It is a chilling look at the world of Satan from the perspective of a young boy who attended the Bible club this year:

> The first time Robert came to the Children's Enrichment Program at Menchaca Housing Project, he was so excited that he just couldn't quite make himself sit still. Robert is an attractive 8-year-old boy, who's usually neat and clean. Little did we know what was in store as Robert had to be taken out of that very first Good News Club screaming threats and obscenities all the way.
>
> Robert came back sporadically and eventually became involved in the reading tutoring program, as well as the Bible club. Recently, Robert was sitting with his tutor and as the session was about to start, he shouted, "No! I don't want to pray! I don't want to pray!" The tutor went on to begin the tutoring session with prayer, as always, and then continued the session. Before long, Robert interrupted, "Can I draw the debo's (devil's) sign?" The tutor answered, "No, Robert, why would you want to draw such a sign?" Robert went on to say, "Because I want to! I like to talk about the debo. I like the debo. We even call up the debo. We say, 'Debo,' and he appears in the mir-

ror. He tells us what house to go to steal. There's 14- and 15-year olds who go with us."

Robert went on to describe occult rituals he had been involved in recently . . . . [and] continued to say, "I like the debo 'cause he protects me." The tutor then presented the gospel to Robert and gave him an opportunity . . . to trust Jesus Christ as his Savior. When asked if he'd like to receive Jesus, Robert said, "Yeah. (Pause.) I mean No. No! The debo will kill me!" The tutor went on to counsel Robert and finally asked Robert a second time. Praise God, Robert trusted the Lord Jesus Christ at that second opportunity. Robert has been showing up regularly. He comes in full of enthusiasm and filled with questions. During the Bible stories, with his big round eyes, and his mouth half open, he is a portrait of attentiveness (Zapata 1).

Does Robert have an overactive imagination? Was he fabricating the story about the devil? Was he trying to scare the tutor? No. Satan is at work influencing even young children like Robert.

HOLD FAST THE FORT

Satan may be at work, but as James has shown us, we can stand up to him (4:7). We don't have to take any of his guff. He is a defeated enemy, thanks to the cross and the empty tomb of Christ.

In the meantime, let's be encouraged by Jesus' words to one of the early churches, "Nevertheless, what you have, hold fast until I come" (Revelation 2:25 NASB). Our orders are not to retreat, but to hold our position and do battle. As these lyrics by Philip P. Bliss illustrate, we are required to "hold the fort."

Ho, my comrades, see the signal
Waving in the sky!
Reinforcements now appearing,
Victory is nigh.

See the mighty host advancing,
Satan leading on;
Mighty men around us falling,
Courage almost gone!

See the glorious banner waving!
Hear the trumpet blow!
In our Leader's name we triumph
Over ev'ry foe.

Fierce and long the battle rages,
But our help is near;
Onward comes our great Commander
Cheer, my comrades, cheer!

"Hold the fort, for I am coming,"
Jesus signals still;
Wave the answer back to heaven,
"By Thy grace we will."

Points to Ponder

1. What are the "big three" James warns us against? In your own words, describe each of these enemies. Refer to James 4:1,4,7, as you answer.

2. Of the "big three," Satan is perhaps the most insidious, manipulative, and hurtful. Discuss ways in which people make the mistake of underestimating Satan, of taking him too lightly. What can practically be done to correct this?

3. What, according to James, is the source of "conflicts and quarrels" among believers? What does the Lord promise us in 4:10 if we humble ourselves? What did this mean in the case of Mary, the mother of Jesus? What might it mean for you?

9

Who's in Charge Here?

James 4:13-17

Independence. Get up and go. Self-reliance. The ability to stand on your own two feet. Those qualities are highly valued in our culture. We admire men and women who appear to keep things under control. Tough, feisty, spirited, spunky—their rugged individualism appeals to us.

From Day One of young adulthood, we are taught to take charge of our lives. Parents, high school teachers, and coaches urge us to take responsibility for ourselves, budget our time, develop self-discipline. Silently whispered prayers are breathed that we will someday be able to hold down jobs and function responsibly in society.

We grow up physically, learn a trade or study for a profession, and leave the nest to fly on our own. In the "real world," the ability to make decisions and to work independently is praised. In some cases, salary increases and promotions come our way as we prove how self-confident and capable we are. You wouldn't want your house built, your spleen removed, your teeth filled, your tax return done, your case tried, your children taught, by anyone who wasn't confident in her or his own ability, would you? A doctor who wouldn't make decisions, a dentist who had to be talked through a procedure, a teacher who couldn't take charge of a class, a judge who didn't know the law—we shudder at the possibilities. We look for competence and confidence in those we deal with.

Part of growing up in most cultures means learning to be independent. But there is a twist when Christ comes into the equation; reaching Christian maturity calls for something different. The truth is, growing up in Jesus Christ means learning to be *dependent.*

The idea of dependence is contrary to every red-blooded American notion we know. It bothers us. We don't like to be thought of as dependent on anything or anyone. One of the worst things about growing older, we tell ourselves, is that we may be forced to be dependent on others. That's also why we hate being sick, jobless, or beholden to anyone. We would rather be our own bosses than the employees of someone else. We would rather handle the controls and determine our destinies.

DEPENDENCE ON THE DESIGNER

Who ought to be in charge of our lives as Christians? Not us, if we are doing things God's way. We must learn to be dependent on someone greater than ourselves if we are to grow to maturity in Jesus Christ.

I recently read a vivid illustration of this principle. In *Men from Earth,* astronaut Buzz Aldrin recalled the circumstances surrounding the first landing on the moon. As the lunar module containing pilot Neil Armstrong and Aldrin rapidly descended toward the moon's surface, warning signals flashed across the top row of the astronauts' on-board computer screen. The data screen went blank. All Armstrong and Aldrin could do was to wait for mission control to decipher the alarm. Both astronauts eyed the large red ABORT STAGE button on the panel in front of them. A touch of the finger, and the upper stage of the lunar module would instantly be blasted toward the safety of the mother craft *Columbia.* Tension mounted as they awaited the decision of mission control. A strained voice informed them to proceed. The guidance officers on the ground had judged the problem an acceptable risk. Suddenly, another alarm went off inside the module. Again, mission control judged the risk acceptable and commanded Armstrong and Aldrin to continue. The astronauts obeyed, although there was no time for explanations from below. A third time the alarm went off, and the module's computer data screen again went blank. If it had happened during a simulation back at the Cape, the astronauts would probably have aborted. But for a third time mission control said go, and as Aldrin put it, "We *had* to trust Mission Control." Later, the astronauts would find out that the alarms had merely signaled data overloads, and were not serious. But aboard the lunar module, they had no idea what lay behind the warning signals. They had no recourse but to keep on, depending completely on directions given 238,000 miles away. And the *Eagle* landed successfully (Aldrin 194, 200-202).

As believers, we have to be dependent on another's directions. We won't know all the details. We won't understand why every alarm sounds. But we must learn to be dependent anyway on the designer, God himself. Our dependence starts with our admission that we cannot save ourselves and must turn to Jesus Christ for salvation. It is a big step for those of us who pride ourselves on controlling our earthly destinies to acknowledge that we must depend on another source, another power, for the future. That step is only the beginning.

The Christian family should ideally be a portrait of dependence—husbands and wives living in the shelter of the loving leadership of God, turning to the Lord and his word for guidance and direction, children looking to parents as models even as they themselves come to terms with the Lord Jesus Christ. Does that sound like a fairy tale? A pipe dream? A fantasy? It needn't be.

Make no mistake. James 4:13-17, like much of this letter, is tough medicine at first. Ultimately the life of submission to God is a life of peace and power. "God helps those who help themselves"—so goes the old saying. But that is not what the Bible says. A more accurate statement is that God helps those who allow themselves to be helped by him. He is looking for men, women, and children who willingly look to him for direction. He desires that we become dependent, experiencing the fulfillment of living under his control. He wants us to acknowledge who is really in charge.

DOES LEANING MAKE YOU WEAK?

"Learning to lean, learning to lean, / Learning to lean on Jesus; / Finding more power than I'd ever dreamed; / I'm learning to lean on Jesus," wrote composer John Stallings.

Maybe you find the idea of submission to anyone or anything, including God, unsettling—even disturbing. Men especially have trouble digesting this dependence stuff. Every time I have taught James 4 to a group of men, the message has made some of them uncomfortable. They don't like it. They struggle against it. They worry that becoming submissive to God will somehow make them lesser men. They are concerned that they will lose the respect of their wives and families if they show they have to lean on God. They are afraid of being vulnerable, terrified of appearing weak, reluctant to admit need or inadequacy. They just don't believe me when I tell them that it is when we are dependent on God that we show our power, leadership, and love as never before. We receive the respect of our families as we drop the superman facade and acknowledge our desire to be led by the Lord.

I will never forget Frank. I stayed with him and his family while in another city conducting a study series on James. The presentation of this chapter on dependence had its usual effect on the men in the crowd. Some soaked it in. Some squirmed or looked skeptical. Frank was one of the squirming skeptics. But later that evening he must have wrestled with the concepts and come to different conclusions, since the next morning he was a sight to behold.

Frank's wife, kids, and I sat down at the breakfast table. Our small talk ended abruptly as he entered a few minutes later, a man with a mission in mind. He sat down and greeted our good mornings with these words: "We are going to pray today, because we are going to start this day right." I was shocked. His wife nearly fainted. His kids' wide eyes and gaping mouths registered shock. I'm sure they were thinking, "Good grief! Dad's going to pray? Has the world come to an end?" Then Dad led us in prayer. It was the sweetest conversation with God I had heard in a long time—simple, honest, straight from the heart, free of theological buzz words. Frank committed the day to the Lord, saying, "Father, today is yours. We are your children, and we are ready to be led by You. Amen."

I wouldn't have traded the experience of being there for just about anything in the world. That father's dependence on God meant more to his wife and kids than he could know. As he admitted his need of direction, he became more powerful than he had ever been before in the leadership of his home. It was the first time he had acknowledged his daily dependence on God, and shown that dependence to his family. He rose miles in their estimation because of it. The air was thick with admiration and respect. I was deeply moved.

It may seem easy to live life independently, to act like the person with all the answers, the one with everything all squared away. It seems easy; that is, until life slaps us with the unexpected. Real strength comes from reliance on God.

As James will show us, we discover God's plan for our lives when we are willing to submit ourselves to his leadership. We find fulfillment. But dependence requires a constant choice. It requires choosing to be under the control of the new nature instead of the old. It means learning to lean on the Spirit to activate that new nature. The life of dependence is Spirit-controlled, not self-directed. All this and more we will see as we turn to the practical teachings of this passage, and see what James said about the principles of leading lives of leaning on the Lord.

Avoid Overplanning—James 4:13-14

> Come now, you who are saying, "Today or tomorrow, we shall go into that city, and we shall spend a year there, and we shall carry on business and make a profit." You are not knowing what will happen tomorrow and what character is your life. For you are a mist which is appearing for a little time and then disappearing.

To show us how to become dependent on God, we are warned what not to do. Principle number one is to avoid overplanning. James first described people who smugly overplan (4:13).

Avoiding overplanning does not mean that we should never make goals for ourselves and our families. It is okay to mark this year as the year we get into shape physically and start to grow spiritually. It is okay to make it a family goal to move, or to participate more in the school system, or to hold family devotions, or to spend the dinner hour talking over the events of the day. It is okay to set goals for our businesses and employees. It is fine to work toward that big account, to aim for a record profit, to attempt to reduce overhead by twenty percent, and so on. James was not criticizing free enterprise and individual initiative. Neither was he suggesting we drift along through the years while our kids grow up without any family goals or direction. It is okay to plan. It is okay to aim.

What James was warning against is overplanning. Overplanning leaves us inflexible—and God desires that we be open to his leading and to the new, unexpected directions it might take us.

More important, and more dangerous, overplanning can make us overdemanding of God. We begin to expect him to fulfill the goals we have set for ourselves. We make our plans and then tell him about them. "Okay, Lord," we pray. "Here's what I'm going to do. You've got to bless it." We become manipulative sheep, dictating to the shepherd what we think He ought to do. We presume far too much when we do that. Like spoiled children, we expect to get our way, and we throw tantrums when we don't.

In *Ordering Your Private World*, Gordon MacDonald described what he calls "driven" people, listing eight characteristics of these men and women. They . . .

. . . are most often gratified only by accomplishment.
. . . are preoccupied with the symbols of accomplishment.
. . . are usually caught in the uncontrolled pursuit of
        expansion.
. . . tend to have a limited regard for integrity.
. . . often possess limited or undeveloped people skills.
. . . tend to be highly competitive.
. . . often possess a volcanic force of anger.
. . . are usually abnormally busy (MacDonald 33-38).

Driven people drive themselves. They overdemand of themselves, their families, their associates, their God. They assume that *their* plans will meet with success. If they are believers, they presume that God will bless them. But God is never obligated to bless the plans we make for ourselves. We are to leave the "driving" to him, as these verses reveal:

> But God said to him, "You fool! This very night your soul is required of you; and now who will own what you have

> prepared?" So is the man who lays up treasure for himself, and is not rich toward God (Luke 12:20-21 NASB).

> Then Jesus said to His disciples, "If anyone wishes to come after Me, let him deny himself, and take up his cross, and follow Me" (Matthew 16:24 NASB).

> But seek first His kingdom and His righteousness; and all these things shall be added to you. Therefore do not be anxious for tomorrow; for tomorrow will care for itself. Each day has enough trouble of its own (Matthew 6:33-34 NASB).

DAILY DEPENDENCE ON THE SPIRIT

Sidestepping God's purpose and doing things on our own does not please him. It does not move us toward maturity. So how do we avoid overplanning? It starts with each new day, each new hour, each new minute. Self-planned lives are not Spirit-controlled lives. So, overcoming overplanning calls for a moment-by-moment walk in the Spirit.

How many times have you awakened in the morning, ready to start the day in submission to the Lord's purpose and plan? "Father, show me where You want me to go and what You want me to do," you say. So far so good. But when the first problem pops up, and one usually does pretty soon, you take over the controls.

Wives, say your four-year-old spills his milk. You have already told him to leave the container in the fridge till you get there to help him, but he doesn't hear or ignores you, and he tries to take out the plastic jug anyway. Splash! An ocean of white spreads quickly over the kitchen floor. This was not on your agenda for the morning. You need to get the kids dressed and there are shopping and errands to be done and doctors' appointments to make.

What is your reaction? If you are like most of us, the flesh or old nature punches in and you holler at the kid, sending him off to his room while you angrily mop up the mess, steam blowing out your ears. Under the control of the Spirit, you might have responded differently. Had you breathed a prayer, counted to ten, closed your eyes and said, "Help, Lord!" you probably wouldn't have yelled at your son. You would have handed him a towel and had him start wiping. If his grabbing the milk in the first place was intentional disobedience, you would have handled that properly too. You would have responded, not reacted.

Husbands, think about the last time you took the boat out to the lake to fish. The launch goes smoothly enough. Your oldest boy holds the boat steady while you climb aboard and then help him in. Both of you use the oars to push away from the ramp. Then you turn to the motor. You pull the cord. Putt, putt, putt, the engine turns over . . . then sputters and dies. Again you pull. Again the motor spits and sputters. Again and again you pull. No success. You open the choke just a little. Another pull. The smell of gasoline indicates that the engine is now flooded. Nothing to do but wait. As you kick the gas can, the boat drifts steadily away from the launch, and you sit down and stew. Your boy stays pretty quiet. No telling what you say. Things are out of control and you're hot! Actually, you have allowed your old nature to kick in and deal with the situation. You have removed yourself from the control of the Spirit.

THE STRESS FACTOR

Our society is infected with the disease of hyperspeed, or stress. The dangers of stressed-out lifestyles are real. In *Is It Worth Dying for? A Self-Assessment Program to Make Stress Work for You*, Dr. Robert S. Eliot and Dennis Breo wrote that in our pressure-cooker culture:

• The tranquilizer Valium is the leading brand-name drug prescribed in America.
• 13 million Americans are problem drinkers; alcohol ranks as America's most perennially abused drug.
• The current recreational drug of choice, besides alcohol, is cocaine, a stimulant that relieves stress by causing the same kind of high we get from accomplishing something great in life.
• One out of every four American adults has high blood pressure, a potentially serious disease that can be both caused and aggravated by stress.
• America's number-one killer is heart disease, also caused or aggravated by stress.

• According to the American Medical Association, half of this nation's annual 250 billion dollar tab for medical care is the result of unhealthy lifestyles (Eliot and Breo 14).

What is the chief cause of stress? Eliot suggested, "after eighteen years of research on stress and the heart, I am convinced that the question, 'Is that all there is?' is the best clue to the cause of harmful, long-term stress: the sense of being trapped, hopeless, and helpless to get what you really want out of life" (Eliot 18). Solomon voiced much the same question in Ecclesiastes: Is that all there is? It's a query originating from a mind and heart neither tuned in to God's purpose nor aware of his power and presence.

Ideally, believers should never feel trapped, hopeless, or helpless. They should consistently live in the confident knowledge of God's control. They should trust that daily He will open the doors He wants them to enter, and close the ones He wants them to avoid. As for life goals, they can be set, but always with the reassurance that God will have the option of altering the course. The life of dependence is devoid of much unhealthy stress, because it acknowledges that the buck stops not with the believer, but with God. Regrettably, that ideal Christian lifestyle is seldom the one we live.

Stress for a Christian is a production number of the flesh, signaling a switch from relationship to performance. In *Healing Grace* David A. Seamands wrote:

> Pressure is a key element of life in the performance trap. There is the pressure of trying to live with a self we don't like, a God who seems hard to love, and others we can't get along with. Put all together, it's the *pressure of feeling caught in a trap where we are expected to live up to unrealistic and impossible demands put upon us by God, ourselves, and other people* (Seamands 168).

But God does not place impossible, unrealistic demands on us. We do it to ourselves, or allow others to do it to us. When we do, we willfully remove ourselves from the security of trust and dependence.

Overstress reveals we are no longer under the control of the Spirit. As Archibald Hart pointed out in *The Hidden Link between Adrenalin and Stress,* Jesus' life was a model of "calmness and peace—the very opposite of overstress." In Mark 4:37, a great storm blew up. Waves washed into the disciples' ship, nearly filling it with water. What did Jesus do? He fell asleep in the back of the boat. The disciples panicked; the Lord rested. When in their terror they finally roused him, He calmed the sea with, "Hush, be still," and asked his men, "Why are you so timid? How is it that you have no faith?" (Mark 4:39-40 NASB). Hart wrote:

> Surely our lack of faith must be behind most, if not all, our stress. Most of the time we just *don't* believe that God is in control! If we saw our world as Jesus sees it, would we be as frantic as we are? If we loved the world as he loves it, would we be as frenzied in our quest for self-fulfillment? I believe not. But then, we are only imperfect followers who must do the best we can to emulate his life and to live in faith (Hart 208).

When we simply don't believe that God is in control, we set ourselves up for tremendous stress. We panic in the storm, forgetting that Christ is also with us. The stress load can permanently be eased only by the life of dependence. That must be, as we have discussed, a life in the control of the Spirit.

SHORTENING THE GAP: GOAL-SETTING WITH GOD'S PURPOSE

One secret of living under the control of the Spirit is to shorten the gap between the time you take over control of a situation until you relinquish control to the Spirit and allow him to lead and direct you. The more you are conscious of responding to the Spirit, the more sensitive you become to various needs as you walk through each day. From the moment of your conversion, you have received the capacity to serve God in righteousness. You may still choose to serve the old sin nature, but that is your choice. Because many Christians leave God out of their thinking so much of the time, their lives are never what the Lord wants them to be.

Avoiding overplanning means rethinking our reasons for being. We are not put on this earth just to be good mothers, fathers, accountants, ministers, nurses, lawyers, laborers, teachers, neighbors. We are not put here for seventy-plus years only so we can have a humanitarian impact on the world. We are not necessarily here to "do something" or to "be somebody" in the world's estimation. We are here to glorify God daily and throughout the course of our lives. "Whether, then, you eat or drink or whatever you do, do all to the glory of God" (1 Corinthians 10:31 NASB).

We glorify God first by coming to faith in his Son. Then we glorify him by letting him take charge of us. When establishing goals for family and work, we must ask ourselves, "How will this goal glorify God?" That is one way of shortening the gap between self-control and Spirit-control.

We must dig into God's word for answers. We must spend time in prayer to discern his will. Professionally, we may well set a goal that our company will generate a million dollars in sales next year. That's fine. But we had also better figure out how that goal will glorify God. Maybe we will be able to increase our church contributions. Maybe we will be able to employ more people who need work. Maybe we will have more free time to be with our children. Then we must move toward achieving that goal with the attitude that God *may* bless it, if it is his will. We must never presume that He *will* bless an endeavor, but be grateful when He does. We must also be open to other options He may show us. It may become evident that reaching a million in sales is going to be too detrimental to family life because Dad will be away from home too much of the time. So the goal must be modified.

We may well go into that city which James spoke of and do business (4:13). We may well stay there for a year. We may well come away with a huge profit. But we had better not assume that because we said it, God will make it so. We had better not close ourselves off to other indications of his moment-by-moment leading. We had better not overlook our opportunities to live daily for him. We cannot afford to overplan.

WHY OVERPLANNING IS OUT

James gave a reason why overplanning is foolish: "You are not knowing what will happen tomorrow and what character is your life. For you are a mist which is appearing for a little time and then disappearing" (4:14). Proverbs 27:1 contains similar sentiments,

Do not boast about tomorrow,
>for you do not know what a day may bring forth
>(NIV).

Both writers had the same message in mind. The character of our lives is temporary. We may think we have seventy-plus years in which to operate, but the truth is that we are like a mist. Like the morning fog, we appear but for a short time, then pass away.

Seventy-plus years seems like a very short time to the person who is there. Where did the years all go? Somehow, sometime, some way, we get old. Our kids are middle-aged. It all happens so fast. And many of us never live even to see seventy. We are a fragile humanity existing on the earth for a brief span of time, and existing eternally in heaven or hell, depending on the choice we make about Christ when we have the chance.

If you don't think that life is fragile, you don't know much about life. Besides raising five kids of my own, I have worked extensively with teenagers during much of my ministry. I can confidently tell you that most teens do not think life is fragile. It is purely by the grace of God that some of them make it to twenty-one. Sometimes the reality of life's frailty becomes shockingly clear.

I will always remember Jerry, a special friend who has gone home to be with the Lord. When Jerry was a teenager, I was his youth pastor. Fresh out of seminary over thirty years ago, this assignment at a church in the Northwest was my first full-time ministry. As I got involved with the church program and began to know the kids in the youth group, I found that some of them were uncommitted. A group of the fellows would sit at the back of the meetings and cut up, tell jokes you wouldn't want repeated, and generally tear up the proceedings. They were tough and they didn't care about the Bible or me. Jerry was one of them. I gravitate to those types, because I have found out that if you can grab their attention and make them leaders, the whole group follows. The commitment of even the committed kids, the ones who have all the answers, increases when the tough guys get involved.

It was a battle to win Jerry over. The turning point came when his leg was broken, and he was going to have to miss out on the time-honored tradition of Senior Skip Day. When I found out he couldn't go waterskiing with the rest of the guys, I called him up and said, "Let's go fishing." We had a fabulous day together, our relationship started to build, and Jerry's relationship with God began to become closer. Events soon happened to accelerate the process.

One evening the phone's ringing shattered the silence of our home. It was one of those late night calls that probably means bad news. Apprehensively I picked up the receiver.

"Don, Jerry is dead!" cried his girlfriend. Amid heaving sobs she caught her breath enough to tell me that she had just driven past a terrible accident. Jerry's body lay on the ground. Two cars were crushed. Flashing lights and police and ambulances were everywhere. She couldn't even stop. But she knew it was Jerry, and she recognized the smashed car as one that belonged to his buddy, also a member of our youth group.

I jumped into the car and rushed to the hospital. Two orderlies and a nurse were rolling Jerry into the emergency room. I uncovered him and he looked up at me and smiled. His bloodied face parted right in two. He had been thrown head first through the windshield in that horrible accident. I stayed with his folks until nearly dawn as the doctors stitched the battered kid back together.

As long as I live, I will never forget the remark made by one of the dads also waiting there, the father of the boy who had been driving the vehicle and who also lay injured. "I cannot believe how life changes in a split second." You see, the accident had been his son's fault. The woman riding in the other car was dead. She had been seven months pregnant, and the baby was dead now also.

Human life is incredibly delicate. We hang by the slenderest threads of God's grace. We are but a mist that soon, too soon, will surely vanish. As I said earlier, Jerry has already gone home. A survivor of the crash, he was claimed by cancer while in his thirties.

Do you see how our human frailty makes overplanning futile and foolish? We risk missing God's best for our lives as we focus on what we alone want to do, where we alone want to go, whom we alone want to know. If the Lord wants us to be dependent on him (and He does), we don't have time to waste being independent of him. Our graduation day to eternity might be sooner than we think. We had better be about the Father's earthly business while we have the time on earth.

Proverbs 14:12 says, "There is a way that seems right to a man, but in the end it leads to death" (NIV). *Tomorrow* cannot be found on God's calendar. *Tomorrow* is the road that leads to the town called Never. *Tomorrow* is the locked door that shuts people out of heaven. *Tomorrow* is Satan's word. Those who expect to repent tomorrow usually die today. "Now is the time of God's favor, now is the day of salvation" (2 Corinthians 6:2b NIV). Those who think they will become dependent on God tomorrow usually wind up frustrated today.

AVOID OVERESTIMATING—JAMES 4:15-16

> Instead of you saying, "If the Lord wills, we shall both live and do this or that." But now you are glorying in your arrogance. All such glorying is evil.

IF THE LORD WILLS

It is wrong to leave God out of our daily lives. It is wrong to overplan. It is wrong to overestimate our humanity (4:15-16). This is a second principle of life in the Spirit.

We have already seen some of the dangers of overestimation in 4:14. We have seen that our earthly lives are transitory. We are not going to last forever. It is wrong to make big plans without taking God into consideration. The *instead* in 4:15 marks a contrast. A proper way to look at any undertaking—and all of life—is with this attitude: "If the Lord wills, we shall live and also do this or that" (4:15).

"If the Lord wills, we shall . . . " You fill in the blank. Buy a new home? Begin a new job? Go back to night school? Take a vacation? Contribute more money? Make an investment? Start that Bible study? Sell our stocks? Trust God with our finances? Do short-term mission work? Teach that class? Assume that office? Help that couple?

WHAT DEPENDENCE MEANS

When we depend on God, we neither overestimate ourselves, nor underestimate him.

Our relationship with the Lord thrives as we learn to be

dependent on him. It means we start adopting the attitude, "If the Lord wills, we will do this or that." It doesn't become a trite phrase to be rattled off, but a living reality to go by and grow by.

Charlie Jones said that the three most important decisions in life are these: Whom will you live your life with? What will you live your life in? What will you live your life for? Can you imagine the power, the relief, the victory of becoming dependent on God in these areas? Of turning things over to him? How our beliefs and behavior might change if we were following his lead before taking the plunge.

I can't tell you how many times I have been privileged to teach Bible classes where couples have either trusted Christ or renewed their commitment to him. More than once, a husband and wife who have taken that leap of faith, have reflected on what they have been doing, and regretted that they hadn't let God direct them earlier. Some have spent years scraping and saving solely for the temporal.

For one couple, a genuine dreamhouse was the center of their existence. Filled with antiques and designer upholstery and draperies, they had poured at least a half-a-million dollars into the home and its furnishings. Then, soon after completion, they both trusted Christ as Savior. Imagine what a relief it was to be able to turn that house and its contents over to the Lord for his use. No, they didn't move out and donate the place to a church or Christian organization. They still lived there, but they began to view their home as a place to be used for God's glory. They were generous in allowing others to use it for Bible studies, discipling groups, prayer and praise groups, social functions. They even opened the doors to teenagers. Youth groups often splashed in their pool after meetings. A weighty burden was lifted as my friends turned that home over to God in this way. As they liked to put it, they had no choice.

Would they have built the house if they had been Christians at the beginning? No. After trusting Christ, they were appalled at the time, money, energy, and effort they had sunk into it. They were kicking themselves over devoting so much to something so temporary. But God turned their regrets to rejoicing as they saw their home being used for him.

I have seen similar freedom bloom in the corporate world.

Sid spent much of his adult life fighting his way to the top. He trusted Christ, turned around, and said, "Lord, this is your business. I'm turning it over to you. You run it through me for your glory, and the success that comes from it is yours." There is liberation in submission, in letting the Holy Spirit lead us, in allowing God to make use of everything we have and inspire everything we hope.

GLORYING IN ARROGANCE

The reverse of the issue is that when we refuse to depend, when we live life independently of the Lord and consistently do our own thing without acknowledging his right to control, we are sinning. In James's words, "But now you are glorying in your arrogance. All such glorying is evil" (4:16). What does it mean to glory in arrogance? Philippians 3:18-19 may give us a clue.

> For, as I have often told you before and now say again even with tears, many live as enemies of the cross of Christ. Their destiny is destruction, their god is their stomach, and their glory is in their shame. Their mind is on earthly things (NIV).

What were these men and women glorying in? They were taking pride in what they had been able to do without God in their lives. Their god was their stomach. They had lived on the level of their physical desires, and they were proud of it.

How often we believe that our lives are better without God than with him. We want to do things on our own. The fact is that very soon what we have done on our own is going to turn to ashes and dust. Our castles will crumble. And when we get on the other side of eternity, we are going to see just who was the wisest in this situation. We will wish we had been humble enough to depend on the designer instead of on ourselves. We will know the truth of the words of James in 4:6, "But God is resisting the proud and giving grace to the humble." We shall wish that we had trusted in the Lord with all our hearts, and not leaned on our own understanding, while we still had time (see Proverbs 3:5-6).

Glorying in arrogance—it's a tough habit to break. Some of us men glory in our cars and trucks, don't we? We worry about the paint job on the Mercedes (in my case, the Chevy)—the thought of a nick or dent plagues us. We hate it when we're not in the driver's seat. What a relief it is to give that car over to the Lord and know that He will take care of it. If He wants his car dented, it will be dented. So what? It is his car, isn't it?

We also glory in our bodies. We strive to keep fit so we can live long lives. We agonize over which of cancer's seven warning signs will pop up first. We worry about how long we'll live, how well we'll live. We dread going to the doctor because it might just show some hidden ailment. We have all read in the paper about how a man in his mid-thirties, a nonsmoker, suddenly collapsed and died of lung cancer totally undetected before. We fear that it will happen to us. Our hearts are just waiting to rebel. Our livers are on the brink of malfunctioning. What an enormous relief it is to turn our bodies over to God. "Okay, Lord, it's not much to look at, but it belongs to You, so do with it what You want. If You want to take it to the grave early, go ahead. If You want it to live to a ripe old age and accomplish your objectives, fantastic. It's all yours."

Imagine the freedom of saying, "Lord, thank You for supplying my needs. Please use me to your glory. Give me an assignment at the office today. Help me to do a good job. Show me those people You would like me to influence for You. Give me strength to be honest, fair, and uncritical. Let me know if the time is right to share news of your Son with Mike who works with me. Give me an insight with which to comfort Sally, whose husband is so ill. Use me to meet people's needs, including their eternal ones." Talk about a life of freedom. That is the result of depending on the designer.

Avoid Procrastinating—James 4:17

> Therefore, to the one who is knowing how to do good, and is not doing it, to him it is sin.

Now comes the worst-tasting part of the medicine. How I wish I could take James 4:17 out of context and smooth over its meaning. It wouldn't cut us so deeply or hurt us so much.

The truth is, the word *therefore* signifies a conclusion. James has told us about the necessity of being dependent on the designer. The conclusion of that is that if we know we must depend, and we are not dependent, we are sinning. We are going against God's standards.

We know what doing right means. It means becoming a Christian and, through the power of the Spirit, living like one. We're sinning if we're not. So what are we waiting for?

STEPS TO START WITH

Let me leave you with a few steps to start with in living lives of dependence. These are methods to make you remember who is in charge.

Step 1: The moment of surrender. If you haven't trusted Christ, now is the time. If you have, then choose to do what Paul exhorted in Romans 12:1-2:

> I urge you therefore, brethren, by the mercies of God, to present your bodies a living and holy sacrifice, acceptable to God, which is your spiritual service of worship. And do not be conformed to this world, but be transformed by the renewing of your mind, that you may prove what the will of God is, that which is good and acceptable and perfect (NASB).

Step 2: The progressive letting go. After you have become willing to surrender your life to God, begin by handing him whichever area He puts his finger on. Is your job killing you? Prayerfully give it to him. Are your children causing you anxiety? Give them up to God. Dependence is a process, not an overnight sensation.

> So then, my beloved, just as you have always obeyed, not as in my presence only, but now much more in my absence, work out your salvation with fear and trembling; for it is God who is at work in you, both to will and to work for His good pleasure (Philippians 2:12-13 NASB).

Step 3: The daily walk. Commence, or continue, to spend time daily getting to know the Lord Jesus Christ more deeply, more intimately. Walking with God fuels dependence on the designer. In characterizing himself as a life-giving, strength-supplying vine to branch believers, Jesus said,

Abide in Me, and I in you. As the branch cannot bear fruit of itself, unless it abides in the vine, so neither can you, unless you abide in Me. . . . If you abide in Me, and My words abide in you, ask whatever you wish, and it shall be done for you (John 15:4,7 NASB).

Every believer should be singing Frances Ridley Havergal's hymn:

Take my life, and let it be
Consecrated, Lord, to Thee;
Take my hands, and let them move
At the impulse of Thy love.

Take my feet, and let them be
Swift and beautiful for Thee;
Take my voice, and let me sing
Always, only, for my King.

Take my lips, and let them be
Filled with messages from Thee;
Take my silver and my gold,
Not a mite would I withhold.

Take my love, my God, I pour
At Thy feet its treasure store;
Take myself and I will be
Ever, only, all for Thee.

Points to Ponder

1. What do 4:13 and 14 tell us about the futility of overplanning? What right attitude is described in 4:15?

2. Is it wrong to set goals? Discuss some practical goals that can be set in your spiritual life, family, and work. How can you know if these goals are in accord with God's will?

3. What does 4:17 say about the Christian who is not dependent on the designer? What ramifications does this have to your own life?

10

You Can't Take It with You

James 5:1-6

The name Donald Trump is the late-twentieth-century equivalent of King Midas. These days, wherever you see Trump's name affixed to a building, corporate conglomerate, television network, ship, airline, or real estate holding, you can be sure "there's gold in them thar hills." The man has it all, from the world's point of view. In an article entitled "Flashy Symbol of an Acquisitive Age," *Time* magazine described Trump this way: "Young, handsome and ridiculously rich, Donald Trump loves making deals and money, loathes losing and has an ego as big as the Ritz—er, Plaza."

The *Time* article contained several quotations from Trump, words revealing the motivation behind his push to acquire and accomplish:

"Who has done as much as I have? No one has done more in New York than me."

"I love to have enemies. I fight my enemies. I like beating my enemies to the ground."

"My style of dealmaking is quite simple and straightforward. I just keep pushing and pushing and pushing to get what I'm after."

"I like thinking big. If you're going to be thinking anyway, you might as well think big."

"Nobody pushes me around, you understand? I don't want to do it [litigation], but nobody is going to push me around."

"A little more moderation would be good. Of course, my life hasn't exactly been one of moderation."

(Friedrich 48-54).

Although he is far richer than probably ninety-five percent of his contemporaries will ever be, Trump represents many of the goals, desires, and dreams of the generation of the '80s. In a material world, he is the ultimate yuppie, the darling of young urban professionals everywhere whose reputations as single-minded pursuers of loot, luxury, and indulgent lifestyles have provided cannon fodder for many a potshot.

It's a yuppie who is credited with saying: "I really don't want a lot of money. I just wish we could afford to live the way we're living now."

Like it or not, the sometimes misguided idealism of the '60s and the introspection of the '70s have surrendered to the gross materialism of the '80s and '90s. Secretly, many of us wish we were Donald Trumps. If not plastering our names across every mega-project, we at least wish we could have enough cash to buy whatever we want when we want it. We wish our bank balances were three times our credit limits, instead of the reverse. While this is the mindset of our secular culture, how tragic that it is also often the mindset of the church.

"But don't you ever get scared?" the *Time* interviewer asked Donald Trump.

"No, I'm a fatalist," Trump replied. "I don't think anything scares me. There's no great way to die. My general attitude is to attack life, and you can't attack if you're frightened. Besides, my pilots are the best, and I pay whatever it takes. When it comes to pilots, doctors, accountants, I don't chisel" (Friedrich 54).

The fact that he employs high-priced pilots and physicians signals that Donald Trump agrees with some of what James said in the last chapter: namely, that life is temporary (4:14). There the similarities seemingly end; their two approaches to life are totally different. People like Trump opt to attack life, to seize and squeeze the moment. Since nothing is forever, let's get all we can, can all we get, and shell out whatever it takes to keep us getting and canning. In James's way of thinking, since life is temporary, we can't afford to waste our time living independently of God (4:15).

We are losing our lives with every breath we take. The question for the Christian must be: For whom am I losing (and living) my life? Myself? Or God?

In James 5 we'll learn that, like life, wealth is also temporary, transitory. James came down hard on Christians who were using wealth the wrong way.

Money can be a tremendous hindrance toward spiritual maturity. Too much money has never been a problem that the Lord has chosen to give me, however. Often I have wished He would try me out, but I guess He knows me too well. I have seen money's effect in the lives of many believers, often positive, many times negative.

James's statements should not be taken as an indictment of wealth in and of itself. God does not disapprove of earthly wealth. To the contrary, it is God who is the giver of everything we have, including our financial resources. It is okay for believers to be rich, although there is no guarantee that we will be. Earthly prosperity was not a part of the atonement. As we will see, what God disapproves of is the misuse of money by his children.

CRY, THE BELOVED BANK BALANCE—JAMES 5:1-3

> Come now, you rich, wail and cry aloud over your tribulations which are coming upon you. Your wealth has rotted away, and your clothes have become moth-eaten. Your gold and your silver have become corroded and their rust shall be a witness against you and shall eat your flesh as fire. You stored up treasure in the last days.

The story is told of a strange discovery made when the ruins of the ancient city of Pompeii were excavated. Preserved in the lava were the skeletal remains of a woman who had evidently been fleeing the city as Mount Vesuvius erupted. Still clutched in her hands were pieces of precious jewelry and a sack of gold coins. One wonders if she might have made it to safety had she not paused long enough in her flight to collect her valuables. Perhaps if she had left it all behind, the molten lava would not have overtaken her.

James began his comments on wealth with a warning to all who are wealthy. Actually, this was a warning to all Christians, since the message of this letter was primarily directed at Jewish believers. How strange that James would compare wealth to tribulation or trouble (5:1). Money isn't trouble, is it?

Actually, money can be big trouble. Acquisition leads to complications. Money brings huge worries and inflames ulcers. The lives of poor people don't rise and sink with Dow Jones. It is the wealthy who tear open the morning papers to read the financial section. It is the wealthy who look at each overseas political development as a potential personal threat. Those of us without investments in Southeast Asia, the Middle East, or Central America don't find our bank balances hinging on the political stability of those areas. We may be concerned and sympathetic, but we aren't going to be financially ruined if Dictator X or King Y is toppled from power, so we don't worry about the periodic coup. The fortunes of poor or middle-class folks are not directly linked to the level of the prime interest rate or to international currency fluctuations. The price of oil may hit us at the gas pump, but it doesn't usually wipe us out. We are not often the targets of lawsuits. We know who our real friends are; nobody I know likes me for my money. People don't gold-dig where there is no gold to dig.

One of the richest men of all time, King Solomon, had much to say about the frustrations of great wealth:

> Whoever loves money never has money enough;
> > whoever loves wealth is never satisfied with
> > > his income.
> This too is meaningless.
>
> As goods increase,
> > so do those who consume them.
> And what benefit are they to the owner
> > except to feast his eyes on them?
>
> The sleep of a laborer is sweet,
> > whether he eats little or much,
> but the abundance of a rich man
> > permits him no sleep
> > > (Ecclesiastes 5:11-12 NIV).

When it came to knowing about riches, Solomon was without equal. He had more money, possessions, and property than any of his peers. Even someone like H. Ross Perot or Donald Trump would be hard pressed to have competed with him. Besides, Solomon also had a harem of over a thousand women. He had it all, according to the world's standards. When a man like that says that money is a hassle, it's our cue to listen.

A MATTER OF ATTITUDE

The worst problem with wealth has nothing to do with sleepless nights, ulcers, or financial worries. The worst problem with wealth is the attitude it often generates. Jesus addressed this issue when He encountered a wealthy young man who was searching for the secret of eternal life. This rich young ruler approached Christ with a question, "Good Teacher, what shall I do to inherit eternal life?" (Luke 18:18 NASB).

After finding out that the young man was moral and upright, the Lord told him, "One thing you still lack; sell all that you possess, and distribute it to the poor, and you shall have treasure in heaven; and come, follow Me" (Luke 18:22 NASB). After Jesus said this, the rich young ruler walked away in sorrow, "for he was extremely rich" (Luke 18:23).

Many times this parable has been misinterpreted to suggest that the young man had to earn his way to heaven by his works, that somehow his selling everything would buy him a ticket to glory. That is not what Jesus meant. The young ruler could never be good enough, by himself, to get to heaven. Jesus pointed out the one area the young man could not bring himself to give up, to show him his inability to "do" anything on his own to earn eternal life. Because he couldn't give up his gold, the ruler, like the rest of us, was going to need God's grace to be righteous enough for heaven.

The episode with the rich young ruler also illustrates the principle that wealth can interfere with our coming to Christ. How often riches are more important to people than a relationship with God. Silver is often chosen over the Savior.

In dealing with us, the Lord will always put his finger on the main issue in our lives. For Nicodemus, it was his birth. For the woman at the well, it was her lifestyle. For the rich young ruler, it was his money. For Jacob, it was Benjamin. For Abraham, it could have been Isaac, but it wasn't. Abraham willingly climbed the hill and laid Isaac on the altar. What does the Lord have his finger on in your life right now? Pride? Prestige? Habits? Relationships? Lack of growth? Physical desire? Money? Will you let him have it?

An immigrant who had risen to prominence in America said, "When I came to the United States, I had a loaf of bread under this arm and sixteen cents in the other hand. Look at what I've been able to do without God." Like him, wealth gives many of us a false sense of self-sufficiency. It lulls us into thinking that we can be good enough for God, and that He's lucky we're interested in him. It convinces us that we don't really need him. When the world is financially our oyster, how quickly we can forget about the Father. It is incredibly tough for successful persons to realize that in their most important venture in life, preparing for death, they must depend on someone greater than themselves.

Wealth can keep us from Christ. If by God's grace we admit our need of him for salvation anyway, the potential for problems remains. There is often still cause for us to "wail and cry aloud" over our "tribulation," because our money can keep us from going on to spiritual maturity. It is easy for us to let the dollar occupy the place that should really belong to the Lord.

Paul told Timothy that some Christians had even "wandered away from the faith" because of their "love of money" (1 Timothy 6:10 NASB). Contemporary believers, too, often find that money provides comfort, creates diversions, makes them feel adequate and in control, and fills them with the pride of success. In the divine plan, God should be that comfort. God's work should be that diversion. God should be in control. God should receive our awe-filled gratitude as the author of every success.

TRANSIENT GLORY

Ultimately the amassing of wealth is futile (5:2). Perhaps James had Jesus' words from the sermon on the mount in mind. "Do not lay up for yourselves treasures upon earth, where moth and rust destroy, and where thieves break in and steal. But lay up for yourselves treasures in heaven, where neither moth nor dust destroys, and where thieves do not break in or steal" (Matthew 6:19-20 NASB).

Wealth and the things we buy with it are temporary. Riches do not last. There is no guarantee that a person who is rich today will be rich a year from now, or ten years from now. Ask former Texas governor and U.S. Secretary of State John Connally. With the oil crunch, real estate disasters, and bad investments, bankrupt former millionaires are a dime a dozen in Texas these days. In 1987 Connally and wife Nellie showed great character in dealing with the difficult situation; they were forced to auction off personal memorabilia and possessions at their South Texas ranch in an attempt to generate capital.

Even if wealth remains with us throughout our earthly lives, it won't follow us to the grave.

"I wonder how much he left," mused one man at the funeral of a wealthy businessman.

"All of it," replied the person sitting beside him.

A friend of mine put it this way: "There are no Brinks armored cars in funeral processions." We die; our wealth remains, perhaps to be squandered by our heirs. As Solomon wrote, "I hated all the things I had toiled for under the sun, because I must leave them to the one who comes after me. And who knows whether he will be a wise man or a fool?" (Ecclesiastes 2:18 NIV).

"You can't take it with you," an old saying goes. Treasures buried with Egyptian pharaohs to ensure the deceased's comfort and security in the netherworld were often stolen by grave robbers. Occasionally we will read of a will stipulating that the dear departed be buried in a valuable sports car or with a treasured antique. But even 'round-the-clock security at the cemetery won't prevent rust, corrosion, and decay. How foolish to live our lives for things like that. As Christians we've got to think beyond the temporary and transient. It is our responsibility to do so.

AT THE INCINERATOR

The language of James 4:3 is strong and descriptive: powerful in its imagery. "Your gold and your silver have become corroded, and their rust shall be a witness against you and shall eat your flesh as fire. You stored up treasure in the last days" (4:3). It is a warning against the improper use of wealth by the believer, a caution that too much emphasis on storing up "treasure" can result in severe consequences.

When Christians misuse money—hoard it, consistently spend it selfishly, use illegal or immoral means to get and keep it—they are in danger. Are they in danger of hell? No, not in light of the rest of scripture, not if they have genuinely trusted Christ—although a question about the reality of their salvation may arise, given their conduct.

Believers who abuse wealth are in danger of suffering for that abuse. Gold and silver can rise up to eat one's flesh like fire.

At the judgment seat of Christ (2 Corinthians 5:10), discussed earlier in this book, our works as Christians will be evaluated and either rejected or rewarded. They will be tested by fire.

> Now if any man builds upon the foundation with gold, silver, precious stones, wood, hay, straw, each man's work will become evident; for the day will show it, because it is to be revealed with fire; and the fire itself will test the quality of each man's work. If any man's work which he has built upon it remains, he shall receive a reward. If any man's work is burned up, he shall suffer loss, but he himself shall be saved, yet so as through fire (1 Corinthians 3:12-15 NASB).

One way we ensure that our works will not be incinerated at the judgment seat is by handling properly everything the Lord gives us. "It is required of stewards that one be found trustworthy" (1 Corinthians 4:2b NASB). The bottom line on your computer printout at the judgment seat of Christ will reveal what you have given of your time, treasure, and talents, and what you have made of your marriage and family.

Regrettably, it is possible for believers to live for what is temporary. But in God's eyes it is always wrong to esteem something temporary over what is eternal.

Misusing money is a sin. Judas Iscariot chose money over the master, and betrayed Jesus Christ for a mere thirty shekels of silver. In the traitor's hands, those silver coins burned as hot as hell when he realized the horrible mistake he had made in selling out the Savior. Judas cast the coins at the feet of those standing at the temple who had paid him off. Yet his act of remorse could not assuage his guilt. He hanged himself on a tree atop a lonely hill outside Jerusalem.

During his earthly ministry, Christ painted a vivid picture of misused wealth and its consequences. In Luke 16 we read of a diseased beggar named Lazarus who lay at the door of a wealthy man. As Lazarus remained prostrate on the ground, longing for scraps from the rich man's table, the dogs would come and lick his open sores. Finally, according to Jesus, the beggar died, and was carried by the angels to be with Abraham in the place of the righteous dead. The wealthy man also died and was buried, but his soul went to hell. There in torment he saw Lazarus in the far distance with Abraham. "Father Abraham," he cried, "have mercy on me, and send Lazarus, that he may dip the tip of his finger in water and cool off my tongue; for I am in agony in this flame" (Luke 16:24 NASB). His request was denied.

The point of Jesus' parable? The Lord was not teaching that the rich man could have earned his way to heaven by showing mercy to Lazarus on earth. Such a claim would have contradicted his other teachings (John 3:1-21; 5:24; 3:36). Rather Jesus was showing his followers that miserly, merciless conduct is wrong, and those who sin thus with money and never come to faith in Jesus, will find hell a horrendous place. Imagine pain so scorching, thirst so searing, that even a drop of water would seem to bring relief. No, thank you. We'll avoid it if we are Christians, even if we are skinflints. But the parable of Lazarus and the rich man tells us exactly what the Lord thinks of such selfishness. If we want to please and honor him, we had better take stock of our behavior where the almighty dollar is concerned. Money management is serious business to God.

GUIDELINES FOR THE GODLY USE OF MONEY

Some of the best advice in scripture concerning the use of our finances comes from what the apostle Paul wrote to the younger man he considered like a son.

> But godliness actually is a means of great gain, when accompanied by contentment. For we have brought nothing into the world, so we cannot take anything out of it either. And if we have food and covering, with these

we shall be content. But those who want to get rich fall into temptation and a snare and many foolish and harmful desires which plunge men into ruin and destruction. For the love of money is a root of all sorts of evil, and some by longing for it have wandered away from the faith, and pierced themselves with many a pang.

But flee from these things, you man of God; and pursue righteousness, godliness, faith, love, perseverance and gentleness. . . .

Instruct those who are rich in this present world not to be conceited or to fix their hope on the uncertainty of riches, but on God, who richly supplies us with all things to enjoy. Instruct them to do good, to be rich in good works, to be generous and ready to share, storing up for themselves the treasure of a good foundation for the future, so that they may take hold of that which is life indeed (1 Timothy 6:6-11,17-19 NASB).

Notice, Paul said it is the love of money, not money itself, that is the root of all sorts of evil. We should look at wealth as a wondrous gift from God, a sign that He knows He can trust us with it. But not all Christians will become wealthy. Indeed, relatively few will—despite the current deluge of health-and-wealth religious speakers who argue to the contrary. God has more ways of blessing us than with big bucks, fancy cars, and luxury condos.

The apostle stresses three principles that should characterize Christians' attitude toward whatever wealth they have.

1. Recognize that wealth is temporary. As Paul put it, we came into this world with nothing, and that's how we're going out.

2. Remember that as Christians we will be called to give an account of how we have used our wealth. Proper, generous use of wealth stores up "real treasure" for us in heaven.

3. Realize the wisdom of investing money well, because the time is short. Paul recommended investing in people's lives, to store up the treasure mentioned in principle 2. As we see from Christ's parable about the talents, it is also acceptable to invest our money to accrue more money (see Matthew 25:14-30). But we must not forget that with more money comes more responsibility. Accountabil-

ity usually increases in direct proportion to our bank balance.

Wealth is temporary. We are accountable. We must use it wisely because the time is short. Remember those three principles the next time you have a financial decision to make. And keep Colossians 3:1-2 in mind as well: "If then you have been raised up with Christ, keep seeking the things above, where Christ is, seated at the right hand of God. Set your mind on the things above, not on the things that are on earth" (NASB).

GOD'S PRIORITIES—JAMES 5:4-6

Behold, the wages of the workers who mowed your fields which you have kept back are crying out, and the cries of the harvesters have entered the ears of the Lord of hosts. You led a life of self-indulgence upon the earth and lived luxuriously. You've fattened your hearts in a day of slaughter. You condemned, you murdered the upright person, and he is offering you no resistance.

NAKED AND OPEN TO HIM

We Christians sometimes get the erroneous idea that we can conceal our actions from the eyes of God. Actually, that assumption is typical of just about all people. We all like to think we can sin in secret and get away with it. As long as nobody knows and we are not caught, it's okay. We forget that someone always knows. The fact is, God is not an uninterested spectator in our lives.

The Bible says, "All things are naked and opened unto the eyes of him with whom we have to do" (Hebrews 4:13b KJV). God knows exactly what is going on. We cannot play hide-and-seek with him. Adam and Eve tried it in the garden after their disobedience, and of course the Lord found them. Guilt-ridden and fig-leaved, they approached him in shame. The Lord always gets his man or woman. The hound of heaven inevitably sniffs us out.

James was describing a wealthy individual who had accrued his riches at the expense of others. This unscrupulous boss had not paid the workers who mowed his fields, or the laborers who worked in the harvest. Their cries "have entered the ears of the Lord of hosts" (5:4). Basically, James was pointing out that if we have used or abused others to gain our wealth, we are doing wrong—and God knows all about it.

Nothing escapes the Lord. Nothing slips by him. God knew that Adam and Eve ate the fruit, that Cain slew Abel, that David sinned with Bathsheba, that Achan kept back booty from the city of Jericho, that Gehazi took the gifts, that Jezebel had Naboth murdered, that Ananias and Sapphira lied about the price of a field. When we are unethical or we use poor judgment concerning our finances, God knows that too. Don't kid yourself that He doesn't.

PERILS OF PROSPERITY

From making it clear that God knows what goes on, James continued to describe a wealthy man who had unscrupulously worked his way to the top (5:5-6). His statements point out four perils of prosperity, roadblocks to spiritual growth, four reasons why some Christians never make it to maturity in their walk with the Lord.

Peril 1: Leading a life of self-indulgence. What does wealth permit us to do? To get more and more things for ourselves. To acquire. To indulge. "Now that we've got it, we might as well enjoy it," we tell ourselves. And there is nothing wrong with enjoying money. The danger is in enjoying it and enjoying it and enjoying it. If we are not careful, thoughts of God are soon replaced with fiscal concerns. I have seen many Christians so wrapped up in what they have, and want to have, that they forget their first allegiance. They begin to look on their wealth as something only for their own personal comfort, and not as an instrument to do what God might have them to do.

Peril 2: Living luxuriously. The self-indulgent person usually lives luxuriously. Luxurious living is filled with the nonessential. Lifestyles of the rich and famous don't do much to honor God. The Lord will hold us accountable at the judgment seat of Christ for how we spend our money—I should say, the Lord's money, because everything we have really belongs to him, if we have truly committed our lives to him. Do you, standing before Christ, want to have to admit, "Lord, I'm sorry. I was a poor spender in the way I used the funds you gave me"? I don't.

How can you learn to live a little less luxuriously? Before you make that next purchase, ask yourself, "Why am I buying this? Is it something I really need, or is it just something I want? Is there anything better I could use this money for?" As with all things, there is a balance. We are not necessarily called to live Spartan lives. We are called to serve the kingdom, not the creature, with our resources. Indulging till you're bulging is a sure-fire way to stall spiritual progress.

Peril 3: A fattened heart in the day of slaughter. The judgment seat of Christ is just ahead—sooner, perhaps, than we think. A healthy appreciation of our future accountability is essential for handling our money correctly, and for growing up in Christ.

Peril 4: Condemnation and murder. James mentioned a heinous crime: the condemnation and murder of an upright person (5:6), the picture of Cain and Abel. People go to unimaginable lengths to accumulate wealth. The love of money makes us step on others to acquire it. We may not physically murder them, but we may smear reputations or destroy careers. We may bring financial ruin on others. It happens every day, even among believers, as we take one another to court, stab one another in the back at the office, or grab for glory and promotion for ourselves. When we are clawing and scraping to get ahead, we can't be spiritually growing.

NOT ME

Maybe you're thinking, "This can't happen to me. I'm a believer. My lifestyle will never be one of self-indulgence. I am not going to get enmeshed in luxurious living at the expense of others." Yet I know Christians who have been derailed at this very point and have lost many friends and family relationships because of it. A once-solid Christian minister I know allowed greed to dominate his life. Like Gehazi, he is experiencing the leprosy of the soul. How tragic when compassion is replaced by the continual search for advantage.

"I am not going to forget that the judgment seat of Christ lies just ahead," you say? But Christians forget that all the time. Like unbelievers, they think they have forever and they are caught at the end with pockets full of good intentions. Jesse always meant to endow a seminary chair with an ample gift from his estate. Lu planned to revise her will to leave a sizeable amount to a local Christian children's home. Neither ever made it to the lawyer in time. Both perished with their plans unfulfilled.

"I will never step on anyone to get to the top," you insist? Yet I know plenty of believers who do that. One Christian business-man invested the money of friends and family members in ventures that turned sour. He walked away from the fiasco, leaving empty office buildings, unsold tracts, a floundering ser-vice company, and unproductive oil wells in the hands of the banks and the original investors. He had sunk little of his own money into any of the deals. In his case, although he did not reach the top, he stepped on a lot of people in the attempted ascent.

The Lord pronounced judgment on the nation of Israel with these words:

> Woe to you who are complacent in Zion,
>> and to you who feel secure on Mount Samaria,
> you notable men of the foremost nation,
>> to whom the people of Israel come!
> Go to Calneh and look at it;
>> go from there to great Hamath,
>> and then go down to Gath in Philistia.
> Are you better than those kingdoms?
>> Was their land larger than yours?
> You put off the evil day
>> and bring near a reign of terror.
> You lie on beds inlaid with ivory
>> and lounge on your couches.
> You dine on choice lambs
>> and fatted calves.
> You strum away on your harps like David
>> and improvise on musical instruments.
> You drink wine by the bowlful
>> and use the finest lotions,
>> but you do not grieve over the ruin of Joseph.
> Therefore you will be among the first to go into
>>> exile;
>> your feasting and lounging will end
>> (Amos 6:1-7 NIV).

God was talking to his special people with those words of warning. They were failing in the area of finances. They were eating, drinking, and making merry to excess, leaving things that were God's intentions unattended.

Today, we in the body of Christ are in danger of failing too. Beds of ivory have been replaced with waterbeds, music with home entertainment centers. Preachers rail at us to give, give, give, so that we might receive, receive, receive. Speaking from multimillion-dollar media soapboxes, they promise us health, wealth, and prosperity in exchange for a few dollars—the abundant life on a block for sale. God never said it should be so. One health-wealth-prosperity guru claimed that if he gave his million dollars to the Lord, the Lord would give him two million. Nothing in scripture suggests that God offers two-for-one money-back guarantees to encourage giving.

On the contrary, the Bible teaches us to be content with what we do have. Paul wrote to the Philippians:

> Not that I speak from want; for I have learned to be content in whatever circumstances I am. I know how to get along with humble means, and I also know how to live in prosperity; in any and every circumstance I have learned the secret of being filled and going hungry, both of having abundance and suffering need. I can do all things through Him who strengthens me (Philippians 4:11-13 NASB).

QUESTIONS AND ANSWERS

Invariably, when I teach this passage from James, many questions crop up. Here are a few of the ones most often asked.

1. How do I know I'm in God's will in the use of my wealth? Try checking in with him daily. "Lord, I'm available, and what I have is yours, and I want you to use me today." Let that be your prayer. You can count on him, as long as you are being submissive, to direct you in the decisions you must make that day. When opportunities come along to use your finances to bring glory to his name, you will be ready.

Try praying, also, before making major purchases. Be sure of your motives. Realize that God does not oppose your enjoying yourself and obtaining material possessions, but you must not become so wrapped up in the "gotta haves" that you forget him as the source of it all.

Don't acquire at the expense of others. If a family need is

pressing or God has laid on your heart the idea of helping someone who is hurting financially, now is probably not the time to make that big purchase for yourself. I know a young family who did just that, foregoing a terrific deal on a pop-up camper that would have provided many special vacation memories, so they could assist their parents financially. In your case, maybe the new car—or whatever you are about to buy—can wait. Maybe there are better, more God-honoring ways to spend your money. Think spiritually before you sign on the dotted line.

2. Is it possible to lose everything once we turn our wealth over to the Lord? Yes, it is possible. If something in your life has a hold on you and takes your attention away from the Lord, He may pull the rug out from under you. He may take it all away, to show you that you must put him first. He wants you to trust him although you have nothing. The clincher is, it is amazing what He can make of nothing.

Many years ago I found myself out of a job with no place to go and nothing to do. I was angry at God. I felt I had been trusting him for everything and now I had nothing. He had let me down, to my way of thinking. He allowed me to reach the point of total human futility before He began to bless me financially. He can put his finger on our wealth and get our attention very quickly, and He knows that.

3. Should a Christian sue someone else over matters of money? According to the apostle Paul, believers should not settle their differences in society's legal system, but within the church.

> If any of you has a dispute with another, dare he take it before the ungodly for judgment instead of before the saints? Do you not know that the saints will judge the world? And if you are to judge the world, are you not competent to judge trivial cases? Do you not know that we will judge angels? How much more the things of this life! Therefore, if you have disputes about such matters, appoint as judges even men of little account in the church. I say this to shame you. Is it possible that there is nobody among you wise enough to judge a dispute between believers? But instead, one brother goes to law

against another—and this in front of unbelievers! (1 Corinthians 6:1-6 NIV).

If we are to follow Paul's teachings, we will not take other believers to court, but will bring these issues for settlement before the body of Christ. As for taking an unbeliever to court, that is another matter—although I would advise much prayer before doing so. Search yourself and your motives to see if the action will glorify God.

4. Much is made of the tithe. Biblically, how much should I be giving to the Lord's work? It is common to think of the biblical concept of the tithe as ten percent of our income. Ten percent may be a good rule of thumb. But as a Christian you are under grace and not under the law. You have the freedom to give as the Lord wants you to do. If you give fifteen percent, that's okay. Nine percent? Fine. The amount you give is between you and the Lord. If you are open to him, He will show you where your money needs to go. He is looking at your heart.

> Now this I say, he who sows sparingly shall also reap sparingly; and he who sows bountifully shall also reap bountifully. Let each do just as he has purposed in his heart; not grudgingly or under compulsion; for God loves a cheerful giver (2 Corinthians 9:6-7 NASB).

5. What about giving to other Christian organizations in addition to the church? There is much debate over where the bulk of our giving should go. Should it all go to the church? What about other worthwhile ministry organizations which God is using and blessing? At the Ministries, part of our income comes from the two churches we staff, and part comes from contributions from individuals.

Let us remember, we are giving to the Lord, for the Lord's work. Any organization that does the Lord's work should qualify for our giving. You must not, however, neglect your local church. That is the ministry in which you are probably most directly involved. Yet if you have decided to give ten percent of your income to God, I wouldn't worry if that ten percent were divided between your local church and other organizations. You are the one to make that decision; it is a personal matter.

I would caution all Christians to bear in mind their account-ability before God for the use of their finances. Many believers belong to churches affiliated with the National Council of Churches, and similar groups. In the '70s, the National Council allegedly provided defense funds for liberal activists like Angela Davis and I do not see how a Christian can justify giving to that. If your local congregation is a member of a wider group, presbytery, synod, or region, it is probably possible for you to designate where the money you give goes. If necessary, you can designate that your contributions be used for the operating expenses of the local church, for example. Then you fulfill your responsibility to use your resources in a godly manner.

AND GREAT WAS THEIR FALL

Bill Bright, in his book *Revolution Now*, recounted the following about an unusual group of men. Movers and shakers all, they were among the wealthiest men of their generation.

> In 1923 a very important meeting was held at the Edgewater Beach Hotel in Chicago. Attending this meeting were nine of the world's most successful financiers: Charles Schwab, steel magnate; Samuel Insull, president of the largest utility company; Howard Hopson, president of the largest gas company; Arthur Cotton, the greatest wheat speculator; Richard Whitney, president of the New York Exchange; Albert Fall, a member of the President's cabinet; Leon Jesse Livermore, the great "bear" on Wall Street; and Ivar Krueger, head of the most powerful monopoly.
>
> Twenty-five years later, Charles Schwab had died in bankruptcy, having lived on borrowed money for five years before his death. Samuel Insull had died a fugitive from justice and penniless in a foreign land. Howard Hopson was insane; Arthur Cotton had died abroad, insolvent. Richard Whitney had spent time in Sing Sing; Albert Fall had been pardoned so that he could die at home. Jesse Livermore, Ivar Krueger, and Leon Frazier had all died by suicide. All of these men had learned well the art of making a living, but none of these had learned how to live (Bright 44-45).

Is wealth temporary? You had better believe it. Does it bring happiness? Not in the long run, as the lives of the nine men above so graphically tell. Why would a Christian need it? For only one reason: to glorify God.

Great was the fall of each of those magnates. It has been said that money is a universal passport to everywhere but heaven. It is a universal provider of everything but happiness. Modern examples abound. Just look around.

Texas billionaire H. L. Hunt once said, "People who know how much they are worth generally aren't worth very much." Lately his two sons Nelson Bunker and William Herbert have had to find out exactly how much they are worth. A 1980 estimate placed Bunker's net worth at $2.4 billion, Herbert's at $1.52 billion. Tax returns for 1988 show that their assets have dwindled significantly, thanks to bum investments and ventures gone bad. Bunker now claims to be worth some $258.83 million, and Herbert reports his assets as totaling $169.38 million. Further, the brothers are being sued by the IRS for nearly three times the respective net worths of each. The case is currently being moved through U. S. Bankruptcy Judge Harold Abramson's court, and may well end in the liquidation of much of the Hunt holdings—the wealth of one Texas dynasty disappearing in the second generation (*San Antonio Express-News* 7A).

Money is not forever. Nothing money can buy is forever either. God has given us principles for using our resources—or, shall we say, *his* resources? May we never forget the giver of every good and perfect gift . . . including the bottom line.

Points to Ponder

1. In 5:1, James compared wealth to trouble or tribulation. In what ways can money bring trouble? In what ways can money present problems, especially for Christians? What are some guidelines for godly money management? You might want to look at 1 Timothy 6:6-11,17-19 as you answer.

2. What principles can we learn from 5:4-6 concerning our treatment of other people in our climb to the top economically? Why, in your opinion, is it particularly bad for Christians to use and abuse people as they try to become wealthy? Explain your answer.

3. Rephrase 5:2-3 in your own words. What do those verses teach about the futility of acquiring material possessions? What did James mean when he said that gold and silver "shall eat your flesh as fire"? Refer to 1 Corinthians 3:10-14 as you answer.

11

We Interrupt This Broadcast

James 5:7-12

The still quiet of a suburban community was suddenly jarred as a car jumped a curb and careened onto the front lawn of a home. So unnerved was the homeowner sitting on his porch at the time of the incident that he suffered a massive heart attack and died. The lawyer for the family of the victim secured a one-million-dollar decision against the driver for causing the death.

This is just one of the many cases I have read about since starting this book. Other headlines have revealed that a college coed was awarded a million-dollar judgment against a former boyfriend who shot illicit footage of her and showed it to his fraternity buddies. Suit was also filed by a woman against a pro-basketball star for alleged breach of a marriage contract. The jilted woman accused the athlete of reneging on his end of the deal so that he could marry a taller woman who would give him tall sons (*in utero* NBA power forwards, I guess).

Without commenting on the integrity of the cases above, they do illustrate a truth about our litigious society. We Americans are lawsuit happy. We are taking one another to court in record numbers. When we feel that our rights have been trampled on, we raise our hackles and do more than cry *foul*. We counterattack.

Sometimes the results of our quests for retribution are bizarre, as in the case of the state district judge who, incensed that a neighbor's son had broken one of her son's toys, pulled a gun on the offending child's mother. Or the municipal judge who, angered because an ambulance had taken his parking space, blocked access to the emergency vehicle. Paramedics were unable to unload a stretcher needed to evacuate a sick employee. And it wasn't too long ago that the anchorman of a major network newscast refused to appear on the air for six minutes because a tennis match had pre-empted the start of the evening news (Curtis 64-73). Sometimes we go to great—and unreasonable—lengths to get even.

Draw what conclusions you will from the situations described above. The fact is, from pre-Constitution days, we Americans have been very concerned about protecting and preserving our rights. Standing up for ourselves is a time-honored tradition with us. The problem comes when we transfer this tradition to the church.

ME-FIRST ON SUNDAY?

There is a disturbing trend in evangelical churches today. Too many of us are walking around clothed in me-first attitudes. We are spending too much time worrying about our individual rights and privileges within the body of Christ.

Me-firstness in the church is nothing new. It has been around since the days of James and John—when those two sons of thunder, their mother, and the rest of the disciples argued about who would be first in Christ's kingdom (Mark 10:35-45; Matthew 20:20-28). But today, in many of the churches I encounter, me-firstness is reaching new heights—make that, new depths. Somewhere along the way we have gotten the message that what we prefer is what we deserve.

"Pass the plates," say some. "Collect the offering in the rear," say others. "Give an invitation." "Don't give an invitation." "Support my missionary." "I'll teach Sunday school, but I don't need to come to any meetings or use the curriculum you chose." "There's only *one* way to baptize." "Plant a church?

Are you kidding? Let's build." "Add on? You're kidding! Let's plant a church." "I think the new carpet ought to be blue." "Red." "Beige." "Let me handle it my way, will you?" The unselfish sharing seen in the early church stands as a rebuke to this kind of me-firstness:

> And everyone kept feeling a sense of awe; and many wonders and signs were taking place through the apostles. And all those who had believed were together, and had all things in common; and they began selling their property and possessions, and were sharing them with all, as anyone might have need. And day by day continuing with one mind in the temple, and breaking bread from house to house, they were taking their meals together with gladness and sincerity of heart, praising God, and having favor with all the people. And the Lord was adding to their number day by day those who were being saved (Acts 2:43-47 NASB).

Pride and personal likes and dislikes didn't interfere with the fellowship of those Christians. They were of "one mind," and their hearts were filled with gladness and sincerity—quite a switch from our modern propensities to argue about plans, programs, and pulpit practices.

FORGETTING THE FUTURE

Perhaps one of the reasons that pride plays so large a role in Christendom today is that many Christians neglect the eternal perspective. They are caught up in the here and now. They don't want to miss out on anything they think this life has to offer. Living for the present causes us to forget the promises Christ has made.

> In My Father's house are many dwelling places; if it were not so, I would have told you; for I go to prepare a place for you. And if I go and prepare a place for you, I will come again, and receive you to Myself; that where I am, there you may be also (John 14:2-3 NASB).

That's nice, if you're interested in pie in the sky by and by, you say. But we've got to live now. True, but when we get caught up in protecting our "rights" within the church, we generally overlook the call to serve, submit, and sacrifice for the spiritual wellbeing of others. While every fiber of our flesh is screaming, "Stand up for yourself!" God just may be quietly saying, "Cooperate."

We have already looked at ten pointers for progress in the Christian life. James has shown us that growing-up Christians are becoming taller through testing and are dealing properly with temptation. They are vitally interested in God's word. They are learning to love without partiality; good works are flowing out of their lives because of their love for God. They are learning tongue control and are developing good judgment based on the wisdom from above. They are actively engaged in a battle on three fronts: a spiritual warfare against the world, the flesh, and the devil. They are becoming increasingly dependent on the designer, God almighty. They are learning to make proper use of their finances.

In James 5:7-12, we also see that growing-up Christians are also keeping the eternal perspective. Specifically, they are living life in view of Christ's imminent reappearing. They know that the Lord's direct re-entry into human history is right on schedule, first with a call for the church and then in his second coming to establish his kingdom. Those events might begin very soon—next week, tomorrow, even a minute from now.

Living with that eternal perspective washes away me-firstness and replaces concern for our rights with joyful expectation. What a motivator toward maturity it is to realize that Christ's reappearance might come with our next breath.

> Beloved, now we are children of God, and it has not appeared as yet what we shall be. We know that, when He appears, we shall be like Him, because we shall see him just as He is. And everyone who has this hope fixed on Him purifies himself, just as He is pure (1 John 3:2-3 NASB).

> Since we have these promises, dear friends, let us purify ourselves from everything that contaminates body and spirit, perfecting holiness out of reverence for God (2 Corinthians 7:1 NIV).

IN THE MEANTIME

In a sense, we believers are living in the *meantime*—sometime before the reappearing. We are doing the work Christ assigned us before He ascended into heaven:

> Go therefore and make disciples of all the nations, baptizing them in the name of the Father and the Son and the Holy Spirit, teaching them to observe all that I commanded you and, lo, I am with you always, even to the end of the age (Matthew 28:19-20 NASB).

Those were his final instructions to us in what we call the great commission. We are to be telling others about the Lord and his good news of salvation, and we are to be encouraging other Christians in their walk with God. In all our busyness, may we never lose sight of those objectives. May we never become so enamored of the here and now that we forget we are living *in the meantime.* We exist on the edge of eternity.

So in the meantime, what do we do? James said that if we are growing up in Jesus Christ, our lives should be characterized by patience, persistence, and peace. As these qualities manifest themselves in us, they mark our maturity, showing that we are living in light of Christ's imminent re-entry.

BE PATIENT—JAMES 5:7-8

> Have patience, therefore, brethren, until the coming of the Lord. Behold, the farmer is waiting expectantly for the precious fruit of the earth, waiting patiently over it until it receives an early and a late rain. You also be patient, strengthen your hearts because the coming of the Lord is near.

A major component of Christian growth is patience. We have already seen this in chapter 1. "But let patience be having its complete work in order that you may be fully developed and complete, lacking in nothing" (1:4).

Each year I have the pleasure of speaking with many new believers. They are usually tremendously enthusiastic about the Lord. It is a thrill to be around them. Their excitement about their faith is catching.

Many times, however, I find that these new believers are also frustrated. They look at Sanctified Sal who has been a Christian for fifteen years, has completed thirty-nine personal and group

Bible studies, has memorized hundreds of scripture verses, has assumed leadership of the children's Sunday school program—and they feel inadequate. They are not in that league; they will never be that capable and spiritual.

The frustration of these new believers is compounded as they discover that their lives are still not perfect. Problems still exist. Old sins still need to be discarded. Often new believers find it discouraging that they are still so spiritually immature in some of their attitudes, so childish in the faith. They long to grow up overnight, and something keeps tripping them up.

What do I tell young Christians in that predicament? First of all, I warn them against making comparisons. Older Christians like Sanctified Sal haven't always been as spiritual as they now seem. Years of living with the Holy Spirit make a difference. Almost every believer's growth is sporadic. Sometimes we make great strides in our faith; other times it's as if we are dead in the water. Besides, if you were to scratch below almost anyone's surface, you would find that the Holy Spirit still has lots of territory to conquer. We may be well on the way, but we have not "arrived," spiritually speaking. Nobody has.

Finally, I tell young Christians that growing up in Jesus Christ is a slow process. *Maturity* is a time word. We do not reach it overnight. Just as it takes time to grow up physically, it takes time to grow up spiritually.

GLIMPSING THE FINISH LINE

"Have patience . . . until the coming of the Lord" (5:7). Did James pause from discussing the marks of Christian maturity, as he caught a glimpse of the tape at the finish line of the Christian life? The "coming of the Lord" is our goal and, as has been said, we are getting closer to its reality with every breath we take.

What is this "coming of the Lord"? James was not referring to the second coming of Christ, but to a prophetic event known as the rapture of the church. Paul described this coming event in letters to the Thessalonians and Corinthians:

> For the Lord Himself will descend from heaven with a shout, with the voice of the archangel, and with the trumpet of God; and the dead in Christ shall rise first.

> Then we who are alive and remain shall be caught up together with them in the clouds to meet the Lord in the air, and thus we shall always be with the Lord (1 Thessalonians 4:16-17 NASB).

> Behold, I tell you a mystery; we shall not all sleep, but we shall all be changed. . . . For this perishable must put on the imperishable, and this mortal must put on immortality (1 Corinthians 15:51, 53 NASB).

In a moment, in the twinkling of an eye, the Lord will descend from heaven with a shout, with the voice of an archangel. From their graves Christians already deceased will burst forth. Then the living believers will join the ascending throng. Clothed in new, immortal bodies, the perishable shall put on the imperishable. It is the next event on God's prophetic calendar.

Soon the world may be hearing a news flash. Imagine the anchorman's thinly concealed shock: "We interrupt this broadcast to tell you that vast numbers of men, women, and children have mysteriously disappeared. The phenomenon appears to be worldwide. Estimates are that as much as a fifth of the population in some cities is now gone. Cemeteries are reporting unusual activity too. The government has announced that a member of the White House press corps will shortly issue a statement. Stay tuned—we'll update you on the situation as more details are available. Meanwhile, we return to our regularly scheduled programming."

IS THE RAPTURE THE SECOND COMING?

Many people get the rapture confused with another future event, the second coming of Christ. The rapture of the church is not Jesus' second coming. In his holy word, God revealed that He has a special program for the nation of Israel and a separate special program for Christians, or the church. His special program for the church on earth as we know it concludes with the rapture. Then his plans for Israel resume, and the Jews, many of whom will come to faith in Christ, must suffer along with the rest of the world through a time of wrath and judgment. Many Jews will realize what their ancestors missed, and will come to faith in Christ during the seven-year period called the tribulation, described in Revelation 6–19. At the end of that tribulation period, Jesus Christ will come again to defeat the kings of the earth at Armageddon, a battle that will be won by the Lord before it ever really begins. After this the Lord will establish his thousand-year (millennial) kingdom on the earth (Revelation 20).

There is much debate over these coming attractions. My conclusions are based on a literal interpretation of the biblical text. What is especially important for us to realize is that Christ is going to call for his own. The cry of the archangel could be heard before you finish reading this chapter, this sentence.

Still here? So why is the Lord's reappearance significant? I think, first, it should motivate us to grow. Then, it should prompt us to seek every opportunity to tell others about Jesus and to learn to know him better. One of two events, our rapture or our physical death, could happen today to end all such earthly opportunities. We may be going up, or God may be turning out the lights. We must live in the knowledge of these final truths.

The Garden from God's Point of View

Not only should we be motivated to grow while awaiting Christ, we should accept the *meantime* with patient expectation. James likened the process of waiting on God to that of a farmer tending his fields (5:7). Daily the farmer checks his new-planted crops. In contrast to the gardens I've planted lately, this man fully expects his seeds to sprout and the plants to grow. He has planted the seed, hasn't he? He has no doubt that fruit will eventually be produced. His expectations are not uncertain, but full of confidence. That's how we Christians should be anticipating Christ's reappearing—without anxiety, but full of confidence.

In many ways the farmer reminds us of God too. The master gardener, God looks into his garden, us, and desires to see growth. He knows that He is fully capable of producing fruit in us. We must be patient, knowing that the Lord has promised to produce fruit if we are faithful, knowing that the Lord is the one who has planted us. An early rain, a late rain. Someday we will bloom. God will use us down here, and one day He will take us to glory. What a way to go!

TAKE HEART, THE COMING IS NEAR!

In the moment Christ calls for us in the clouds, and our bodies are instantly changed, we shall become just like him. "Beloved, now we are children of God, and it has not appeared as yet what we shall be. We know that, when He appears, we shall be like Him, because we shall see Him just as He is" (1 John 3:2 NASB). That's worth waiting for, isn't it? The king will be calling! "You also be patient; strengthen your hearts because the coming of the Lord is near," echoed James (5:8).

The coming of the Lord is near. What an incredible thought. I am reminded of NASA space shuttle missions. Thousands of miles into space the orbiting rocket plane ascends, only to re-enter the atmosphere at a designated time and achieve a pin-point landing at a specific airstrip. Even with computer technology, a successful shuttle mission is astonishing.

The Lord is coming, and that's miraculous. Of course, He's been here before. "But when the fulness of the time came, God sent forth His son, born of a woman, born under the Law, in order that He might redeem those who were under the Law, that we might receive the adoption as sons" (Galatians 4:4-5 NASB). Just like a shuttle craft on target, Jesus came the first time at the exact moment and at the specific place predesignated by the Father. The fullness of time will arrive again, when God will once more send his Son to intervene in human history and fulfill biblical prophecy. In view of these truths, we must be patient and we must, as James urged, strengthen our hearts.

Would you like some heart-strengthening verses? Try these:

> Wait for the Lord;
>   be strong and take heart
>   and wait for the Lord (Psalm 27:14 NIV).

> [So that you may be] strengthened with all power, according to His glorious might, for the attaining of all steadfastness and patience, joyously (Colossians 1:11 NASB).

> I can do all things through Him who strengthens me (Philippians 4:13 NASB).

> But they that wait upon the Lord shall renew their strength; they shall mount up with wings as eagles; they

shall run, and not be weary; and they shall walk, and not faint (Isaiah 40:31 KJV).

And He has said to me, "My grace is sufficient for you, for power is perfected in weakness." Most gladly, therefore, I will rather boast about my weaknesses, that the power of Christ may dwell in me (2 Corinthians 12:9 NASB).

Notice, the heart strengthener in each of the above verses is God. He will help us, cried the psalmist. His grace is sufficient, his strength is perfected in our weakness, wrote Paul. His glorious power and indwelling strength will renew us. Growing-up Christians are not only patiently awaiting the call of the Lord, they are experiencing God's strength to meet whatever demands come their way.

In 1988, some well-meaning believers published a booklet warning that the rapture was going to take place that year. I would agree with them that with the establishment of the state of Israel and the tension in the Middle East, events on God's prophetic clock do seem to be ticking down. But at this writing, 1990 is upon us, and the rapture has not yet taken place.

Let's not get bogged down in determining when the Lord will call us home. Christ said, "It is not for you to know times or epochs which the Father has fixed by His own authority" (Acts 1:7 NASB). Instead, let's simply have the confident expectation that it is going to happen, and as we wait, let's remember our walking orders to make disciples.

The Christians at Thessalonica so anticipated the imminent reappearing of Jesus that they quit their jobs and sat down to wait for him. The apostle Paul had to write them to correct their error in judgment. "For we hear that some among you are leading an undisciplined life, doing no work at all, but acting like busybodies. Now such persons we command and exhort in the Lord Jesus Christ to work in quiet fashion and eat their own bread" (2 Thessalonians 3:11-12 NASB). "Occupy till I come," Christ advised in a parable on money usage, giving a similar principle (Luke 19:13b KJV). God is on schedule, as far as his plan is concerned. Since we are not privy to the details of his strategy, we must do as Christ did, and "work the works of Him who sent Me [Christ], as long as it is day; night is coming, when no man can work" (John 9:4 NASB).

BE PERSISTENT—JAMES 5:9-11

> Stop complaining, brethren, about one another in order that you may not be judged. Behold, the judge is standing now before the doors. As an example of suffering and patience, brethren, take the prophets who spoke in the name of the Lord. Behold, we are considering fortunate those who showed endurance. You heard of the patience of Job and you saw the outcome which the Lord brought about because the Lord is sympathetic and compassionate.

According to James we should be waiting, watching, and working until Christ comes—not just waiting for the bridegroom, but watching at the window, and preparing ourselves and others for his arrival. We do our working largely by allowing him to work in us. "For I am confident of this very thing, that He who began a good work in you will perfect it until the day of Christ Jesus" (Philippians 1:6 NASB). We are to be persistent in pursuing the things of God. We are to be persistent in seeking to grow.

James urged us to be persistent by first mentioning one roadblock to maturity. He issued a warning: "Stop complaining, brethren, about one another that you may not be judged" (5:9). So much for complaining about others! So much for worrying about our rights within the body of Christ! So much for bitterness!

Evidently the Jewish Christians James was addressing had similar problems in keeping an eternal perspective. They griped and complained. They allowed themselves to be controlled by the flesh rather than by the Spirit. The hair on the backs of their necks stiffened when their rights were offended. So many of us in the church today are just like them.

I remember an older man who attended a study series several years ago. After hearing this passage on James, he came up to me with arms outstretched. A huge man, this staunch and usually reserved Lutheran gave me a big hug, and in his German brogue exclaimed, "Thank you! Thank you! Don, you've helped me discover the truth. For many months, I've been bitter and hateful toward a brother, and it's been a matter of pride. I've read the statement, 'Father, forgive them for they know not what they do,' and never understood that

Christ's words on the cross could also be spoken by me. I know I've been wrong to insist on my rights."

"I don't know what he said to you," his wife commented later. "But he's had a rough time these past six or eight months. Something happened at church, and for over half a year he's had no interest in spiritual things. The Lord must have really gotten to him tonight." I thought her insight was accurate. My words may have piqued his interest, but the Lord stirred him, and the Holy Spirit continued working on his heart to cause him to want to forgive and forget. There was no longer a place for me-firstness in his theology.

A sobering fact, which should shut our mouths and start us looking for ways to serve others, is that "a judge is standing at the door" (5:9). As soon as the rapture takes place, we Christians will be with the Lord. There we shall face the judgment seat of Christ mentioned in earlier chapters of this book. At the *bema*, no gold, silver, or bronze medals will be awarded for complaining.

So, part one of being persistent calls for persistence in godliness.

> Do all things without grumbling or disputing; that you may prove yourselves to be blameless and innocent, children of God above reproach in the midst of a crooked and perverse generation, among whom you appear as lights in the world (Philippians 2:14-16 NASB).

TWO EXAMPLES OF PERSISTENCE

Part two of persistence is found in 5:10, where we have examples of men who patiently endured. They were willing to be submissive rather than to complain. They grew better, not bitter, with trial.

The first examples of the beauty of endurance are the prophets, men and women who knew how to keep on in their calling despite tremendous adversity. Jeremiah, for example, spent a lifetime telling others of God's coming judgment. No one would listen.

> Oh, that my head were a spring of water
> and my eyes a fountain of tears!

I would weep day and night
for the slain of my people (Jeremiah 9:1 NIV).

We call him the weeping prophet, so frequent were his tears and so bitter his rejection. But Jeremiah continued to preach God's message faithfully.

A second example of endurance is found in 5:11. Job, remember, lost his children, livestock, property, and possessions within a matter of minutes. Soon his entire body was diseased, covered with sores and boils, so that his emotional suffering was nearly equaled by his physical torment. As we read the prologue to the book of Job, we see that all these problems were preplanned in the councils of heaven to test Job's faithfulness. With the intention of comforting him, Job's friends said all the wrong things. They looked on with incomplete knowledge, as did Job's grief-stricken wife whose anger at her "do-nothing" husband mounted as he refused to become angry with God. It wasn't until Job turned his eyes to God that he could say, "Though he slay me, yet will I hope in him," (Job 13:15a NIV). Nothing could destroy his trust in God. The grand finale of the story sees Job again a wealthy man. His property has been restored to him twofold, and God has given him the same number of children (Job 42:10-17). Yet Job did not emerge from his ordeal unscathed. His older children were with the Father and could not be replaced, although surely the younger ones now brought him great joy.

The patience of Job—we use that phrase to describe anyone who keeps his cool through impossible circumstances. It is a supreme compliment. But I think the trust of Job is more miraculous than his patience, although the two go hand in hand.

Through the account of Job, God shows us that he is worthy of our trust. Let us not forget the "outcome [of Job's ordeal] which the Lord brought about because the Lord is sympathetic and compassionate" (James 5:11). When the final chapter of any test is written, we will see the Lord's compassion and sympathy. We will find that we are richer somehow for the experience, perhaps not materially, but emotionally or spiritually.

BROKEN HEARTS—FIRM FOUNDATIONS

Often I've seen that before the Lord can use people, He has to break them. When we pray for patience, we can almost count on the Lord's sending us some trouble so that patience might be produced in us. When we pray to be more loving, the Lord will try us so that the fragrance of his love can flow through us. We pray for joy, and there will probably come tears as we learn the true meaning of his joy in the midst of difficult circumstances. God is sovereign. He knows how to produce the qualities we pray for. "Not me! I don't want trouble! I'll ask for nothing!" you exclaim. Trials will come anyway, if for no other reason than to get you to the point of prayer. How much better to face those trials with God in your corner than in defiant independence.

One woman whom God has enabled to grow better through brokenness is my mother. Mom is over eighty now. Dad has been gone for a couple of years, his loss still a difficult reality for her. How proud we all are of Mom, and all she has done and is doing in the wake of tragedy. Besides caring for Dad through his long bout with cancer, Mom has undergone cancer surgery herself and suffers from arthritis. Despite it all, she just keeps on, ministering to others, attending her church, sharing her meager funds with people in need. She inspires all of us because she refuses to feel sorry for herself. She has chosen to fix her primary focus on the Lord and on the needs of others. I pray I grow old just like her.

BE AT PEACE WITH OTHERS—JAMES 5:12

> But especially, my brethren, stop swearing either by the heaven or by the earth or by any other oath, but let your yes be yes and your no be no, in order than you may not fall under judgment.

A third quality of a life lived in expectance of Christ's reappearance is peaceableness.

PEACE IN COMMITMENTS

We are to be honest and straightforward in our dealings, and not make empty vows. We are to let our yes be yes, and our no be no. Jesus said much the same thing when He cautioned believers against making vows:

> But I tell you, Do not swear at all: either by heaven, for it is God's throne; or by the earth, for it is his footstool; or

by Jerusalem, for it is the city of the Great King. And do not swear by your head, for you cannot make even one hair white or black. Simply let your "Yes" be "Yes," and your "No," "No"; anything beyond this comes from the evil one (Matthew 5:34-37 NIV; see also Ecclesiastes 5:1-5).

It is crucial that Christians be people who can be depended on to do what they say they will. We should be the kind of persons of whom others say: "Al's word is his bond." "If Sarah said she would, you can count on it." "Pete? Don't worry. He won't let you down." There is no need for us to make rash, meaningless vows. There is a pressing need for us to be solid, stable, and reliable in our dealings with others.

Peace without Profanity

James's injunction against the taking of oaths may also apply to the use of profanity by believers. Acts 4:12 says, "And there is salvation in no one else, for there is no other name under heaven that has been given among men, by which we must be saved" (NASB). The name by which we are saved is the name of Christ. Let us not make the mistake of using his precious name in vain. We show misplaced priorities when we do.

We Shall Behold Him

The growing-up Christian recognizes that Christ's reappearing is on schedule, in his time. It behooves us to live lives of purity until He appears. Perhaps, as we wait, watch, and work, we might pray a prayer like this one:

Our Heavenly Father,

Help us to be urgent. Teach us how to number our days and apply our hearts to wisdom. Teach us how to be busily engaged capitalizing on the opportunities you give us. Help us to be faithful, living the lives you want us to live, and to be patient, realizing that you are at work conforming us to the image of your Son. Lord, we pray that we might be faithfully plodding along. May there be a quality of endurance about our lives so that no matter what happens, we will trust you. Encourage us, Father.

In your precious Son's name we pray, Amen.

The excitement of his return is clearly communicated in Dottie Rambo's song:

> The sky shall unfold, preparing His entrance;
> The stars shall applaud Him with thunders of praise.
> The sweet light in His eyes shall enhance those
>   awaiting;
> And we shall behold Him then face to face.
>
> The angels shall sound the shout of His coming;
> The sleeping shall rise from their slumbering place.
> And those who remain shall be changed in a moment;
> And we shall behold Him then face to face.

Points to Ponder

1. Reread 1 Thessalonians 4:16-17 and 2 Corinthians 5:51-52. Describe in your own words what you think the rapture will be like.

2. From James 5:9 and 5:12, we see that attitudes of me-firstness had infiltrated the early church. Are these attitudes prevalent today in modern Christianity? Do you know of any areas in your spiritual life where you are manifesting me-firstness? Be honest. Is there some area in your relationship with God or with other believers where you are putting your own needs before the needs of others? What can be done about your me-first attitude? What should be done about it?

3. The passage is a call to keep on keeping on, patiently awaiting the upward call of Christ, strengthening our hearts in the meantime. What are some practical ways Christians can keep on keeping on in their spiritual lives while they await Christ's reappearing? How can this passage be put into practice? How can our hearts be strengthened?

12

Tell Your Daddy Where It Hurts

James 5:13-20

The wanted man met with his cohorts one last time. They accompanied him a short distance to a city park. The ringleader was bone tired. He knew that a price was on his head, and that it was only a matter of time until someone close to him tipped off the police as to his whereabouts. There was nowhere to run and nowhere to hide in the steamy, bustling city. Besides, He was ready to surrender.

While He awaited the arrival of the SWAT team, He did something unusual for a common criminal: He isolated himself and prayed. His buddies who were supposed to be keeping watch at the park gate fell asleep on the job, and as He woke them the third time, a former friend burst in with a riot squad. As if He had known it would happen, the ringleader allowed himself to be arrested, offering no resistance and instructing his men to do the same.

What had the accused criminal prayed while awaiting his arrest? We know his very words, even though they were uttered nearly two thousand years ago in an obscure corner of a teeming, tourist-filled city.

> My Father, if it is possible, let this cup pass from Me; yet not as I will, but as Thou wilt (Matthew 26:39 NASB).

> My Father, if this cannot pass away unless I drink it, Thy will be done (Matthew 26:42 NASB; see also 26:44).

Yes, Jesus knew all about the power of prayer. As He earnestly prayed in Gethsemane, He broke into a heavy sweat (Luke 22:44). In times of extreme anguish or strain a condition can occur which physicians term "hematidrosis," a mingling of blood with sweat. Jesus was in such agony of spirit as He fervently prayed that great red drops of perspiration fell to the ground. In his divinity, Jesus knew that Judas would shortly lead his captors to their prey. In those difficult hours He turned to the Father, knowing that his triumph in the circumstances would be based on his communion with God.

Throughout the night and the mockery of a trial, Jesus largely kept silent. By nine the following morning, the soldiers were pounding nails into his hands and feet, pinning him to the cross. His splayed back scraped against the beams. With each blow of the hammer, the nails were thrust more deeply through his body and embedded in the unyielding wood. Then the rugged cross and its dangling victim were jolted upright and thrust into the ground. What did Jesus do in those moments of agony? He prayed. "Father, forgive them; for they do not know what they are doing" (Luke 23:34 NASB).

Six hours later the sun's light failed; darkness fell over the whole land (Luke 23:44-45). The Father withdrew his fellowship from the Son. Jesus suffered complete isolation as He was made sin for us. Total separation from the Father brought pain more excruciating and intense than the physical torment. And Jesus prayed. "Eli, Eli, lama sabachthani? . . . My God, My God, why hast Thou forsaken Me?" (Matthew 27:46 NASB). Moments later his agony ceased and his earthly life ended as He again prayed, "Father, into Thy hands I commit My spirit" (Luke 23:46 NASB).

If Jesus placed such importance on prayer, can we afford not to do the same?

PRAY WITHOUT CEASING?

"Pray without ceasing" is the command of the apostle Paul in 1 Thessalonians 5:17. John Foster reflected as he approached physical death:

> I never prayed more earnestly nor probably with such faithful frequency. Pray without ceasing has been the sentence repeating itself in the silent thought, and I am sure it must be my practice till the last conscious hour of life. Oh, why not throughout that long, indolent, inanimate half-century past?

Aware as we are of the importance of prayer, so often we allow hours, days, weeks, even months, to slip by without spending significant time on our knees. We stay lukewarm and lethargic, turning to earnest prayer only when we lose power over our circumstances. We pray without ceasing when we can do nothing else. Tim Hansel said it well:

> I got up early one morning
> And rushed right into the day;
> I had so much to accomplish
> That I didn't have time to pray.
>
> Problems came tumbling about me
> And heavier came each task;
> "Why doesn't God help?" I wondered;
> He answered, "You didn't ask."
>
> I wanted to see joy and beauty
> But the day toiled on gray and bleak;
> I wondered why God didn't show me;
> He said, "But you didn't seek."
>
> I tried to come into God's presence,
> I used all my keys at the lock;
> God gently and lovingly chided,
> "My child, you didn't knock."
>
> I woke early this morning
> And paused before entering the day;

> I had so much to accomplish
> That I had to take time to pray.
>
> (Hansel 142-143)

WHEN ALL ELSE FAILS

James did not wait to pray until all else failed. He was first and foremost a man of prayer. Legend has it that he spent so much time on his knees talking to God that they became calloused as a camel's; he was sometimes called "Camelknees"—a well-deserved nickname for all the time he spent kneeling before the Father.

When Peter was miraculously delivered from prison and was reunited with some of the believers at the home of Mary, the mother of John Mark, he made a point of saying, "Tell James and the brothers about this" (Acts 12:17 NIV). Why? I'm sure Peter knew that James would be in constant prayer, and would need to be interrupted with the good news that his prayers had been answered with a resounding *yes*. Such was the quality of James's life.

Given James's personal convictions about prayer, it is not surprising that he chose to conclude his letter with an exhortation to pray. The growing Christian is a praying Christian, and vice versa.

PRAY IN AND OUT OF TOUGH TIMES—JAMES 5:13

> Is anyone among you suffering misfortune? Let him keep on praying. Is anyone cheerful? Let him keep on singing praises [making melody].

Paul referred to believers as adopted children of God, with the privilege of calling the Lord "Abba! Father!" (Romans 8:15). The aramaic word *abba* indicates a relationship of tenderness and intimacy. Today we might translate it "daddy." James began his comments on prayer by urging each of us to pray in the midst of adversity. "Tell your daddy where it hurts," he might just as well have written.

As we have seen, Jesus prayed in the tough times. Many times the tough times are the only times we ever come to the end of ourselves and sink to our knees. From James we learn that it is good to pray in the midst of trial, when we are "suffering misfortune" (5:13a). His words contain a warning:

When we are experiencing difficulty, the one thing we cannot afford to do is to withdraw from fellowship with the Father. We need the Lord's consistent company to make it through the fiery furnace. We need our daddy.

I have often observed the reverse. Many believers face crises, and the distance between them and the Lord seems to widen. The gap becomes greater. They do not pray fervently; they can hardly bring themselves to talk to God at all. It's as if they've convinced themselves that they can avoid him. They can turn off the reality of his presence by refusing to acknowledge it.

Why do people turn off God, rather than turn to him, when they're in a crunch? I can think of at least two reasons.

1. Many people have a wrong concept of suffering. They believe they are experiencing difficulty because God is angry at them. He is sending the trial to vent his disapproval and anger.

Just as children avoid annoyed parents when a rule has been disobeyed, so believers run from God because they believe they have made him angry. They are afraid things will only get worse, so they pretend they can ignore him. They opt to steer clear of him, forsaking the comfort of his presence in the midst of cancer, job loss, church turmoil. The apostle Thomas was one of them. He disappeared after Christ's crucifixion. Off by himself, he missed the first appearance of the resurrected Lord to the disciples.

2. Many people refuse to pray in difficult situations because they are angry at God. They blame him for bad weather, ruined crops, wayward kids, an ungrateful boss, financial reversal. They want nothing to do with him. Who wants to communicate with someone you blame for ruining your life? So they huff and puff and avoid the one thing that might give them peace: prayer in the presence of the Father.

KEEP ON PRAYING

Mature Christians do not let their communion with God be affected by the circumstances of life. We prove our level of commitment and spirituality by our ability to stay in fellowship with the Father apart from the good and the bad of human existence. Remember, James's instructions in case of adversity were: "Keep on praying."

How dramatically that principle is depicted in Acts 16. Paul and Silas answered the missionary call to go to Macedonia. When they got there, what happened? After brief opportunities at ministry, they found themselves severely beaten and thrown into prison. What was their response? At midnight they sat in jail exhausted, their hands and feet locked in stocks, their backs open with gaping wounds from the floggings they had received—and they sang praises and prayed to God, rejoicing in the situation. "About midnight, Paul and Silas were praying and singing hymns of praise to God, and the prisoners were listening to them" (Acts 16:25 NASB).

Paul and Silas's attitude in stress should be the goal of every growing-up Christian. Spiritual maturity means it doesn't matter what the world does to us; our joy and communion with the Lord will not be affected. And remember, there were witnesses to the event. Fellow prisoners heard the prayers and praises of Silas and Paul, and knew of the superhuman joy that only the Lord can bring. We read this account, and know too.

BENEFITS OF STAYING IN TOUCH

When the world seems to be falling apart, the best thing we can do is to stay in touch with God. Some see disappointment as God's appointment, as one poet has said. I can think of at least three benefits of staying in touch in the thorny thick of things:

1. Staying in touch prevents loneliness. It is a comfort to realize that no matter what, God is there. We have a constant, caring friend in him.

2. Staying in touch reminds us that God is in control. We cannot come and talk to him without thinking about his sovereignty and power over even the toughest situation.

3. Staying in touch enables us to see things from God's point of view. It is through fellowship with him that we begin to see what He is trying to do in our lives. His thoughts are not our thoughts, his ways not our ways, as scripture teaches (see Isaiah 55:8-9). Too often we have relegated prayer to the act of petition. We ask for things, petitioning for our needs and thanking him for answers. Prayer is more than that. Prayer is communication. Prayer is constant communion growing out of relationship. Prayer sensitizes us to God. Slowly his thoughts begin to become our thoughts. We understand some of the *why* behind the *what*.

The late Joe Bayly wrote:

> I cry tears
> to you Lord
> tears
> because I cannot speak.
> Words are lost
> among my fears
> pain
> sorrows
> losses
> hurts
> but tears
> You understand
> my wordless prayer
> You hear.
> Lord
> wipe away my tears
> all tears
> not in the distant day
> but now
> here.
>
> (Bayly 90)

FOR THE GOOD TIMES

The good times of our lives should not be empty of prayer either. We are to pray in and out of stress (5:13). Don't think you have to wait for trauma or trial to drop to your knees. Prayer is an ongoing exercise independent of circumstances. It is the key to deepening the relationship between you and God.

Pearl and I have made it a practice to pray regularly for each of our children. Our severely diabetic daughter, Becky, whom I mentioned in an earlier chapter, has been the subject of more crisis prayers than the other kids, simply because she has suffered through more physical and emotional trauma than the other four. More than once in her short life, Becky has been on the brink of going home to be with the Lord. Today we continue to pray for the functioning of her transplanted kidney and the preservation of her eyesight.

Through Becky and the other children, we have learned the value of steady prayer, in good times and bad. Ongoing prayer has sustained us in the crunch. From the day Becky's diabetes was diagnosed, we have truly not known what a day might bring forth for her. We have learned to be grateful for each day the Lord gives her. We have learned to commit her to God's care daily, hourly. Because of her frailty, she has taught us the immense value of prayer without ceasing, no matter what the circumstances. We sang praises and rejoiced on the Easter Sunday when she was married to our son-in-law Ray. We sing praises and rejoice each day that she continues to be with us. Because we have committed her to the Lord so consistently in prayer, we truly have peace concerning her condition. God does have the whole world, including our daughter and her brothers and sisters, in his hands.

PRAY FOR OTHERS—JAMES 5:14-15

> Is anyone among you sick? Let him call the elders of the assembly and let them pray over him, having anointed him with oil in the name of the Lord. And the prayer of faith shall make the sick person well, and the Lord shall raise him up, and if he has committed sins, they shall be forgiven him.

We are to turn to prayer in the midst of affliction. Prayer may not remove the affliction, but it will certainly either transform it or transform us to endure it.

Prayer has some specific purposes, one of which is to deal with disease (5:14). James's words give us the procedure to follow when praying for someone in the local congregation who is afflicted. The ill person should call the elders together. The church leaders are to come, anoint the sick person with oil, and pray over him. In James's day, the oil had medicinal purposes and would have been used by doctors. Oil also is symbolic of the Holy Spirit; its use signifies the elders' awareness of the operation of the Holy Spirit in the healing process.

Even today physicians will tell you they do not know why some people get well and others do not. Identical diseases, identical treatments—one recovers, the other develops complications and doesn't make it. The will to live is cited as a critical factor in some cases. Often overlooked is the matter of God's will for the patient. We may not want to accept it, but sometimes it is God's will for an ill person to go home to be with him instead of going home to her or his family. When our days are up, no medical procedure, regardless of its success rate, can save us (Psalm 31:15).

Donnie Guion was a tremendous friend, a faithful member of the Ministries board. He, his wife Pat, Pearl, and I traveled together and shared many good times. He looked fit and trim at our annual board meeting in September of 1985. By the following January the doctors had diagnosed that a spot on his lung was cancer. A few short months later he was gone. The anointing of oil and all the prayers on his behalf were stamped "No! I have a better plan!" Sometimes that's the way it is, and there is nothing we can do about it.

WHAT DOES GOD WANT?

Many believers today do not want to accept the fact that physical illness is sometimes incurable: "God wants me to be whole." "God promised me an abundant life. He doesn't want me to lie in this hospital bed any longer." "I know I can walk again, if only I have enough faith!" "I am going to be healed." "It's not God's will for me to be sick."

I can't tell you how many times such statements have been spoken with confidence by people I have visited in hospitals and sickrooms. Not only do they expect to get well, they believe that their recovery is a foregone conclusion, that it has been promised by God, that every Christian's life should be characterized by good health. This mindset is a reflection of our age, when Christian television and radio, and many of our churches, promote men and women who claim to have the gift of healing. If only we have faith enough, we are told, we can be healed of whatever malady plagues us. Sounds great, doesn't it? The problem is that it is not biblical.

The apostle Paul suffered from what he called "a thorn in the flesh," evidently some physical ailment. Although he prayed three times to be relieved of that handicap, God chose instead to show him that his grace would be sufficient (2 Corinthians 12:7-8). So, until the end of his life, as far as we know, Paul lived with his disability. If anybody ever had enough faith in God's ability to heal, it was Paul. Yet God chose to allow him to remain afflicted.

Nowhere in God's word are we told that healing is the inevitable outcome of faith in every situation. It is always a possible outcome. Nowhere are we told that if we do not recover from an illness, it is because we do not have enough faith. Many of the individuals with the so-called modernday gift of healing argue otherwise. They often cite James 5:14-15 as proof, saying that sick people fail to recover because their faith is weak. Let's examine what those verses really say about the issue.

First of all, about the matter of the sick person's faith, notice who is to be praying (5:14). The elders are to offer up "the prayer of faith" (5:15). It is the faith of the elders, not the faith of the sick person, to which James referred. How sad that there are people who promise to heal for X amount of dollars, and then blame their failure on the sick person's lack of faith. James said nothing about the faith of the afflicted. He referred only to the faith of the elders, who are to pray over the ill. The elders cannot legitimately blame the poor sick person for lack of faith if he or she fails to get well.

What is the "prayer of faith"? It is the elders' believing prayer to bring the sovereign God into action to provide healing, if healing is the Lord's will. The elders should pray fully convinced that God can heal, if He chooses. The option not to heal remains with the Lord, and that should be recognized also.

If it is the Lord's will to heal in a situation, we can be assured that the individual will be healed (5:15). We must not interpret that statement as an absolute promise that every time a sick person is prayed over in faith by a group of godly elders, healing will occur. Such a conclusion contradicts the rest of scripture. We have already considered Paul's experience. Second Timothy 4:20 tells of one Trophimus whom Paul left sick at Miletus. In the twentieth century, Christian speaker, writer, and artist Joni Eareckson Tada has not been healed of her paralysis. Our daughter Becky, as radiant a Christian as you'll ever encounter, is still a diabetic—and her disease has nothing to do with lack of faith on anyone's part. People don't always get well.

If God chooses not to heal, we must take it on faith that He knows better than we do. It is his prerogative to take us home whenever He desires. We must not make the mistake of thinking we can manipulate him into healing someone if that is not his plan. We cannot control God.

James 5:15 evidently refers to sins the person has committed which have made him sick. It is not a blanket statement of forgiveness for all of the individual's sins.

Notice three truths about the principles of healing:

1. The elders' prayer of faith can result in the sick person's being made well.

2. The Lord will raise him up. God ultimately controls the situation.

3. If the afflicted person has committed sins resulting in sickness, he or she will be forgiven.

PRAY IN THE POWER OF PURITY—JAMES 5:16-18

> Be confessing therefore your sins to one another, and be praying for one another that you may be healed. The effective prayer of a righteous person is able to do much. Elijah was the man with the same nature as we, and he prayed earnestly that it might not rain, and it did not rain upon the earth for three years and six months. And he prayed again, and the heaven gave rain, and the earth produced its fruit.

In 5:16 we have guidelines for pursuing the power of prayer, which is the key emphasis in our study of this passage. What did James mean when he urged us to confess our sins to one another?

Today whole groups organize themselves for this purpose. It is fashionable to hang out our dirty laundry so everyone will know what we have done and how many times we have done it. We are supposed to find spiritual therapy in this group sharing. I have known Bible study groups who have stressed sharing their individual sins and struggles openly and honestly among themselves. Total honesty brings relief, they tell me. Maybe momentarily, I generally answer.

There is no advantage in trucking around confessing our sins indiscriminately in the body of Christ. Scripture doesn't ask us to, and we don't need to. There *is* a place for accountability to other believers in the Christian life, but there are basic problems with mass confession.

Constantly sharing the nitty gritty keeps us focused on ourselves, for one thing. We are continually thinking about what we can say, how much we dare own up to. Although that kind of confession is supposed to bring greater intimacy, embarrassment, strained relationships, and awkwardness often result.

Another problem with talking about struggles and sin is that doing so is discouraging to others. It does not edify, exhort, or encourage. The focus of such a meeting is on temporal problems instead of on the person of Jesus Christ.

What did James mean when he urged us to confess our sins? First of all, we have a responsibility to confess our sins to God. Confession means agreeing with God that something is sin. It is vital to our spiritual growth that we recognize sin as sin.

"If we confess our sins, He is faithful and righteous to forgive us our sins and to cleanse us from all unrighteousness" (1 John 1:9 NASB; see also Psalm 32 and 51). Agreeing with God that we have sinned against him is critical to our walk with him. If we do not confess, we will still have a relationship with him. Nothing can change that. We are saved forever at the moment of conversion. But if we allow sin to remain unacknowledged, it grows, and our friendship with God will be affected. We won't sense his presence or his blessing. We won't experience the sweetness of his fellowship. When we feel distant from God, it is because we have moved. He remains the same. Confession keeps us closer. It forces us to realize that we can start afresh. It prevents us from getting bogged down with guilt, and keeps us effective in what we do for God. When we confess, we won't be telling God anything He does not already know about us, but we will be acknowledging that we have done wrong.

If our disobedience has offended somebody else, we probably should confess our sin to that person too, unless doing so will make matters worse. For example, if we have thought something derogatory about a friend, we have sinned against him, but it won't make the situation any better if we confess those critical thoughts to the person. "Hey, Sandy, I need to confess something to you. I've secretly resented you for six months now, ever since you became president of the women's association." "Bill, I need to be honest. I've thought you were a stuffed shirt for twenty years. I've been privately critical of the way you've handled your kids too. I'm sorry." Confess wrong attitudes to God. Leave Bill and Sandy alone, if confession is only going to make things worse.

Three Obstacles to Confession

Confessing our sins to God and, where reasonable or possible, to those we have humanly offended, is essential for spiritual growth. If we are unwilling to confess, it may mean that some things are getting in the way.

Why do we sometimes find it so difficult to own up to what we have done? The first reason is pride; we never want to admit that we are vulnerable or wrong; we equate confession with weakness. A second reason is fear; fear comes along and mocks us; fear suggests that our confession will be greeted with boos, hisses, and I-told-you-so's. Finally, dishonesty also gets in the way; we just won't admit to ourselves or anyone else that we have failed. Pride, fear, and dishonesty, singly or in any combination, are enemies to keep us from following the prescription of confession and praying for one another.

That You May Be Healed

Why is it essential that we confess and pray? "That you may be healed" (5:16). Healing refers here to mended relationships with other people and a healing in our walk and fellowship with the Lord. We are in relationship with one another, and we are accountable in those relationships.

Unconfessed sin hinders our ministries. I remember one day several years ago. My Wednesday morning breakfast class was a wash-out, and I didn't know why. The mostly-businessmen audience and I just didn't connect. We were all relieved when the hour was over. Wednesday lunch wasn't much better. The women who attended had been in a three-hour seminar all morning, and they sat glassy-eyed, unable to absorb anything from the book of John which I was teaching. It was like talking to a roomful of folks who would rather be taking a nap. I couldn't blame them either. With the morning seminar, they had been saturated with information and needed a break before they could soak up anything else. After surviving the hour, I returned to my host's home to lie down and rest until dinner and the evening session, all the while wondering what went wrong, why I wasn't more sensitive to those women, why my usually receptive group of men had seemed cold and distant.

"Anderson," a voice seemed to say as I lay resting, "if you had dealt with the problem, I could have used you a lot more effectively in those two classes today." It wasn't an audible voice, but somehow as I was thinking about the fruitless morning, the Lord spoke to my heart and opened my eyes to the real reason for the day's struggles.

"Lord, I wasn't aware that there was a problem," I thought in reply.

"Oh no? What about last night on the telephone?"

It was as if a ton of bricks had slid off the truck and onto my conscience. Last night? I remembered what I had said to Pearl over the phone.

"Anderson, get back to that telephone and get this situation straightened out, if you expect me to use you at the university class this evening," came the message straight to my heart. I picked up the receiver immediately. Collect call—long distance in the middle of the day when the rates are high—it didn't matter. I had to talk with Pearl.

"Honey," I said when Pearl answered. "Remember when I told you I had invited those people over, and you were upset because we had so many other obligations that weekend?"

You bet she remembered. "Yes," she said without hesitating.

"I am really sorry. I realize my timing was awful, and I should have consulted you first. It has even affected my ministry today. I want you to forgive me. And listen, we can take Bill and Betty out for dinner instead of your having to cook."

Pearl, gracious as ever, forgave me—and I attribute the success of that evening's class at the university to the fact that I followed the biblical prescription for confession. I was cleansed, ready to meet the needs of others, without the urgent cry of an unchecked offense getting in the way. Answered prayer came in a renewed relationship with Pearl and an evening Bible class full of interested, questioning, searching college students. Talk about a living, breathing fulfillment of scripture—the words and warning of 1 Peter 3:7 became real. "You husbands likewise, live with your wives in an understanding way, as with a weaker vessel, since she is a woman; and grant her honor as a fellow heir of the grace of life, *so that your prayers may not be hindered*" (NASB, italics mine).

THE PROPHET WHO PRAYED

One of my favorite statements in scripture is this one of James: "The effective prayer of a righteous person is able to do much" (5:16b). When properly harnessed, the power of prayer can do incredible things. Oh, God won't give us Rolls Royces or fat bank accounts on demand. And as we have discussed, He won't necessarily cure us of all disease. But He will answer with anything that is in his will. He will strengthen us. He will encourage us. He will use us for his purposes.

What a pity it is that we don't pray more. In the book, *The Kneeling Christian*, we read this about prayer:

> Why are so many Christians so often defeated? Because they pray so little. Why are so many church workers so often discouraged and disheartened? Because they pray so little.
>
> Why do most men see so few brought "out of darkness to light" by their ministry? Because they pray so little.
>
> Why are not our churches simply on fire for God? Because there is so little real prayer. The Lord Jesus is as powerful today as ever before. The Lord Jesus is as anxious for men to be saved as ever before. His arm is not shortened that it cannot save, but He cannot stretch forth His arm unless we pray more—and more. We may be assured of this: the secret of all failure is our failure in secret prayer (An Unknown Christian 14).

"Be anxious for nothing, but in everything by prayer and supplication with thanksgiving let your requests be made known to God (Philippians 4:6 NASB). First Peter 5:7 recommends "casting all your anxiety upon Him, because He cares for you" (NASB). We are God's personal concern. Nothing in our lives is too great for his power or too small for his care. The prophet Elijah knew all about that, and James used him as an example to illustrate to his Jewish Christian readers the value and power of prayer.

Elijah was a righteous man whose prayer accomplished much (5:17-18). We have spoken of him briefly earlier in this book; now is the time for more details.

The account of Elijah is found in 1 Kings. Elijah was the prophet of God when evil King Ahab ruled the land of Israel. Not only was Ahab utterly degenerate, he was married to an exceptionally wicked woman, Jezebel. It is no accident that even today her name suggests vileness and deception.

Commanded by the Lord to speak his word, Elijah came to Ahab with a severe warning. "As the Lord, the God of Israel, lives, whom I serve, there will be neither dew nor rain in the next few years except at my word" (1 Kings 17:1 NIV). Because of Ahab's sinful ways, for three-and-a-half years he would know the meaning of a dry country. Not a drop of rain would fall. The three-and-a-half years passed with no rain. There were no herds in the fields, no water for them to drink. It was a national disaster, designed to teach the king, his queen, and the people who had fallen into idol worship the ABCs of the power of God.

After three-and-a-half years of drought, Elijah returned with God's instructions for a showdown. Let's call it the Carmel Convention. Elijah challenged the prophets and priests of the false god Baal to a stand-off. The confrontation would show whose god was the true God. At the top of mount Carmel, Elijah summoned 450 priests of Baal, plus 400 prophets of the god Asherah.

At Carmel, Elijah presented the game plan.

> I am the only one of the Lord's prophets left, but Baal has four hundred and fifty prophets. Get two bulls for us. Let them choose one for themselves, and let them cut it into pieces and put it on the wood but not set fire to it. Then you call on the name of your god, and I will call on the name of the Lord. The god who answers by fire—he is God (1 Kings 18:22-24 NIV).

The challenge sounded easy to the prophets and priests of Baal, because Baal was the god of the sun. The altar to Baal was erected. At about nine in the morning, the false prophets started praying. Soon they were wailing and whooping, shouting and dancing. By high noon there was still no smoke, and Elijah rubbed it in. "Shout louder!" he said. "Surely he is a god! Perhaps he is deep in thought, or busy, or traveling. Maybe he is sleeping and must be awakened" (1 Kings 18:27). Those taunts whipped the priests into a greater frenzy. They shouted louder and slashed their wrists till blood flowed. Round and round the altar they ran, pleading for Baal to send fire. There wasn't a spark to be seen. By three in the afternoon, they fell to the ground in total exhaustion.

In contrast to the false prophets, Elijah came coolly onto the scene. He quietly rebuilt the altar of the Lord which had fallen into disrepair from disuse. He directed that four barrels of water be brought and poured on the altar and sacrifice. Then he commanded this act to be repeated twice more. The sacrifice and altar and surrounding ground were soaked. It was obvious to all, beyond a shadow of a doubt, that no one could kindle a fire there for many hours. But Elijah's faith in God was complete. He knew that God could get the job done.

Do we trust the Lord that much? Don't we often ask something of God, and then make all sorts of human effort to remove the obstacles so that He can answer our prayers? Don't we try to make things easier for him? Go out of our way to talk to So-and-So, and pave the way for that promotion or donation? But Elijah needed none of that. He esteemed God as God, totally powerful, totally capable.

The altar and sacrifice were ready. Elijah prayed a prayer of faith, quiet confidence, and assurance.

> O Lord, God of Abraham, Isaac and Israel, let it be known today that you are God in Israel and that I am your servant and have done all these things at your command. Answer me, O Lord, answer me, so these people will know that you, O Lord, are God, and that you are turning their hearts back again (1 Kings 18:36-37 NIV).

Instantly a megabolt of fire flashed from the sky and ignited the animal sacrifice and the altar. The water standing in the trench cut around the altar evaporated in the heat. "The

Lord—he is God! The Lord—he is God!" came the cry from the throngs of Israelites witnessing the miracle. The prophets of Baal were slaughtered. Elijah cautioned Ahab to head for the hills. Rain was coming, and the king took off. What did Elijah do then? Again he prayed.

Elijah walked up the mountain a bit and began to talk to God. He asked God to supply the needs of the people by sending water again. Fully expecting his prayer to be answered, understanding that the purpose of the drought had been fulfilled, since the hearts of the Israelites were once more tuned to God, Elijah sent his servant to the top of a hill to give a weather report. Six times the servant went and looked, but saw nothing black and threatening in the horizon. Finally, the seventh time, the servant came back with the report that there was a cloud the size of a man's hand. That was all Elijah needed to know. They left for Jezreel, and got caught in the rainstorm along the way.

Elijah's prayers were answered prayers, in God's will and in his time. What is especially striking about the prophet is that James called Elijah "a man with the same nature as we." Elijah was as human as any of us. He prayed, and a three-and-a-half-year object lesson in depending on God commenced for his people. He prayed again, and the heavens gave forth rain and the earth was again fruitful. He was no better or worse than any of us who know the Savior, yet the Lord answered his prayers, because the prayers were in accordance with God's will.

PRAY TO BE FAITHFUL—JAMES 5:19-20

> My brethren, if anyone among you wanders away from the truth, and someone brings him back, let him be knowing that he who turns a sinner from the error of his way shall save his soul from death, and shall turn from sight a host of sins.

God is looking for Elijahs. Through his prayer, the prophet saved a nation, rescued the Israelites from the practice of idol worship, and taught the followers of Baal a lesson about whose god was God. As the Israelites had wandered from the truth, so too have many of us. The spiritual remains of Christians lie decaying along the road of life. Many people begin their journey of faith aflame for the Lord. They prove to be only short-distance sprinters, not marathoners, and they drop along the wayside.

As discussed in an earlier chapter, there are many reasons why believers don't finish well. Perhaps they are left to their own devices, and no one of spiritual maturity ever disciples them. They have no foundation on which to build. Perhaps they are led away by their lusts, saying yes to the world, the flesh, and the devil, instead of struggling against them. Whatever the reason, none of us can afford to become cocky about our spirituality. Like Demas, a man discipled by none other than the apostle Paul, we too may fall away from the faith, lured by the evils of this present world.

"My brethren," James began his final remarks. But obviously, Christians can wander away. They can walk straight out of fellowship with God. It is a constant danger to guard against, for ourselves and for others within the body of Christ.

If anyone wanders from the truth, we are to seek out the straying sheep (5:19b-20). We are to look for those who have lost their way. We are to lead them back to the fold.

You probably know a Christian who has fallen out of fellowship with the Lord. Think about it a minute. What about your college roommate? You remember how enthusiastic he was about God at school, always witnessing to other students on campus. He even got you involved in that Christian organization where you met your future wife. He's had some rough times in his career and with his folks' health failing. How is he doing spiritually? Hadn't you heard he had quit going to church? Why don't you give him a call?

What about that Sunday school teacher you once had? He really failed, didn't he? You couldn't believe it when he left his wife and children for his secretary. What a disappointment. You thought he had it all together. I'll bet he hasn't cracked a Bible in years. Why don't you look him up and encourage him to seek God's forgiveness and to pick up the pieces?

Don't forget Charley's wife, Sue. She was so shaken by his illness and early death. What a blow. It has been over a year, and she is trying not to be bitter at God. Wouldn't it be easier for her if she were studying his word with a group of single women like herself? Maybe you could introduce Sue to an older widow at church. Maybe you could tell her about Bible Study Fellowship or another organization where she wouldn't feel like a fifth wheel without Charley.

And there's Cliff. He rarely comes to church these days—just to usher, really. Could you phone him and ask if he would like to start meeting regularly for lunch? You two could go over a passage of scripture or do a Bible study together.

The straying sheep are there to be found. Christians who are in danger of not finishing well are all around us. You shouldn't have to look far to see one who is falling by the wayside.

When you do notice spiritual slackness, it is time to encourage your friend to get it together and get back in fellowship before things go from bad to worse. Start praying for opportunities right now, if you're serious. During one study series where I spoke on the book of James, within a two-week period at least four people expressed such sentiments as these: "The Lord is back. I'm in fellowship again; I just know it. I sense his presence." It wasn't by chance that these four found their way back to God. People told me about them, and I began diligently praying for them, friends invited them to class, and the Lord took care of the rest.

In Relationship, Out of Fellowship

When one of us brings a sinning brother or sister back into fellowship with the Lord, we "save his soul from death and remove from sight a host of sins" (5:20). Does this mean that a Christian who backslides can lose his salvation? Is James speaking of eternal death? The answer to both questions is no.

Christians have eternal security and everlasting life, no matter what. So-called believers whose lives never give any evidence of changed behavior may not have ever truly trusted Christ (James 3), but the Lord alone knows that. It is possible for true believers to live lives out of the will of God. It happens all the time, and it is not without its dangers.

The "death" (5:20) is not spiritual death or separation from God; it is physical death. If we persist in moving in our own direction, apart from what God desires, away from the truth, the Lord has the prerogative to say, "Time's up. Come on home before you wind up in any more trouble." He can easily snatch us to heaven. A car accident, an undetected aneurysm, a rapidly spreading cancer, even a lightning bolt—within seconds, the quiet hum of a heart monitor signals that it is all over. It may well be all over if we disgrace his name with our conduct. He isn't looking for ambassadors on earth of whom others say, "Well, look at that. If Joe's a Christian, I want no part of it." He wants lights to shine in the darkness, not lamps that flicker, fade, or illumine the wrong path.

Let me remind you of some scriptural proof that believers can fall out of fellowship and suffer physical death as a consequence. In Ephesians 6 we see that obedience to parents is rewarded with a long life. In 1 Corinthians 11 we read of believers who are "sick and weak" and a few of whom "sleep in physical death" because they have not dealt with sin in their lives. It happens.

How do we turn our Christian brothers and sisters back to the right path? Galatians 6:1 tells us. We are to admonish, or confront, the believer with what is wrong. We then instruct him in what is right. We help him return to the fellowship of the Lord, encouraging him to pray and to discard the behaviors getting in the way of growth. We do this humbly and gently, not judgmentally or critically. And before we ever make a move, we pray. We pray while we are with him. We pray after we leave. We pray, pray, pray. We cannot pray too much for the wayward brother or sister. Restoration starts on bended knee. So do all good things.

SANTA (SCROOGE) IN THE SKY

Bingham Hunter wrote, in *The God Who Hears*, "You can easily envision God being interrupted by you as he manages the universe and saying into the phone: 'It's been good to hear from you, kid. But listen. Next time, don't call Me, I'll call you'" (Hunter 41). We too often look at God as a Scrooge in the sky—unwilling to listen, not wanting to help, too busy to care.

Then there's the other extreme—God as the ultimate sugar daddy, a heavenly Santa waiting to open the bag full of goodies and shower us with our requests whenever we ask.

Both images are wrong. Prayer is evidence that a relationship and fellowship with God are possible.

Prayer is a manifestation of relationship. Prayer is talk

between a child and a father. God hears the prayer of an unsaved soul who cries for salvation. Only then does He become a daddy to that soul.

Prayer is a manifestation of fellowship. Prayer becomes effective only when we have confessed our sins, and fellowship with God and man is restored. Prayer is communion and communication between caring parties.

More than a list of requests, proper prayer rejoices in good times. It expresses gratitude. It follows God's will. It comes in words. And sometimes, when we do not know how to pray, it comes in a sigh, a tear, an upward glance, a single unspoken thought, a solitary utterance: "Help."

When my children were toddlers, sicknesses meant feverish foreheads, glazed eyes, runny noses, and lots of tears. Into our arms they nestled, heads cradled against us. They couldn't tell us where it hurt. But we could often tell. Swollen gums meant teething. Red ears signaled infection. Poor appetites indicated upset stomachs. We often knew where it hurt. Often we knew what to do, just as we usually knew what to do when they were fighting, playing, laughing, pouting, or sleeping.

Pearl and I usually knew what to do. God always knows what to do. May we never forget it.

Points to Ponder

1. What does James 5:13 tell us about *when* we should pray to God? What is significant about this verse in light of the fact that James was writing to Christians? What are some practical ways we can "pray without ceasing," as Paul instructed us in 1 Thessalonians 5:17?

2. What does Elijah's example tell us about the effectiveness of prayer that is in the will of God? Refer to 5:17-18 as you answer.

3. What are James's instructions in 5:19-20 concerning believers who have wandered away from the faith? What should Christians do about these individuals? Does someone you know fit into this category? What are some ways you might seek to restore this brother or sister to fellowship?

A Passion for Excellence

The really good things run contrary. Take proper eating, for instance. We know it's better for us to consume low fat, high fiber, low cholesterol foods. But somehow broccoli, oat bran, steamed wild rice, and yogurt don't appeal to us as much as chocolate syrup, ice cream, yeast rolls, and T-bone steaks—at least not until we become accustomed to eating them.

What about exercise? We all know that cardiovascular workouts are important. We all know we ought to be cycling, attending aerobics classes, jogging, or walking. We know it even as we lie on the sofa, couch potatoes with good intentions and minimal motivation. After all, we mowed the grass. That ought to be enough for today. It is only after we force ourselves to stick to a fitness regimen that we become hooked on its benefits, and it becomes a vital part of our lives.

We don't want to eat right. We don't want to exercise. And biblically, the good things run contrary too. We don't really, naturally, want to do any of the things James exhorted us to do in his letter. Think about it.

1. *Growing taller through testing*—How many of us joyfully anticipate being wrung through the wringer, knowing that the experience will be filled with lessons from a loving God? No,

thank you. We prefer smooth rides on pumped-up tires to rocky roads and flats.

2. *Resisting temptation*—Do we really want to say no when we know we ought to say no? Be honest. Isn't it really our natural inclination to peek at crib notes, lie about our age or weight, deny that we touched the ball before it went out of bounds?

3. *Working out in God's word*—How natural is it to want to read the Bible? To study scripture? A thirst for God's word isn't a longing we are born with or develop on our own. It goes against the grain.

4. *Loving without partiality*—It is much easier for us to shower affection on people we like, people who appeal to us or feed our egos or return our gestures of kindness, than it is for us to love the unlovely. Give us the cream over the crud any day, the beautiful over the boring, banal, battered, bleeding.

5. *Bearing fruit*—We like to do good works when others know about it. It isn't all that unusual for us to donate to charity, as long as our donation is public record. Sure, we will help out with Special Olympics, collect for the American Cancer Society, go with a group to visit crippled children, if those activities aren't secret. We don't ask for headlines, but if the boss and a few friends know, it won't hurt. People should see how giving and unselfish we are.

However, when it comes to manifesting the Galatians 5 fruit of the Spirit in our lives—love, joy, peace, patience, and the rest—those things really aren't normal. Self-control? It's a learned response. Goodness, gentleness, faithfulness? Naturally, we are always looking for an angle. Unselfish do-gooders who neither seek nor desire human recognition and reward are rare outside the control of the Spirit.

6. *Controlling the tongue*—Clamping the mouth shut comes hard. We would rather chatter. The world deserves our two bits worth.

7. *Growing in good judgment*—God's thoughts aren't our thoughts. Christ-minded Christianity and the world's wisdom conflict. Naturally, we consider the things of Christ, like service

and sacrifice, to be bleeding-heart sentimentalism —stuff for Mother Theresa, Peace Corps volunteers, and missionaries. Not for the real world.

8. *Battling the big three*—God's ways aren't our ways either. It is far easier for us to say yes to the flesh, go along with the world, and pal up with Satan, than it is to engage in warfare on all three fronts.

9. *Developing dependence on the designer*—We would rather stick to our guns than admit our dependence on someone greater than ourselves, even God. Our society exalts self-reliance. The human heart craves independence.

10. *Handling money correctly*—Naturally, our finances are our concern, the results of our efforts, the rewards of our labors. Thinking about Christ before we say, "Charge it," or sign on the dotted line is unusual.

11. *Living in light of Christ's re-entry*—Even the most committed Christian has a tough time with this one. It is just plain difficult to keep the eternal perspective when so much of life demands massive amounts of our time and attention. Thinking about heaven when bills pile up, kids rebel, products beg to be purchased, deadlines pressure us, doesn't come easy.

12. *Pursuing the power of prayer*—Getting on our knees is inconvenient, downright uncomfortable. Pausing in our busyness to pray and to confess isn't natural. We would rather read books or attend seminars on prayer than actually pray.

Yes, the really good things do run contrary. Maybe that's why James presented twelve of the really good things as marks of maturity in the Christian life. We know we are making strides spiritually if some of these points of progress are making their way into our lives. Isn't one of the functions of the Holy Spirit to energize the new nature? He makes it so that the good things won't run quite so contrary.

No Change—No Gain

Remember the story of Puff, the magic dragon in the song by folk artists Peter, Paul, and Mary? You know Puff, who "frolicked in the autumn mist in a land called Ho-nah-Lee." Puff frolicked alone, until a boy named little Jackie Paper came along to play. Complete with strings, sealing wax, and fancy stuff, Puff and Jackie sailed the seas of the imagination. They conquered pirates and entertained princes and kings . . . until one day, when Jackie grew up:

> A dragon lives forever, but not so little boys
> Painted wings and giant rings make way for other toys.
> One gray night it happened, Jackie Paper came no more
> And Puff, the mighty dragon; He ceased his fearless
>   roar.
>
> His head was bent in sorrow, green scales fell like
>   rain.
> Puff no longer went to play along the cherry lane.
> Without his life-long friend, Puff could not be brave
> So Puff that mighty dragon, sadly slipped into his
>   cave.   (Leonard Lipton and Peter Yarrow)

As that song illustrates, change is the essence of growing up. Like little Jackie Paper, we believers leave behind our toys and games and old pre-Christ selves. For Christians, the dragons of pre-Christ behaviors hopefully steadily withdraw into their caves. The new man gets put on, bit by bit, piece by piece. And yet the fact remains that the old dragons never entirely go away. The new self in Christ never entirely gets put on, at least not until glory. The process is what's most important. James issued a call to take a reading on our lives, to discover where we are in the standings.

GROWING UP GODLY

The grown-up Christian? He or she is a myth this side of eternity. The growing-up Christian? That's another matter. Such a person ought to be any Christian friend of yours. In fact, such a person ought to be you.

Growing-up, godly Christians are implementing what they know of biblical truth in their lives. They are pursuing the pointers that James described. Above all, they are willing to let God make of them whatever He wants to, whenever, wherever, and however He wants to. They are

. . . learning to walk with God
. . . learning to be a servant instead of selfish
. . . learning to seek godly counsel
. . . learning to submit to God's authority
. . . learning to reach out and touch

You can be that growing-up, godly person if you're willing. And believe me, if you are, you are going to be ultimately fulfilled and happy. "But godliness with contentment is great gain" (1 Timothy 6:6 KJV).

Exercise and eating right become habits if practiced long enough. Obedience in the Christian life does too. Practice, prayer, poring over the word, and depending on the Spirit—all help to perfect us. Someday we shall be just like Christ.

Let's pull out the equipment and get cracking. A passion for excellence should characterize more than our academic concerns, business endeavors, athletic pursuits. That passion should permeate our spiritual life goals as we endeavor to allow God to use us for his glory.

A Prayer

Father, the longing of my heart at this moment is to be all You want me to be and to do the things You want me to do.

Teach me to rest in your sovereign purpose. May I become convinced that You are working all things together for my good and growth. I want to avail myself of the grace You have so generously provided, and I desire to relate victoriously to the curriculum of circumstances that You have designed for my development. To You be the glory.

You have taught me to pray: "Lead me not into temptation." Recognizing my weaknesses and vulnerability, I pray that I might not be a victim of Satan's strategy to distract me from the good gifts that come only from You. May I find pure pleasure in your purposes, fulfillment in food from your table and water from your well, satisfaction in your salvation, stability in your strength.

Thank You for the word that cuts and prunes so I might bear fruit. May your Spirit open my eyes that I may behold wondrous things out of your law. May I have not only eyes to see clearly, but ears to hear distinctly what You are saying. Enlighten my mind that I might comprehend the living word, the Lord Jesus Christ, in the written word. May I find time to memorize and meditate on your precepts that I might be a tree planted by the rivers of water bringing forth fruit.

Create in me a heart of compassion that knows no bounds. Motivated by my master, may I minister healing to broken hearts and shattered lives. May I be known as one who gets involved in meeting needs. May I work, weep, and wear out, winning the lost.

It is my hope and prayer that a family likeness might begin to be manifested in my daily life. The fruit of the Spirit is what You long to see, and I want that too. May the evidence of your life permeate my whole being. When others see me, may they be reminded of Jesus. I know that if He is lifted up, He will draw all men to himself. The internal fruit can produce external fruit with eternal ramifications.

Father, my tongue is a problem. I often use it to criticize, condemn, wound, and whip my brothers. Teach me to encourage, exhort, edify, and evangelize by speaking freely of the glories of my Savior. May my praises flow unhindered from lips that have been touched by You.

May it please your heart, as in the days of Solomon, when I ask for wisdom. You have given me the invitation that if I lack, I may ask. Please forgive the times I have so readily leaned on my own understanding.

Thank You for the armor designed to make me effective and victorious in battle. May my shield of faith catch and quench Satan's fiery darts. May the sword of the word cut away the entanglements with the world, and may the power of the Spirit energize me to victory over the flesh.

Lord, I am prone to wander and, like the sheep, I often go astray. Stubborn as I am, I think I know the way and refuse to seek direction, only to find I am on a dead-end street. Help me to learn that dependence does not equal weakness. I know the steps of a good man are ordered by the Lord, and I want to learn to let you lead.

Lord, material things make me comfortable and I find myself backing away from any sacrificial commitment. Teach me to be a faithful steward, generous and willing to share that others might be enriched.

When I awoke this morning, I found myself rejoicing because I am another day closer to your coming. May I work the works of him who sent me. May I press on toward the goal with intensity and excitement, knowing that it is only a little farther to the finish.

Why is it, Father, that I have so little quality time in your presence? Is it because I feel guilty or awkward? Perhaps I know I won't like what You are going to say or tell me to do. Help me to long for those times and to rearrange my priorities to have fellowship with You often.

Father, two things have inspired this prayer. One, I want to fight a good fight, finish the course in championship form, and keep the faith. Second, more than anything else, I want to hear, "Well done, good and faithful servant. Enter into the joys I have prepared for you."

> *In the name of our victorious Savior,*
> *Amen.*

Select Bibliography

Adamson, James B. 1976. *The Epistle of James. The New International Commentary on the New Testament*. Grand Rapids MI: Wm. B. Eerdmans Publishing Company.

Barclay, William. 1960. *The Letters of James and Peter*. 2d ed. Philadelphia PA: Westminster Press.

Colson, Howard P. 1969. *The Practical Message of James*. Nashville TN: Broadman Press.

Gaebelein, Frank E. 1955. *The Practical Epistle of James*. Great Neck NY: Doniger and Raughly.

Gutzke, Manford George. 1969. *Plain Talk on James*. Grand Rapids MI: Zondervan Publishing House.

Heibert, D. Edmond. 1979. *The Epistle of James*. Chicago IL: Moody Press.

Kenyon, Don J. 1959. *The Double Mind: An Expository and Devotional Study from the Epistle of James*. Grand Rapids MI: Zondervan Publishing House.

Lange, John Peter. 1869. *Commentary on the Holy Scriptures: Critical, Doctrinal and Homiletical: James*. Ed. Philip Schaff. Grand Rapids MI: Zondervan Publishing House.

Lenski, R. C. H. 1966. *The Interpretation of the Epistle to the Hebrews and the Epistle of James.* Minneapolis MN: Augsburg Publishing House.

Luck, G. Coleman. 1954. *James: Faith in Action.* Chicago IL: Moody Press.

Mayor, Joseph B. 1978. *The Epistle of St. James: The Greek Text with Introduction Notes and Comments.* Reprint. Grand Rapids MI: Baker Book House.

McGee, J. Vernon. 1983. *Thru the Bible with J. Vernon McGee. Vol. 5, 1 Corinthians—Revelation.* Nashville TN: Thomas Nelson Publishers.

Morrice, William G. 1984. *Joy in the New Testament.* Grand Rapids MI: Wm. B. Eerdmans Publishing Company.

Strauss, Lehman. 1967. *James, Your Brother: Studies in the Epistle of James.* Neptune NJ: Loizeaux Brothers, Inc.

Tasker, R. V. G. 1957. *The General Epistle of James: An Introduction and Commentary.* The Tyndale New Testament Commentaries. Grand Rapids MI: Wm. B. Eerdmans Publishing Company.

Acknowledgments

Aldrin, Buzz and Malcolm McConnell. 1989. *Men from Earth*. New York NY: Bantam Books. Condensed in *Reader's Digest* (July 1989): 30-38, 187-216.

Bayly, Joseph. 1987. P*salms of My Life*. Elgin IL: Cook Publishers, p.90.

Bliss, Philip. "Hold the Fort."

Bodett, Tom. 1987. *Small Comforts: More Comments and Comic Pieces*. Reading MA: Addison-Wesley Publishing Company, Inc.

Bombeck, Erma. 1987. *Family: The Ties that Bind . . . and Gag!* New York NY: McGraw-Hill Book Company.

Bright, Bill. 1969. *Revolution Now*. Arrowhead Springs CA: Campus Crusade for Christ, Inc.

Brown, Stephen. 1988. *When Your Rope Breaks*. Nashville TN: Thomas Nelson Publishers.

Calkin, Ruth Harms. 1988. *Lord, Don't You Love Me Anymore?* Wheaton IL: Tyndale House Publishers, Inc.

Cory, Lloyd. 1985. *Quotable Quotations*. Wheaton IL: Victory Books.

Cornwall, B. V. 1988. "The Vessel." From *Help Lord, My Whole Life Hurts*. Carole Mayhall. Colorado Springs CO: Navpress.

Cosgrove, Francis M. 1980. *Essentials of Discipleship*. Colorado Springs CO: Navpress.

Curtis, Gregory, ed. "1988 Bum Steer Awards." *Texas Monthly* 16:1 (January 1988): 64-73.

Dillard, Annie. 1974. *Pilgrim at Tinker Creek*. New York NY: Harper and Row Publishers.

"Drop the Phone: Busting a Computer Whiz." *Time* 133:2 (January 9, 1989): 49.

Eliot, Robert S. and Dennis L. Breo. 1984. *Is It Worth Dying For?: A Self-Assessment Program to Make Stress Work for You, Not against You.* New York NY: Bantam Books.

Friedrich, Otto. "Flashy Symbol of an Acquisitive Age." *Time* 133:3 (January 16, 1989): 48-54.

Gaither, Gloria and William and Greg Nelson. 1982. "We Are So Blessed." Nashville TN: River Oaks Music Co./Gaither Music Co.

Hansel, Tim. 1988. *Eating Problems for Breakfast: A Simple, Creative Approach to Solving Any Problem.* Dallas: Word Publishing, pp. 142-143.

Hart, Archibald D. 1979. *Feeling Free.* Old Tappan NJ: Fleming H. Revell Company.

Hatch, Edwin. "Breathe on Me, Breath of God."

Havergal, Frances R. "Take My Life, and Let It Be."

"Hunt Brothers Forced to Count Fortune." *The San Antonio Express-News* (June 18, 1989): 7-A.

Hunter, W. Bingham. 1986. *The God Who Hears.* Downers Grove IL: Inter-Varsity Press.

Hurnard, Hannah. 1977. *Mountains of Spices.* Living Books ed. Wheaton IL: Tyndale House Publishers, Inc., 1985.

MacDonald, Gordon. 1984. *Ordering Your Private World.* Nashville TN: Oliver-Nelson.

Miller, Calvin. 1987. *Becoming: Your Self in the Making.* Old Tappan NJ: Fleming H. Revell.

Miller, Keith. 1988. *Secrets of Staying Power: Overcoming the Discouragements of Ministry.* Carol Stream IL: Christianity Today, Inc. and Word, Inc.

Moyer, Larry. "Why Some People Don't Go On for the Lord." *The Tool Box* (Spring 1989): 1,3.

Oatman, Johnson, Jr. "Higher Ground."

Osbeck, Kenneth. 1982. *101 Hymn Stories.* Grand Rapids MI: Kregel Publications.

Packer, J. I. 1987. *Hot Tub Religion.* Wheaton IL: Tyndale House Publishers.

Porch, Ludlow. 1981. *A View from the Porch.* Atlanta GA: Peachtree Publishers.

Seamands, David A. 1988. *Healing Grace.* Wheaton IL: Victor Books.

Sell, Charles. 1987. *The House on the Rock.* Wheaton IL: Victor Books.

Stallings, John. "Learning to Lean."

Swartz, David. 1987. *Dancing with Broken Bones: Blessed Are the Broken in Spirit, for God Can Make Them Whole.* Colorado Springs CO: Navpress.

Tan, Paul Lee. 1984. *Encyclopedia of 7700 Illustrations: Signs of the Times.* Rockville MD: Assurance Publishers.

Unknown Christian. 1945. *The Kneeling Christian.* Clarion Classic Series. 1986 edition. Grand Rapids MI: Zondervan Publishing House.

Zapata, Jerry. "Robert and the Debo." *Shaping Lives* (May 1989): 1.

Popular pastor, teacher, and conference speaker, Don Anderson tours Texas and neighboring states giving Bible classes and business luncheon seminars during the fall, winter, and spring months. Don Anderson Ministries conducts annual couples', women's, and men's conferences, and in the summer operates youth and family camps. Don preaches regularly at a church staffed by the Ministries, and also speaks at conferences in various locations in the United States and Canada. His audiences of business and professional men and women, housewives and tradespeople, testify that his refreshing teaching makes the scriptures "come alive" for them.

Don Anderson graduated from Northwestern College in 1955 with a bachelor of arts degree and received his master's degree from Dallas Theological Seminary. He has recently completed course work toward a doctorate of ministries at Talbot Seminary. Don has been in Christian ministry for over thirty years, serving as a Young Life staff member, youth pastor, program director at the Firs Bible and Missionary Conference, executive director of Pine Cove Conference Center, and since 1972, as director of the nonprofit organization, Don Anderson Ministries, headquartered in Tyler, Texas.

Don Anderson has many audio and video cassette tapes based on his teachings, which are produced by the Ministries and distributed widely. There is also a Ministries newsletter, *The Grapevine*, which reaches about 9,000 homes.

If you would like to enhance your study of James, cassette tapes of this series are available from the author. If you are interested in hearing Don's teachings, please write to this address for a free tape catalog:

Don Anderson Ministries
P. O. Box 6611
Tyler, Texas 75711
214-597-3018